Finding My Way

ALSO BY MALALA YOUSAFZAI

I Am Malala

CHILDREN'S BOOKS

I Am Malala (Young Readers Edition)
Malala: My Story of Standing Up for Girls' Rights
Malala's Magic Pencil
We Are Displaced
My Name Is Malala

Finding My Way

A Memoir

Malala Yousafzai

ATRIA BOOKS

New York   Amsterdam/Antwerp   London
Toronto   Sydney/Melbourne   New Delhi

ATRIA
BOOKS

An Imprint of Simon & Schuster, LLC
1230 Avenue of the Americas
New York, NY 10020

First Atria Books hardcover edition October 2025

ATRIA B O O K S and colophon are trademarks of Simon & Schuster, LLC

Simon & Schuster strongly believes in freedom of expression and stands against
censorship in all its forms. For more information, visit BooksBelong.com.

Some names have been changed.

For information about special discounts for bulk purchases,
please contact Simon & Schuster Special Sales at 1-866-506-1949
or business@simonandschuster.com.

The Simon & Schuster Speakers Bureau can bring authors to your live event.
For more information or to book an event, contact the Simon & Schuster Speakers
Bureau at 1-866-248-3049 or visit our website at www.simonspeakers.com.

Interior design by Davina Mock-Maniscalco

Manufactured in the United States of America

1   3   5   7   9   10   8   6   4   2

Library of Congress Control Number: 9781668054277

ISBN 978-1-6680-5427-7
ISBN 978-1-6680-5429-1 (ebook)

For Abai, Toor Pekai, and all the Shangla girls

Finding
My Way

Introduction

I'll never know who I was supposed to be. Maybe everyone feels that way, curious about the invisible crossroads in their lives, the wrong turns and chance encounters that change everything. But I am haunted by it, the gulf between how I imagined my life and what it became. I can't escape the feeling that a giant hand plucked me out of one story and dropped me into an entirely new one.

On a mild October afternoon, a bullet changed the trajectory of my life, cutting me off from my home, my friends, and everything I loved, spinning me out into an unfamiliar world. At fifteen years old, I hadn't had time to figure out who I wanted to be when, suddenly, everyone wanted to tell me who I was. An inspiration, a hero, an activist. But also a wallflower, a punching bag, a paycheck. To my parents, I was an obedient daughter. To my friends, a good listener. When I was alone, I unraveled—because the hardest thing to be was myself.

My early twenties were a tangle of anxiety and indecision, reckless nights and foggy mornings, friendship and first love. It was never going to be easy, in this wonder-struck season of life, when the world feels full of possibility, to find the path that was right for me. Still, I tried to shrug off other people's expectations and hear my own voice, to reckon with what I had lost and who I might become. What I wanted, more than anything, was to make sense of my story.

1.

If you get up in five minutes, you'll be on time, I bartered with my-self, calculating how long it would take me to brush my teeth and throw on some clothes. Half an hour later, I was still in bed, scrolling on my phone—dorm room décor, virtual campus tours, packing lists. I would start college in just two days, and my brain was buzzing.

New friends! No parents! No rules! I could barely contain my excitement, bouncing on my toes and humming to myself as I got dressed and took the elevator down to a windowless conference room in a midtown Manhattan hotel.

"You're late," the PR woman sighed, "and I'm not even going to ask if you reviewed your talking points."

I smiled and shrugged. Over the summer I'd traveled to four continents, met with nine prime ministers, and spoken at multiple events. Now I was in New York to promote *Malala's Magic*

Pencil, a new children's book—six hours of back-to-back interviews and then an overnight flight home to Birmingham, England. It was my last day of work for a while, but my mind was already out-of-office.

The PR rep left the room and, a few moments later, a child entered. I was about to ask if she was lost when I noticed her polo shirt was embroidered with a magazine logo and *Kid Reporter* underneath it.

"When you were little, what did you want to be when you grew up?" she asked.

"A car mechanic!" I replied, adding that I'd always loved puzzles and figuring out how to put things together.

The next journalist was far less charming. He didn't want to hear about my children's book and tried to shift the focus to hot topics, hoping I'd say something controversial enough to spice up a slow news day. Most of his questions were about the American president: "As the youngest Nobel Peace Prize laureate, what is your message to him on women's rights?" and "You visited the White House to meet with Obama. If the new administration invites you, will you go?" I knew how to avoid having my name plastered across headlines and didn't take the bait.

The last interview was for a morning TV show. The host asked thoughtful questions about my work and day-to-day life. We were close to wrapping up when she leaned toward me, her face full of concern.

"Five years after the attack, do you think about it every day?" she asked.

Inevitable, I thought. *No way I was leaving this room without talking about it.* I wasn't bothered or surprised by questions like this, only by how often people asked them. That part of my life felt so long ago and far away in my mind, yet it always seemed to push past me and fill the air every time I stepped into a room.

∽

I GREW UP in a remote region of Pakistan, in a place called Mingora. My hometown ran alongside the Swat River, surrounded by forests, wildflower meadows, and colossal, snowcapped mountains. Life in our valley wasn't perfect—most families were poor and strict social norms held back progress, especially for women. But it was a stunningly beautiful and peaceful place.

That changed when I was ten years old. Strange men with long beards and assault rifles came down from the mountains and took over our town. The Taliban began bombing hospitals and hotels; executing musicians, teachers, and policemen in the streets; and issuing new rules over the radio several times a day: No TVs or music allowed, no entertainment at all, not even board games for children. Men must not shave their beards. Women must not leave their homes.

As the bombs and gunfire got louder, our lives got smaller. We lived in constant dread of breaking some new rule that we had not yet learned. A man in a nearby neighborhood was killed because the Taliban said the hem of his pants was too long. One day I saw my five-year-old brother Atal digging a big hole in the yard and asked what he was doing. "Making a grave," he replied.

When I was eleven, the Taliban announced that, in three weeks' time, girls would be banned from going to school. Fear gripped my heart. If I kept going to class after the deadline, they might kill me. If I didn't, my life was over anyway. Even at that age, I knew the fate of uneducated girls in my community: marriage in your early teens, several children before you turned twenty, the rest of your life spent behind the walls of your husband's house. It was a future I could not bear to face.

I started writing an anonymous blog for the BBC, chronicling life under the terrorists' rule. *Our school told the girls not to wear our uniforms,* I wrote, *because it might make us targets. We all showed up in our favorite pink and purple dresses. Then they told us not to wear colorful clothes because the Taliban don't like that either.*

As the deadline for girls to leave school drew closer, I went public, declaring to anyone who would listen that education was my right. The Taliban could not keep me from learning, I vowed, no matter how many schools they destroyed. On national TV, I demanded that our leaders stand up and defend us. The fear I had felt over the last two years was replaced by outrage and indignation. I could not let these men take away my future.

Eventually the Pakistani army launched a large-scale military operation against the extremists. My parents, two little brothers and I, along with thousands of others, fled Mingora when the fighting began. After a few months, the army prevailed, and we returned to our homes and life went back to normal. But the Taliban were not gone for good, and they had not forgotten my defiance. When I was fifteen, a gunman boarded my school bus and asked, "Who is Malala?" Before I could answer, he shot me in the head at point-blank range.

In an instant, my entire world changed.

I came out of a coma a week later, waking up to find myself in Birmingham at a trauma center that specialized in complex brain injuries. Before the shooting, I'd never left Pakistan; now I was surrounded by strangers. I spent the next several months there, undergoing multiple surgeries and learning how to walk and talk again.

As my story traveled around the world, people began to describe someone I didn't recognize—a serious and shy girl, a wallflower forced to speak out when the Taliban took away her books. They made me into a mythical heroine, virtuous and dutiful, predestined for greatness.

Sometimes the absurdity of it made me laugh. Growing up in

Mingora, I was a troublemaker. At school, I ferried bits of gossip back and forth between groups of girls and cracked jokes that made my friends laugh and scold me in the same breath. If a class-mate did better than me on exams, I cried bitter, undignified tears at the injustice of it. At home, I was messy, rambunctious. I'd watch John Cena—my favorite wrestler—on TV and try out his moves on my little brothers, then tattle to my father when they fought back. Even on my best day, I was not the reticent saint that everyone now claimed I was.

I was still in the hospital when people came with offers to turn my story into books and films. Journalists jockeyed to land my first interview. Talent agents wanted to represent me, though I wasn't sure what talents they thought I possessed. "Why are you famous now?" Atal asked. I told him I didn't know.

Before I understood what was happening, I was thrust into an unfamiliar, unbidden life—crossing the globe to give speeches and pose for photos, spending most of my time with adults. Backstage at big events, one of them would spin me around by the shoulders and cry, "High energy, Malala! Give them everything!" To these grown-ups, I was a public figure and a product to be marketed; they were blind to the awkward teenager sitting next to them, try-ing to do her homework. In their orbit, I withdrew, becoming the quiet girl they assumed I'd always been.

Everywhere I went people asked the same question: "What do you remember about the shooting?" When I said that I couldn't re-member anything about it, they seemed almost disappointed, as if it was impolite of me not to recall my fear and suffering. As if the worst thing that ever happened to me was the most interesting part of my life. It made me feel like a butterfly with a straight pin through its heart, forever trapped under dusty glass. The living girl in front of them was not as captivating as the one on the school bus, a young dreamer about to die.

⌒

"DO YOU THINK about it every day?"

I blinked at the morning show host. It would be easy to say what she and her audience wanted to hear—that, at times, I felt afraid or that I might never fully recover from my injuries. Why complicate the tidy, tragic narrative that people seemed so drawn to?

But something was changing inside me—I didn't want to play the part anymore. I was ready to be young and free, to go on adventures and make mistakes, to have a life that happened somewhere other than airports and conference rooms. The future was wide open and waiting for me.

"I don't think about it at all," I said. "My life is moving forward."

2.

The night before I left for Oxford University, I sat on the floor, wishing my bedroom door had a lock. It was broken when we moved in, and no matter how many times I'd asked my parents to fix it over the years, they never got around to it. I reached under the bed, pulled out the contraband items I'd been hiding there, and stuffed everything into my suitcase as fast as I could.

My mom and I had been locked in a cold war all summer, ever since she assigned herself the job of assembling my college wardrobe. This wasn't a new dynamic for us: For years, she hung what she wanted me to wear on the front of my closet before I went to bed. When I tried to exert some independence, emerging the next morning in something other than what she'd assigned, she would say, "Do you think Allah approves of daughters disobeying their mothers?" It seemed unwise to try to answer that, so back to my room I'd go.

Wherever I went, my mom insisted that I wear the traditional clothes of Pashtun people, the ethnic group to which my family belongs. That meant only one outfit, the *shalwar kameez*— billowy pants, a tentlike tunic, and a headscarf. In our deeply conservative culture, a woman's clothes must cover all skin above the wrist or ankle; garments are shapeless, giving no hint of the female form.

All summer, my mom assembled her "college collection" of shalwar kameez for me. There were hot-pink paisley trousers and a top with matching pom-poms on the cuffs. A lime-green number with heavy silver beading. Delirious floral patterns that could make you dizzy if you stared at them too long. Black, ivory, and tan were out of the question because, according to her, neutrals were a waste of good fabric.

I can't say I had a clear personal style at the time, but I knew I absolutely could not go to Oxford dressed like a set of neon highlighters. So, while my mom was out shopping, I googled "what to wear to college 2017" and ordered what I saw in the pictures—jeans, striped tees, a quilted bomber jacket. A search for "Selena Gomez casual" led me to oversize cardigans and Adidas Superstars. Chunky knit scarves, embroidered sweatshirts, a black dress with bell sleeves, and several pairs of ankle boots were all squirreled away, awaiting their debut.

I stuffed everything I'd purchased in my suitcase and threw a couple kameezes on top in case my mom decided on a last-minute inspection. I knew she would find out about my new look eventually and wouldn't be happy, but that was a risk I was willing to take.

To me, they weren't just clothes—they were camouflage. The Malala everyone recognized, who stood on stages, signed autographs, and shook hands with world leaders, wore shalwar kameez. At Oxford, I wanted to blend in, just another student in sneakers and jeans. I had to make sure that college was nothing like high school.

⌒

WHEN I WAS released from the hospital and started ninth grade at an all-girls' academy in Birmingham, I assumed I would quickly acquire a gang of friends, Brummie versions of my classmates in Mingora. I imagined us walking home every afternoon, arm in arm, laughing over inside jokes. They would catch me up on all the gossip and tell me which teachers could be sweet-talked and which were strict.

Things didn't turn out exactly as I planned. Most of the girls in my new school had known each other since kindergarten and, years ago, formed tight circles of two or three—not unkind, but not welcoming either. At lunch, I'd take my tray and find the nearest seat, furtively glancing around for friendly faces. If no one spoke to me, I'd take out a book and pretend to read. One day I worked up the courage to ask the other girls a question. Leaning across the table, I pointed to my plate and said, "Sorry, but could you tell me the meaning of 'fish fingers'?" They all looked confused—one of them said, "It's just fish, yeah?"—before returning to their conversation.

If someone told a joke in class, I laughed along with the other girls, pretending I got it too. I couldn't understand any of their references. In Mingora, where almost no one had internet access, we'd only heard echoes of American or British pop culture, those loud enough to ring around the world and land in our valley—*Titanic*, World Wrestling Entertainment, Taylor Swift. What little I knew about life in England came from reading one Jane Austen novel. After my first day at school, I gathered that the book was slightly out of date.

Sometimes photographers turned up at the front gates, trying to snap photos of me going in or out of school. I hated it, and worried the other girls would think I was either full of myself or fake. But no one cared that I was famous, it quickly became clear, because I simply wasn't cool. We all wore uniforms, but the hem of my pleated skirt fell to my ankles, double the standard length. On top of that, my mom insisted that I wear opaque black tights, even in spring, to avoid showing any part of my legs.

My injuries made it worse. I was fifteen years old and wore a hearing aid. The bullet had destroyed my left eardrum and severed my facial nerve, leaving one side of my face paralyzed. My mouth could no longer form a smile, so an uneasy grimace was all I had to offer my new classmates. Despite months of relearning how to walk in rehab, I moved slowly through the riot of teen girls—a hopeful little ghost, trying to rejoin the land of the living.

You're not here to socialize anyway, I told myself after weeks of trying and failing to make friends. *School is for making good grades, so you can get into college.* Then I saw the scores on my first few tests: 41% in English, 57% in Biology, 63% in Geography. Having always been a top student, I was stunned and embarrassed.

In Pakistan, teachers focused on memorization. You didn't need to grasp the underlying concepts as long as you could parrot the textbook. My new school expected critical thinking and analysis, a way of learning that I didn't understand. For a while, my only solid grade was in Algebra, as math seemed to have the same set of answers everywhere in the world.

Eager to restore my academic standing, I studied for hours every night. I read the books my teachers assigned and supplemental reading I assigned myself. When I came across a word I didn't recognize, I looked it up and wrote the definition on a Post-it note. Soon the walls of my bedroom were covered in little yellow squares, scrawled with the meanings of "cat burglar," "crepuscule," and "pensive" in my loopy handwriting.

While my grades steadily improved, my social life did not, and I often found myself watching the clock throughout the day. It was noon in Mingora when I arrived at school in the morning. My old friends were eating lunch, pooling their rupees to buy samosas and mango juice. A few hours later, while I pushed cold peas around a cafeteria tray, they were in front of the TV, catching up on *Shararat*, an Indian knockoff of *Sabrina the Teenage Witch*. Maybe if any of the Birmingham girls thought about approaching me, they were put off by the haunted look in my eyes, the way I always seemed to be somewhere else in my mind.

Every few weeks, I called my best friend, Moniba, and quizzed her on the latest news and gossip. *What Bollywood song is everyone singing on the bus these days? Who got in trouble at school? What are the older girls up to?* I did my famous impressions of our middle school teachers just to hear her laugh. But she always knew when something was wrong. "Why do you never talk about yourself?" she asked.

"Pfft, because everything at my school is boring," I'd demur. "Trust me, you'd fall asleep on the phone." I didn't want to tell her that I was no longer the fun, talkative girl she remembered.

After six lonely months, I decided to take action, trying everything I could to restart my life. On Field Day, I signed up for the fifty-yard dash and came in last place. I ran for student council and lost the election. When the popular girls insisted everyone participate in a flash mob, I did as they commanded, standing on top of my desk and clapping off-beat to a song I'd never heard. It was all as awkward as it sounds.

Then, finally, I made a friend. Alice had fallen out with her best mate, and I was available to fill the role. I clung to her in the hallways and at lunch tables, whispering questions in her ear when I couldn't follow the other girls' conversation. Sometimes she came over for dinner. She liked my mom's pakoras, and I liked feeling normal for an hour or two. When Alice went to parties that I wasn't allowed or invited to attend, she sent pictures so I didn't feel left out.

As grateful as I was for her, I yearned to belong to a group of girls again, to be surrounded by people who understood me and shared my memories. My childhood friends had shaped me in ways I couldn't explain to Alice or anyone else. In primary school, we survived a massive earthquake, huddling together in our classroom as the room began to shake and the floor cracked beneath us. A few years later, the river swelled and flooded our classroom, covering everything in chest-high mud. The odor was awful, but we cleaned the floors and walls together. The school was our world, a place where we could be ourselves, and we wanted to take care of it. On the last day of class before the Taliban's deadline, we stayed in the courtyard long after the final bell rang, playing freeze tag and singing songs. When the teachers told us we needed to leave, we hugged each other and cried. Whatever disasters or dangers we encountered, I always felt safe when we were together.

When the army ran off the Taliban and we went back to school, we were euphoric, unshakable. On a field trip to the mountains, Moniba and I stood under a waterfall, singing "Love Story" by Taylor Swift at the top of our lungs. Later that year, our class traveled to Islamabad, the capital city, where we watched a play, tried duck pancakes at a Chinese restaurant, and marveled at women walking down the street without headscarves. It was our first glimpse of the world beyond our remote mountain town, and we came home with wild dreams for the future.

I thought we would go to college together. At fifteen, I hadn't thought much past that, but I'd never imagined a life without my friends. Now I was heading to Oxford alone, carrying a bag of trendy clothes and dreams for a less lonely life.

3.

On the first day of orientation week, I woke up and surveyed my shabby kingdom. The dorm room carpet had frayed edges and burn marks left by former students ironing their clothes on the floor. Sickly yellow paint was flaking off the walls, and the sink in the en-suite bathroom was no bigger than a soup bowl. But all of it was mine—a place where no one could tell me when to go to bed or what to eat—and I immediately fell in love with it.

I opened my phone and scrolled through Instagram, where other students were already posting about their morning runs, breakfast in the dining hall, or trips to the bookstore. Not wanting to miss any of the action, I hopped out of bed, got dressed, and was halfway down the hall when a voice behind me called, "Wait for us, please!"

"Sorry, guys," I said, spinning around and walking back. In the room next to mine were two Metropolitan Police officers, members of the Specialist Protection unit who provide security to high-profile people. After I came to the UK, the government informed me that they were monitoring threats to my life and offered their services. I was thousands of miles away from Pakistan, but my life was still in danger, as the Taliban periodically renewed their pledge to kill me. Since then, the security team had become part of my everyday life: dropping me off at school, picking me up at the end of the day, and watching over my parents' house at night.

A few weeks before I went to Oxford, the officers laid out their plan: They would bunk in the dorms and walk with me to all my classes. Anywhere I couldn't walk, they would drive me in a bulletproof car. If I went out to dinner or a party, a few middle-aged dads in blazers and earpieces would be there too. *Just what every college girl wants*, I thought. I was grateful for their protection and understood it was necessary, but I hoped they wouldn't create a barrier between me and the other students.

With security following discreetly behind, I walked to the registration center to complete my first task of the day: taking a photo for my Oxford ID. *Smile, make eye contact, be approachable!* Since arriving the day before, I had exchanged hellos with a few students on my floor, but hadn't really talked to anyone yet. Now was the time to get serious about meeting people. *It's everyone's first day. This isn't high school. I don't need to hang around waiting for someone to talk to me.*

After picking up a map and a schedule for the week, I spotted another girl standing on her own and walked toward her. She was short like me, with strawberry-blonde hair, tortoiseshell glasses, and a reassuring smile.

"Hey, I'm Malala," I said, trying my best to sound casual but friendly.

The other girl took a step back and didn't speak. *Not this again.*

"Sorry, sorry! Brain freeze," she blurted out. "I'm Cora—nice to meet you."

"What do you study, Cora?"

"PPE."

"Me too!" I beamed, delighted that I'd met someone else in my major—Philosophy, Politics, and Economics—on my first try.

Cora and I walked together to the Freshers' Fair, a carnival-like event showcasing Oxford's extracurricular activities. The cavernous Examination Hall was transformed into a maze of hundreds of stalls, jam-packed with enthusiastic older students pitching their clubs and wide-eyed newbies trying to take it all in. We followed the flow of bodies in a daze, not sure where to start.

"Do you play any instruments?" Cora asked, as we walked past booths for heavy-metal fans, Irish folk musicians, and a jazz ensemble called the Oxford Gargoyles.

"No," I said. "I like to sing, but I'd be *terrified* to do it in front of other people."

We turned a corner to see a boy in an Oxford Cheese Society T-shirt passing out samples of brie and Gruyère. "A cheese-tasting club? That's a thing that people do?"

Cora laughed. "A thing that posh people do, yeah. Not my idea of a night out, but whatever makes them happy."

In the sports section, I made a beeline to sign up for cricket and badminton, games I had loved to play on the streets and rooftops of Mingora. Then, on a whim, I joined the rowing club too. On the walk to the fair, I'd seen students in little wooden boats meandering down the river that ran through campus, and thought it looked like a dreamy way to spend an afternoon.

The women at the Islamic Society stall called me "sister" and invited me for mocktails later in the week. Next I joined the Christian Union and the Hindu Society, hoping to learn more about the faiths practiced by religious minorities in Pakistan.

I may have also heard a rumor that the Christians brought baked goods to your dorm room and the Hindus threw the best parties.

We hadn't been at the fair for a full hour when the complimentary tote bag I'd received at the entrance was bulging with new-member packets, event flyers, and free pens. I handed over my contact information and money for membership dues to anything that caught my interest—a philosophy reading group, a film club, the Pakistan and South Asia societies. Cora, by contrast, had signed up for only two organizations—the Conservative Association and the pub quiz team. "I definitely want to socialize," she explained. "I'm just not particularly sporty or musical or into whatever speedcubing is."

We both agreed that joining the Oxford Union, one of the oldest debating societies in the world, was essential. As a member, you could attend events and hear well-known politicians, writers, and artists argue over statements like "Celebrity icons have corrupted the feminist movement" or "Democracies should never ally with authoritarian regimes." You even got access to the Union's secret library.

The sign-up queue snaked around the room and out into the corridor. It was so densely packed that I couldn't even see the stall. As Cora and I approached the front of the line, a banner featuring the Union's famous former speakers came into view. I scanned each face: Albert Einstein, Malcolm X, Queen Elizabeth II, Ronald Reagan, and . . . me.

Oh no. My stomach dropped. I had nearly forgotten my first visit to the Union four years earlier. The details of my speech were long gone, but I remembered looking out at the students in their seats, wishing to fast-forward to a time when I could be in the audience, and not at the podium. Now I was finally here, and I had to resist the urge to run away. How was I going to be a normal student with my spotty teenage face blazed across the Freshers' Fair?

If Cora noticed that my cheeks had turned bright red, she didn't let on, though I was sure she'd seen the banner too. I kept my head down while I filled out my membership paperwork, trying not to make eye contact with my younger self.

As we walked away from the table, I noticed a group of girls staring at me and whispering. One of them rushed over. "Can we take selfies with you?" she asked. I was mortified, but declining felt rude, so I smiled and said yes. As soon as they snapped the first picture, I realized my mistake. Other students had noticed what was happening and began to form a line. When they started handing their phones to Cora to take group pictures, my chest tightened, certain that this would be our first and last outing together. Why would she want to be my friend if other students were pushing past her to get to me? But Cora just smiled as the line grew longer. "Maybe I should sign up for photography club," she joked, handing back the last selfie-seeker's phone.

"I'm so sorry," I said, and I meant it. I didn't want Cora to think that I was some sort of diva, the type of person who expects her friends to stay in the shadows while she takes the spotlight.

"Oh, it's completely fine," she said. "Though it must be pretty weird for you, no? Having people stop you like that?"

I gave her a surprised smile—it was rare for anyone to acknowledge the strange conditions of my life. "I mean, I'm used to it," I replied. "But I don't want people to treat me differently at college. I just want to blend in, be a normal student, you know?"

"Yeah, of course. Though I have to tell you . . . when my mom saw the news that you would be studying PPE in my year, she was so obnoxious. She said I should read all about your life in case we met!"

"Oh . . ." I paused. "Did you?"

"No! I told her it would be weird to go into uni knowing

everything about you, like a stalker," Cora said, rolling her eyes. "I figured if we got on, I could just ask you questions."

But Cora never asked about the shooting or the Taliban, meeting celebrities or being famous. In our first days on campus together, we talked about the dining hall food, her life growing up in Wales, the fact that we both had little brothers, what music we liked, whether we'd met any other nice people at Oxford so far. Sometimes we sat in my room, drinking tea and scrolling social media, not talking at all. The more time I spent with her, the more relaxed I felt.

My habit of curating myself and thinking before I spoke—shaped by years of being onstage and in front of cameras—started to fade in her presence. I must have seemed years younger to Cora, who, like most other students, came to Oxford with her first hangovers and heartbreaks already under her belt. But she didn't mock my outsize enthusiasm for every part of college life, from getting my own mailbox to seeing shirtless boys run past us in the park. Whatever I wanted to try, she was ready and willing to be my wingwoman. I even dragged her to Quran Club at one point.

As much as I wanted to get swept up in all the activity on campus, I found I was equally happy taking a long walk or sitting quietly with my new friend. In those early days, Cora gave me what I needed most—a blank page to write whatever story I chose.

4.

On Friday of Freshers' Week, I tumbled into a small, rectangular office two floors above the dining hall. "I got lost—I'm sorry," I stammered. Arriving twenty-five minutes late to our first meeting was not the way I hoped to meet my academic advisor, the professor assigned to monitor my progress for the next three years.

Lara had short brown hair and wore a simple navy frock, no makeup. I guessed she was in her mid-thirties. "First appointments are for finding your way," she said, gesturing for me to sit down.

I suspected I would need a lot more than one appointment to navigate this new world. Oxford is made up of forty-three different colleges—each with its own history, character, and campus—all under the banner of one university. I was studying at Lady Margaret Hall, otherwise known as LMH, a college set in a quiet corner of town on twelve acres that are mostly riverbank, forests, and gardens. I'd had a week to learn LMH's four main buildings, and was still taking wrong turns anytime I ventured out on my own.

In the remaining half hour of our meeting, Lara sped through Oxford's academic mechanics. PPE was a three-year degree. A college year at Oxford comprises three eight-week terms, starting in October and ending in June. Around Christmas and Easter, undergraduates have five-week breaks, but are expected to dedicate no less than twenty hours a week to their studies while they're away from campus.

"Oxford is very different from high school or college as it's depicted in American movies," she said. "We teach through tutorials, not classes, and students are expected to manage their own learning process."

Lara said I would take two courses per term. For each course, I would be expected to do the following every week: Read three or four books, plus academic journal articles and case studies. Write a two-thousand-word essay on an assigned topic; for economics, complete a mathematical problem set and mini-essay. Attend a tutorial—a one-hour meeting with my professor and one or two other students in the course.

"In tutorials, you will demonstrate what you've learned during the week," she said. "You should arrive prepared to participate in rigorous discussion and defend the ideas in your essays. Think of it as education through interrogation." I nodded energetically, like I couldn't wait to be questioned for my intellectual crimes.

"You also have the option of attending lectures on your subject matter," she continued. "These are open to all students in your discipline, from every college at Oxford. Not required, but strongly encouraged."

Lara informed me that undergraduates take exams at the end of their first and third years. The first-year exams, or prelims, determine whether a student is allowed to continue with their degree, whereas final exams determine your academic marks. Prelims, essays, tutorials—none of it counts toward your end result. But if you fail finals, you leave Oxford without a degree.

"Students are not allowed to have jobs during term time," Lara continued. "They must be present on campus and attend all tutorials." She folded her hands and looked at me with concern. "I know you have a lot of competing pressures and requests for your time, Malala. But I hope you will give yourself the space you need to succeed at Oxford."

She sat back and put her palms flat on the desk. "Okay, now that the basics are out of the way, did you bring your first problem set for economics? I would love to take a look at it to see where your math skills are at the starting point."

I felt an electric shock go through my body, followed by a prickling sensation in my scalp, feet, and armpits. *What problem set?*

Lara saw the look on my face. "In June, we sent all PPE students a reading list and mathematical exercises to complete before the start of term. Did you miss them?"

I had nothing to say but "I'm sorry." I'd spent the summer months traveling, giving speeches, and attending meetings. In what little downtime I had, I'd hung out with Alice and shopped for my new college wardrobe, totally unaware that I had homework to complete.

"All right," she said, logging on to her computer and emailing the documents to me. "Do the math assignment and drop it in the box outside my office. And you might want to dedicate the weekend to catching up on some of the pre-course reading."

On the stairs outside Lara's office, I reflexively bit my nails, a nervous habit I'd worked hard to curb in high school. College hadn't officially started, and I was already behind.

⌇

BEFORE WE LEFT Pakistan, I had read only a handful of books, maybe seven or eight. My small collection made its way to me in haphazard fashion—a friend of my father's brought me *A Brief History of Time*; tourists at a local guesthouse had left behind a worn-out paperback of *Pride and Prejudice*. Journalists from the United States and Europe contributed *Oliver Twist* and *Sophie's World*. I can't remember where Moniba and I found copies of the *Twilight* series, only that we read them together and spent many afternoons pretending we were vampires. Until I came to England, I'd never been inside a bookstore or a public library. To me, books were like fireflies—delighting with their unexpected arrival but not something you could see whenever you wished.

My younger self would've been overwhelmed by the library at Lady Margaret Hall, both a cozy refuge from busy student life and a fantasy world of more than eighty-five thousand books. Inside, it looks a bit like an old ship, with bookshelves surrounding the upper and lower decks and a long, open galley in the middle to let in the sunlight. Between every two rows of shelves, the architect placed study nooks that feature built-in desks centered on windows overlooking the gardens and river. When I first saw the library during my prospective student tour, I'd imagined spending hours and hours there, trying to read as many books as possible.

After my meeting with Lara, I was determined to plant myself at a desk in the library until I was caught up on my summer homework. I swung open the heavy wooden door and an eerie stillness hit me immediately. There were no other students or even staff in the room, just the brindle-coated library cat stretching out in the sun. *Quiet is good for concentration*, I reminded myself.

The first few problems weren't difficult—I'd always been decent at math. But farther down the page, they got more complicated, and I realized this was going to take longer than I'd expected. I put down my pencil and stared out the window at the autumn sunset flushing through the trees. On the other side of the glass, students were walking to dinner and riding bikes along the riverbank. A group of friends drifted across the lawn, chatting like they'd known each other for years. Suddenly the library felt claustrophobic and airless. *It's only Friday. Plenty of time to catch up over the weekend.* I tossed the books and papers in my bag, and abandoned the ship.

5.

"So, Club Night—you interested?" Cora asked me at dinner that evening.

I was definitely interested. Not because I intended to drink or go wild—I just wanted to see what it was like. In high school, a few of the girls went clubbing on weekends. They always described it the same way—"soooo crazy"—as if the rest of us couldn't possibly understand. Club Night was the closing event of Freshers' Week, an off-campus dance party at a place called Emporium. From the RSVPs on Facebook, it looked like everyone would be there.

My curiosity was outweighed by my fear of being photographed. British tabloids and Pakistani journalists had been hanging around LMH all week, taking pictures as I walked around campus and asking other students if they'd met me. I figured they would give up when they saw that I was just doing boring things like going to the library and the dining hall. Dancing at a night-club, though—that would be newsworthy.

If I said this to Cora, she would feel sorry for me and stay behind to keep me company. "Ugh, I wish I could, but I promised my academic advisor that I would finish this problem set," I sighed. "I want to hear all about it in the morning, though!"

After half an hour trying to make a dent in the math homework, I gave up and wandered down to the LMH bar, where the Freshers' Week schedule said there would be a pizza party for those who weren't attending Club Night. I arrived to an empty room and checked to make sure I was in the right place. When I confirmed that I was, I didn't know what to do, so I sat down at a table by myself, cringing every time I made eye contact with my security officers across the room.

I was debating leaving when another student arrived and marched over to my table. She had a wide smile and wore a denim skirtall over a white T-shirt and sneakers. To me, she looked like the cheery older girl they put on advertisements for things children don't want to do, like going to the dentist or summer school.

"Not clubbing tonight?" she asked, continuing before I could answer. "Me neither. I'm Hen. Henrica, but only to my mother."

"Hi, I'm Malala," I said, almost laughing in astonishment at her social confidence.

"Nice to meet ya. You shoot pool, or are you more of a Trivial Pursuit person?" We settled on Scrabble and, as we clicked our tiles around the board, Hen talked nonstop—about her favorite YouTubers, why she'd chosen history for her major, the boy she'd met earlier in the day who didn't know how to use the washing machine. She barely seemed to take a breath, and I nodded along, a willing audience for her thoughts. At heart, I'm an extroverted introvert; someone who knows how to be "on," but prefers not to take the lead in social situations. With Hen, I didn't have to say a word, and that alone moved her to the top of my potential friends list.

"Do you want to come up to my room and have some tea?" I asked when we were both full of pizza and bored with Scrabble.

"Lead the way," Hen replied.

We talked for hours that night. I learned about her life growing up in Zimbabwe, how she moved to the UK at age seven and worked the night shift at McDonald's in high school to help support her family. My jaw dropped when she recited her list of life goals: "Graduate Oxford. Get master's degree at Harvard. Become a TV host. Create my own talk show." Hen was only nineteen, but I was fully convinced she would make her dreams come true. I also knew we were destined to be friends. Her openness and energy made me feel included without being overwhelmed—like I could blurt out anything that popped into my head or say nothing at all, and she would understand me either way.

WHEN I INTRODUCED Cora and Hen, they hit it off and we formed a trio. I spent every minute I could with one or both of them—not in the way I'd clung to Alice in high school, like she was a human life raft, but because I loved every new thing I learned about them. Cora liked to blast movie soundtracks at top volume while she studied, and Hen had an elaborate seventeen-step nighttime ritual that could not, under any circumstances, be interrupted. They teased me for eating food past its sell-by date and only cleaning my room when my mom was coming to visit. We borrowed clothes from each other's closets and ate dinner together every night. After a lifetime of brothers, sisterhood felt like going to a foreign country and discovering I somehow already knew the language.

The effortlessness of my first two friendships gave me the courage to add to their number. I met Yasmin early one morning, while I was taking a walk by the river. In the first few weeks of college, I'd picked up the habit of starting my weekly essays the night before they were due and drinking tons of tea to stay awake, desperate to make the 8 a.m. deadline. If I finished early, I'd reward myself with a stroll down to the water to watch the sunrise in my pajamas.

One day I found a girl sitting cross-legged on my favorite bench in her bathrobe. "Did you have an essay crisis too?" I asked her. Yasmin and I kept meeting there once a week, watching the dawn light catch and swirl in the currents, then grabbing hot hash browns from the dining hall before going back to the dorm to catch up on sleep. As we talked, I learned her life story: She was born in Iran, but had fled an abusive father, immigrating to the UK as a teenager. In high school, she'd faced the same hardships as many refugees—the language barrier, poverty, paperwork—but she'd thrived in London, falling in love with indie bands, noodle shops, and detective shows. Now she was studying English literature and hoped to become a writer.

Anisa studied finance, and we were paired as tutorial partners for an economics course. I hadn't even introduced myself when she told me I was stirring my tea the wrong way. "Side to side, without touching the spoon to the mug," she said. "If you swirl it like that, you'll splash on your shirt."

Anisa's parents were from India, and had sent her to a British boarding school where she learned to play polo and shoot clay pigeons. Almost every time I saw her, she was laughing—often at someone else's expense, sometimes at mine. I had lived in the UK for five years at that point, but there were still a lot of things I didn't know. When I asked questions like "What's a bagel?" she called me "categorically thick" or "an absolute broomstick." My

Topshop jeans were "naff" and my taste in music was "moldy." Most of the time, I had no idea what she was saying. I only knew it wasn't nice.

In high school, I stayed as far away as possible from girls like Anisa. But by the time we met, I felt like I could handle the challenge of a mean friend. Sometimes her natural bossiness was an asset. On weekend days when I wanted to be lazy and sleep until 2 p.m., Anisa barged into my room and said, "Get up, we're leaving in ten minutes." She planned itineraries with military precision—brunch at the Jericho Café, browsing the stalls at the covered market, exploring the colleges we hadn't visited yet. And I was always glad I followed her orders.

For the first time in five years, I belonged to a gang of friends again. On my way back from lectures and tutorials, I would stop by each of their rooms to check in, chat, make plans. On weeknights, two or three of them would pile into my room under the pretense of studying together. That usually ended with our textbooks stacked on the floor and used as makeshift tables to hold nail polish or takeout food. The day after essays were due, when no one felt like working, we would go out to a pub or the college bar to chat with other students, or cram ourselves into a twin bed to watch a movie on someone's laptop.

I never went anywhere by myself. Even a routine trip to the grocery store felt more exciting with friends, getting their thoughts on shampoo brands and recommendations on frozen meals. When Yasmin needed new bras, we all tagged along and couldn't stop laughing at the middle-aged dads on my security team trying to figure out where to stand in the tiny lingerie shop. They were supposed to keep eyes on me at all times, but eventually decided it was acceptable, in this particular case, to wait outside on the street.

We were hanging out in Anisa's room one night when I

opened my email to see a message from the Hindu Society. "Oh my god! The members-only pre-sale for the Diwali Ball is open," I announced. "We should all go together! Say yes and I'll get the tickets right now."

"You're in the Hindu Society?" Yasmin asked.

Cora laughed. "Remember when I told you she went wild at the Freshers' Fair? It would be easier to list the clubs she didn't sign up for."

Most Oxford societies and colleges host balls every year. They begin with a fancy dinner, then live music and dancing until the following morning. I was dying to go to one, and the Diwali Ball, with its promises of an Indian food buffet and Bollywood music, sounded perfect.

Three weeks later, everyone gathered in my room to touch up their hair and makeup before we left for the ball. Anisa, Cora, and Hen opted for elegant strapless gowns in satin or crepe. I'd spent a lot of time perfecting my look: a black dress covered in sparkly beaded flowers and a headscarf with little pearls around the hem.

When Yasmin arrived in a sari, I thought she looked beautiful, but Anisa was not impressed. "Your pleating is all wrong," she said.

"It can't be!" Yasmin moaned. "I followed every step of the YouTube tutorial!"

"Yaz, I'm literally Indian. Let me fix it."

Re-draping the sari—and a mad scramble for safety pins— took an hour, which meant the party was in full swing by the time we arrived. I felt lightheaded and giddy as soon as I stepped into the ballroom. Spotlights had turned the cream-colored walls of Oxford Town Hall into a pink and purple fever dream and the ceiling was covered in twinkly stars. Everywhere I looked, there were women in electric-blue lehengas and cherry-red Anarkali suits; gold bangles cascaded up and down their forearms, rattling as they danced. Onstage, a DJ was spinning Bollywood and bhangra hits with occasional Western pop interludes. The music was so loud I could feel it in my chest like a second heartbeat.

"Let's dance!" Hen shouted.

"We just got here, and there's a whole other room to see. With food!" I replied.

"You can eat anywhere—I'm hitting the floor!" And then she disappeared into the pulsing crowd.

The second room had a live band playing Indian folk and classical music, henna stations where guests were getting their hands painted, and a large buffet. As we picked up our plates, I realized we'd lost Yasmin. I scanned the room and saw a tall guy in a suit hovering over her, talking a mile a minute. "Poor Yaz, that guy won't let her leave," I said. "I'll go save her."

Cora put her hand on my arm to stop me. "Check out her face," she said. "Not sure she wants to be rescued at the moment." I put on my glasses and saw that Yasmin was smiling and running a hand through her hair. *We've been here five minutes! How did she already find someone to flirt with?*

After dinner, Anisa and Cora joined Hen on the dance floor. I wandered around the room, taking it all in. After a few minutes of eavesdropping on a group of women discussing South Asian soap operas, I took a step closer and said, "Mind if I join you?" We spent almost an hour cracking up over the ridiculous plotlines— vengeful daughters-in-law, reincarnated husbands who come back as six-year-old boys, random nuclear bombs in corner stores. "It's like, I fully realize how absurd a show is, but then I'm also crying?" one of the women exclaimed.

A little after midnight, my friends finally got tired of dancing and were ready to go. Anisa went to find Yasmin, returning to report that she was at the bar, chatting it up with some boys, but would find us soon. Twenty minutes later, Anisa stomped off again and came back with an apologetic Yaz in tow.

In the coat check line, Hen suggested we stop by McDonald's on our way back to the dorm. "Oh, *now* you're hungry?" the rest of us squawked, before eventually acquiescing to her plan.

The place was packed with students, ordering burgers and fries to sober up or fuel their late-night study sessions. As we stood in the back of the line, I asked, "So, what's good here?"

Hen whipped around to face me. "Wait, wait, wait . . . have you *never* been to McDonald's?"

"Only once. It was in Pakistan and I got something called a 'McArabia,' which is basically just a shawarma. So . . . not too exciting, I guess."

The four of them were completely silent for a moment, then erupted in laughter.

"All right, here's what we're doing," Hen said. "Everybody pick their favorite thing on the menu and order it for Malala." I ended up with two boxes of chicken nuggets, a Big Mac, and a caramel frappé. We took our trays up to the second floor and sat by the window, where we could watch the other students drifting in and out. When Yasmin started showing off her henna to the boy at the next booth, Anisa insisted we call it a night.

The old bell tower on the quad chimed twice just as we reached the gates of Lady Margaret Hall. *Two a.m.!* I had never stayed out this late in my life. After high school graduation, I'd gone to dinner at Pizza Express with Alice and gotten home at eight thirty. At the time, even that small taste of freedom was thrilling for me. Now here I was, roaming around a city with my friends in the early morning hours.

After the Diwali Ball, my excitement for college life bordered on mania—I wanted to try everything. I combed through upcoming campus events, adding as many as possible to my calendar. There's a saying that every Oxford student knows: "College is study, sleep, and social life—but you can only pick two." It didn't take long to decide that one was enough for me.

6.

Rowing club met at sunrise. As I dressed in the dark for our first practice, I already regretted signing up for it in my Freshers' Fair haze. The full extent of my error hit me as soon as I reached the docks. These were not the charming wooden rowboats I'd seen lazing along the river—they were racing shells, long and narrow aluminum tubes with a heavy, twenty-foot oar at each seat.

"First thing you need to know, if you want to be a rower: you can't just step into the boat," the instructor announced. "If you put all your weight in at once, you'll sink. You place one foot on the side farthest from the dock and then squat, lowering yourself down and hovering your other leg over the boat until you're fully seated." I was now sure I did not want to be a rower, but it was too late to run away. Everyone had seen me.

With eight of us inside, the top of the boat was almost level with the water. One wrong move and I would go overboard, drowning in the river in my first month at Oxford. I had neglected to tell anyone that I didn't know how to swim. Just a small, unimportant detail.

The instructor pushed the boat off the dock with her oar. I rowed as hard as I could but did little more than splash the water's surface, alternating between saying prayers and holding my breath for the entire practice. Afterward I went back to my room, collapsed on the bed, and slept for a few hours.

When I woke up, my phone was buzzing with Twitter notifications and WhatsApp messages. Someone had snapped a picture of me walking back to the dorm after rowing practice and sent it to a popular Pakistani Facebook group. From there it spread to other social media platforms, then to Urdu-language news sites and TV channels. In the photo, I'm wearing jeans, a T-shirt, and a nylon bomber jacket. The faint morning light is falling on my headscarf.

Hundreds of people, mostly Pakistani men, voiced their shock that I was wearing jeans instead of a shalwar kameez. There were comments calling me a traitor or a porn star; others claimed my clothes were a sign that I had abandoned my country and religion. A few wrote that it was shameful that I had walked down the street on my own without a father or brother to monitor me. *This is absurd*, I thought. *Because of jeans?* I'd expected some sort of uproar about my college life, but not this soon, or over something so stupid.

My phone rang and I knew who it was without looking at the screen. "Why did you wear those clothes?" my mom demanded. "Our relatives are calling! Everyone at home is talking about you."

My mom's anger always shook me, but I knew I had to stand up for myself. If I gave in now, I'd have to do it again and again for all three years of college. I might as well move back home and let my parents run my life.

"I was going to rowing club, not on a religious pilgrimage, Mom. I'm not a diplomat representing my country or culture. I'm just a student! And I want to have a normal life, at least while I'm at college."

"You are not *just a student*," she hissed, then changed tack. "Zia, you speak to her."

My shoulders relaxed—I'd always had an easier relationship with my dad. "Hello, Malala," he said in a weary voice. "So what will we do about this? People are very upset." Criticism from Pakistan always unnerved him. He desperately wanted to go back home someday, and didn't want to find himself an outcast when he got there.

"Dad, this is so unfair. Look at my brothers, *your* sons— they wear jeans and hoodies every day and no one says they're less Muslim or Pakistani or Pashtun. Men and boys can wear whatever they please, so why can't I?"

I could hear the resignation—and a hint of pride—in his voice. "I suppose you're right about that, Malala," he said. "You are right."

I hung up the phone feeling justified but still frustrated. Jeans are not a crime against Islam and not wearing a shalwar kameez didn't make me any less Pakistani. But too often in my home country, women's bodies are used to measure the strength of our religious beliefs and national identity. Challenge the social norms created and enforced by men, and you disgrace your family and community. That morning, it meant that the patriarchy had grown so fragile that it could be threatened by a pair of jeans. On darker days, it meant a woman could be killed for rejecting a suitor or posting pictures of herself on Instagram. When a man's honor lies in a woman's body, he will take her life to reclaim it.

I was only eight years old when I learned what would happen if I broke these rules. One afternoon my little brother Khushal and I followed some neighborhood kids to a nearby stream. On hot days, we liked to splash around and throw water on each other, soaking our hair and clothes until we cooled off. Walking home, we ran into our teenage cousin. "Where have you been?" he demanded.

"Playing with my friends," I answered, unsure what I had done wrong.

"You bring dishonor on your family," he seethed, "parading around with your clothes tight and sticking to your body for everyone to see." Then he raised his hand above his head and slapped me hard across the cheek.

The shame lingered much longer than the physical pain. For a while, I stopped going outside and kept to my room when we had guests. I felt nauseated when I thought about the slap, yet I couldn't stop replaying it in my mind. It was a brutal introduction to the way some men police women's bodies, protecting their power under the guise of "honor" and "tradition."

My phone kept buzzing; when I picked it up again, I found that the online conversation was spreading beyond Pakistan. Tabloid websites had compiled the most hateful tweets and rushed to publish their clickbait. Thousands of people shared the *Daily Mail*'s story, "Nobel Prize Winner Malala Yousafzai Is Targeted by Vile Trolls for Wearing Skinny Jeans."

Most of the comments were a mix of "her body, her choice" and "leave her alone." I paused at a reply from a reader in the Czech Republic: *It is not the UK or the Western world she needs to impress. They, for the most part, respect a woman's right to education. But her own people expect her to dress the part. No matter what she does or where she is, she will always be an object of interest as well as ridicule. By adhering to a dress code acceptable to her critics, she will get more positive attention for her cause.*

It surprised me that someone who didn't know me or live in

my country could understand the impasse so well. It was true: If I wanted to promote education and equality for girls and women in Pakistan, I had to be inoffensive in every way. I felt responsible for proving that an educated girl is not a threat. As long as I conformed to my culture's rules and dress code, no one in my community could say, "Look how Malala turned out. We are right to keep a tight leash on our daughters."

Every time I gave a speech and mentioned the millions of girls around the world who weren't in school, the same faces ran through my mind: My cousin who came home one day to learn she would never go back to the classroom because her father had arranged her marriage. A friend who had two babies by the time she was fifteen. The child laborers I saw everywhere in Mingora—girls who cleaned houses, sold oranges by the side of the road, sifted through garbage dumps for scrap metal.

To help girls like them, I had tried, for a long time, to obey all the rules — to wear the clothes my mom picked out, to be the deferential daughter that Pakistani parents expect. But maintaining that balance was starting to feel like a trap. I could stand behind a podium all day, calling out the worst abuses perpetrated by men, and it would never stir up the level of media attention that wearing jeans did. So why should I even try to placate my critics?

Choosing what I wore was a small rebellion, but clothes symbolized freedom and anonymity to me. They gave me confidence, especially at Oxford. I couldn't live a normal life if I was always looking over my shoulder, trying not to cause a scandal.

I knew I should turn off my phone for the rest of the day, but morbid curiosity made me open the *Daily Mail* story again. A few commenters were taking issue with my headscarf, claiming it was a symbol of oppression and arguing that I could not be fully emancipated until I erased all traces of my ethnicity and my faith. Those opinions were as unwelcome as the others—I wouldn't justify my choices to the secular mob any more than I would to the denim police.

My scarves reminded me of home and helped me connect to a world I had lost. No matter what the misogynists or Islamophobes said, I wanted girls in Pakistan to know that I had not forgotten them. If I was going to be photographed without my consent, at least they would see that a girl in a scarf could walk down the street on her own, go to college—or even row a boat.

7.

One night in the dining hall, shortly before the winter break, Cora and I chatted with a third-year student. I've since forgotten his name, but I remember the question he asked us: "Have you been to the bell tower?" When we said no, he insisted it was an experience that every Lady Margaret Hall student must try once. "If you're up for it," he said, "meet me in the quad at midnight."

Something about the way he said it told me this would be a covert mission. I informed my security guards that I was staying on campus for the night. If they assumed I meant in the dorm, that was their mistake. Cora and I slipped outside and stared up at the cupola housing an old iron bell that rang every hour. "How do we get up there?" I asked.

"Quietly," our guide whispered. "If the college catches us . . . well, I don't want to say we'd be kicked out. No one has ever been caught, so I'm not really sure what the punishment is, but it likely won't be good." He put a finger to his lips, and we followed him into the building.

On the fourth floor, he opened the door to the student prayer room—a cramped and carpeted rectangle with a small window on the opposite wall. "First step, climb out this window and walk to the corner of the building." I looked below the windowsill to see a narrow ledge, not more than seven inches wide. Below the ledge was a multistory drop to the cobblestone courtyard.

"When you get to the end, there's a short jump to the next section of roof, only about three feet. You can easily make it—just don't look down."

I stuck my head out to watch as he balanced along the ledge, made the jump, and threw his arms in the air to show us how easy it was. Then I looked back at Cora. "I can't," she said, shaking her head.

"That's all right," I replied. "But . . . do you mind if I do?"

Whatever her answer, I knew I would go anyway. People had been watching me my entire life, making sure I followed the rules, obeyed orders, stuck to the script. Since arriving at college, I felt high on independence. Every choice, even the bad ones, belonged to me.

Cora's face shifted from concerned to supportive and back again. "If you're sure. I'll wait for you here and . . . pray, I guess?" She gave a weak laugh, and I went out the window.

A blast of cold December air hit my face. Keeping my eyes straight ahead, I teetered down the narrow ledge and jumped as quickly as I could. As soon as my shoes hit the flat, square section of roof, blood poured through my heart like a whirlpool. I tossed my head back and inhaled, putting a hand on my chest to mark the spot where I needed the air to travel. A few seconds later, I was full of energy and ready to climb higher.

"Good job, you've done the hard part," my guide said. "But the next bit is dangerous in its own way." He pointed to a steel staircase leading up to the bell tower, built for maintenance workers who needed to access the cupola. "We climb up this little slant of roof, lob ourselves over the railing, and then scramble up those stairs. The challenge is those floodlights. Until we make it to the top, we'll be in full view of the whole college, so be quick and silent, okay?" I nodded, and off we went, racing across the roof tiles, up the stairs, and finally into the bell tower.

This rooftop path, I later learned, was likely discovered by the Night Climbers, a secretive student society dedicated to scaling tall buildings and walking high above the sleeping city. Founded in the 1930s, the group has climbed every college landmark, including Radcliffe Camera (140 feet) and Tom Tower (150 feet) at Christ Church College. At roughly 50 feet, the bell tower was a beginner course, though just as punishing if you happened to fall.

All Night Climbers are thrill-seekers, but they have different reasons for taking risks. Some enjoy working out the puzzle of an old building with its jumble of parapets, cornices, and crenellations. There are pranksters who steal weather vanes, and protestors who hang banners against homelessness and war. Others simply love to climb, using libraries and cathedrals in place of mountains. I suspected a few of them were like me, chasing the wonder and endless possibility in the world. Most of my peers couldn't imagine growing old, but I understood how quickly youth escapes, how you could lose it even as a child. I'd seen enough of the adult world to trade my safety for freedom and adventure.

I smiled to myself, imagining what my parents, high school teachers, and all the adults I knew assumed about my Oxford life. In their minds, I was studying day and night, certain to earn academic honors. They probably pictured my friends and me having heady debates about global politics in our free time. *That girl, the one I'm supposed to be, wouldn't take any risks,* I thought. *She wouldn't know what her college looks like from the rooftops. She would never see any of this!*

As I stood in the bell tower, I scanned the horizon, looking out at the dorms, the yellow light shining back at me from almost every window. Behind those walls, my friends were laughing, reading, brushing their teeth before bed, or putting on their coats to go out again. Crossing to the other side of the tower to see the gardens, I watched a group of students huddled together on the grass. I smiled, wondering what secret they were sharing. Beyond them, the River Cherwell lay still and quiet in the moonlight, like a silver ribbon dropped at the edge of the forest.

I want to stay here forever, I thought.

My first term at college felt like living in a constant state of amazement, new wonders and revelations unfolding all around me. I had rowed a boat, stayed out past midnight, and now scaled a rooftop! But the best part was waking up every morning and remembering that I had friends—four friends who were always there, saving me a seat at breakfast or waiting for me to get ready so we could walk together to the lecture halls. For the first time in years, I felt like myself again.

The 1 a.m. bell was about to strike, and my guide said it was time to go. On the way up, I hadn't thought at all about the reverse trip. Instead of hurtling my body onto a flat surface, now I had to make the leap and touch down toes-first on the narrow ledge with nothing to grab on to, no way to steady myself. A shudder ran through me as I looked down, searching for ground beneath four stories of shadows. But the moment I jumped, I knew I would do it again and again.

8.

My parents' doorbell must have rung a thousand times over the Christmas break. Every afternoon guests came for tea; as soon as they left, another group arrived for dinner. My dad, who had always thrived on socializing, loved it. I was less enthusiastic.

When I was in Birmingham, my dad treated our house like an art museum and me like the signature piece in the collection. In his mind, no one would go to the Louvre without seeing the *Mona Lisa*; the least I could do was give our visitors an autograph, a selfie, and a couple of hours of polite conversation. I half expected to come home one day and find our small vestibule converted to a gift shop featuring key chains and postcards with my face on them, maybe a Malala-themed umbrella or snow globe. It was my first break from college, and I wanted to lounge around the house, watch TV, and eat my mom's food. But it's impossible to relax when you're always on display.

With all the commotion, I couldn't devote twenty hours per week to studying over the break as Oxford recommended. I needed time to prepare for "collections," a series of mini-exams undergraduate students take at the start of every new term. They don't count toward your final marks, but professors and academic advisors use the tests to monitor your progress. As I wasn't the most diligent student in my first term, I had hoped to spend the holiday catching up. But between the parade of visitors and finally getting some proper sleep, that seemed impossible.

I went back to Oxford a couple of days early, hoping to somehow master eight weeks of material in forty-eight hours. The dining hall was closed, so I ate dry cereal in my room, not wanting to spend the fifteen minutes it would take to run out for milk. My philosophy study session went pretty well, but I couldn't bring myself to open the economics textbook. If I did, it would only remind me of all the things I didn't understand and couldn't possibly learn before collections.

The next day, I shuffled into the econ test a sleep-deprived wreck. When the professor called time after three hours, my hands were shaking. I had only answered half of the questions, and the finished half was subpar at best. On the walk back to the dorm, I was filled with regret—angry at myself for not staying on top of my coursework, angry at my dad for making it so difficult to study at home.

Hen was waiting at my door. "Yay! You're done with first collections! Mine are tomorrow—tell me everything. How did it go?" she said. I shook my head, went into my room, and cried for the first time at college. Two days later, Lara sent an email asking to meet with me about the results. When I opened her message, I was at the airport boarding a plane for Beirut.

⌒

BEFORE GOING TO Oxford, I didn't think about how being a college student would affect my work for girls' education. In high school, I'd spent my free time on calls or in meetings, dedicating weekends and summer breaks to traveling around the world to advocate for every child's right to learn. But now I had friends, a packed social calendar, a much fuller life. When I was binge-watching TV shows or gossiping with my girlfriends, I sometimes felt guilty for having fun, telling myself that I was wasting time and ignoring my mission. I thought of girls I knew in Pakistan or those I'd met in refugee camps on my travels: *Why should I be here when they are not?* Socializing, and even studying, could make me question my value as an activist, as if having any sort of life while other young women suffered was a betrayal.

In the months after I was shot, thousands of people reached out to ask how they could support me. From my hospital bed, I signed the paperwork to set up Malala Fund, an organization that could redirect all the attention I received into helping other girls go to school. Once I'd recovered, my dad and the staff at Malala Fund encouraged me to take advantage of interest in my story— to speak at events, give interviews, meet with politicians. If I really wanted to help girls, they said, I needed to leverage my public profile and advocate for education in every possible forum.

The pressure—of knowing I could make an impact, yet always feeling like I wasn't doing enough—built inside me, until I started to believe that I was personally responsible for delaying progress. If I wanted to sleep in on a Saturday instead of practicing for an upcoming speech, out-of-school girls would suffer. If I skipped a meeting and went to the movies with my brothers, new schools wouldn't be built for children in need. *God saved my life for a reason,* I reminded myself. *And I must spend it helping others.* I felt compelled to say yes to every invitation, to go wherever people told me I was needed.

I assumed Oxford would offer a mandatory break from work, as students weren't permitted to travel during term time. But the requests kept coming. "Could you miss just a couple of days?" people asked. "If you come to this event, it will really make a difference for girls' education." I couldn't say no. That's how I found myself, in the first week of my second term at college, blowing off essays and skipping tutorials to fly to three countries in eight days.

First I went to Lebanon to give Apple CEO Tim Cook a tour of Malala Fund's alternative education programs for Syrian girls, refugees of their country's civil war. I came back to Oxford for one afternoon to repack my bag. Then I flew to Switzerland to speak on a panel with Canadian Prime Minister Justin Trudeau. In truth, the panel was just a ruse; the team at Malala Fund wanted me to corner Trudeau in the green room and press him to make education aid a priority when Canada hosted the G7 Summit later that year.

Both efforts paid off: Apple's support helped fund education programs in countries like Brazil, Nigeria, and Pakistan; and G7 leaders pledged $3.8 billion to girls' and women's initiatives when Trudeau hosted the summit that year. But I returned to Oxford exhausted and stressed out over missing a few days of coursework.

My friends could sense my anxiety and tried to help. Cora shared her lecture notes and essays with me; Anisa spent a few hours walking me through the week's economics problem set. I studied all weekend, but still hadn't caught up.

On Monday morning, Lara sent a note asking me to come to her office later that afternoon. I watched the hours tick by all day, and felt like a big rock had settled in my stomach as I opened her door. "Well, I would ask why you missed your tutorials last week, but I don't have to because you were on the news twice from two different continents!" she said with a cheeriness that slightly scared me.

"I'm sorry I had to skip, but I felt like it was important for my work," I replied solemnly.

"Malala, your professors and I realize you have responsibilities that your peers do not. But it is our duty to prioritize your education, and we can't do that if you're not physically here."

"I understand," I said, slumping in my chair.

"I know that your work is not a job in the traditional sense, but the end result is the same. You are not focused on your studies."

I shifted uncomfortably in my seat and waited for Lara to continue.

"Your collections results show that your proficiency is not where it should be and, after last week, you've fallen further behind. I can help you regain your footing, but can we agree that you won't travel again during term time?"

The stone in my stomach rolled over. "I, um . . . I have to go to Monaco tomorrow." Lara's face reminded me of a Pashtun idiom I'd heard as a child—she looked like she was "sitting on a sack of pepper."

"I'm going to speak to business leaders about the economic importance of girls' education," I added, as if it were an extra credit project.

It was true, but not the whole truth. I didn't tell Lara that, unlike my trips to Lebanon and Switzerland, the conference organizers in Monaco were paying me for my appearance. When she'd mentioned the "no job" rule during Freshers' Week, I'd pictured working in a bookstore or coffee shop. Getting paid to give speeches didn't seem the same to me. I wasn't sure Lara would agree.

The truth was, I couldn't stop working, even when I wanted to. After my family settled in Birmingham, I became our only source of income. My dad had been a teacher in Mingora, but he wasn't licensed in the UK. My mom couldn't speak English, and my brothers were too young to take jobs. My speaking engagements paid for my parents' mortgage, my brothers' school fees, my take-out dinners—everything we needed to live.

Like Hen and many other first- and second-generation immigrant kids, I was expected to share everything I earned—not just with my immediate family, but with those in our home country as well. We sent thousands of dollars a year to people in Pakistan to buy medicine, food, air conditioners for the sweltering summer months. We paid for cars, livestock, even entire homes. My dad had promised to cover the costs for two daughters of a family friend to study abroad, as their lives were in danger at home. One girl was accepted to college in the United States and one in Canada. When my brother Khushal graduated high school the following year, I would need to make enough money for four college tuitions on top of all the other expenses.

At twenty years old, I was earning more than my family ever had in Pakistan. But we gave so much away that we lived paycheck to paycheck, and I worried about our household bills. I couldn't cancel my speaking engagement in Monaco, and I didn't know how to explain this to Lara.

"So counting last week and this week, you will miss twenty-five percent of the tutorials this term," she said with a heavy sigh. "I will speak to your professors about scheduling some replacement sessions. And you will need to work very hard to catch up."

Lara continued talking, her voice fading in and out in my mind. I could only focus on one thing: For the first time in my life, I was a bad student. Not just struggling, like I had in high school, but unfocused and irresponsible. As I walked away from her office, my legs felt unsteady as if gravity, and everything else I thought I understood, had vanished.

9.

Cora, Anisa, and I were working on our econ problem sets in my room when Hen and Yasmin burst through the door. "Yaz is bailing on me! At the very last minute!" Hen wailed.

Yasmin gave a look that was half frightened, half amused. "I told you I'd go next time," she said.

"There won't be a 'next time'! Malala, you have a Nobel Peace Prize—mediate," Hen demanded.

"Not sure that qualifies me for interpersonal conflicts, but what's the problem?" I asked.

Hen explained that, weeks ago, Yasmin had agreed to go with her to a cooking class with a visiting American chef, an expert in soul food. "You have to have a partner to participate, and now she's saying she can't because some guy said he *might* be free to hang out tonight."

"I could go with you," I offered.

Without looking up from her calculations, Anisa overruled me: "No—you need to study. Also there will probably be ham involved."

"Fair points," I said, looking back at Hen with sympathy. "Yaz, what's the story with this boy?"

She handed me her phone and I scanned her texts with the potential love interest. Over the last week, Yasmin had been trying to keep the conversation alive with jokes, invitations, questions that required more than a yes or no response. She'd send five or six messages in a row. A day or two later, he'd respond with "nice," "sorry, can't make it. essay deadline," or "maybe this weekend if I have time."

It seemed obvious to me that he was signaling disinterest, but Yasmin refused to take the hint. "If you met him, you'd understand why he's perfect for me," she said. "I just need us to hang out more so I can show him that I'd make a great girlfriend." Out of the corner of my eye, I saw Cora wince.

"Yaz, maybe don't get off the train at the first stop," I said gently. "There are lots of boys at Oxford; try meeting as many as you can."

"But I have tried—you've all seen me trying!" Yasmin replied, as the rest of us cackled in agreement. "This guy, though . . . he's different. You're telling me to just give up on him?"

"Give up on *waiting* for him. Make your own plans; keep the plans you already made. You're at college and you have more exciting things to do than audition for his attention."

All four of them gawked at me like they'd just discovered I had a secret superpower. After that night, everyone started asking me for advice. Cora couldn't figure out why her relationship with her high school boyfriend wasn't working anymore. He hadn't done anything wrong, but she'd felt so bored and restless when they hung out over Christmas break.

"It's because you've changed," I said. "Your life is here now, and you want to be free to explore, but you feel guilty about it." They broke up a week later. (He had a new girlfriend within a month, and Cora tried to follow her private account on Instagram. When the girl blocked her, we tried again from my verified profile with more than a million followers. She blocked me too, which both Cora and I had to admit was pretty cool on her part.)

Hen preferred dating apps to meeting a man at college. At night we would sit on my bed and scroll through the latest crop of profiles. *"Looking to meet new people and see where things go,"* I read aloud, rolling my eyes. "Why doesn't he just say he only wants to hook up?" I acted as Hen's unofficial security consultant, weeding out the bad prospects—mainly those who mentioned crypto or posed in front of their car. One time I sensed a guy was trouble and she ignored me; he ended up stealing her debit card and emptying her bank account.

I had somehow become the resident advisor on romance, examining carefully cropped photos, cryptic text messages, and astrological charts with much more intensity than I brought to my textbooks. "How are you so good at spotting red flags when you've never been on a date?" Hen asked me.

I shrugged it off. "I guess I'm a better coach than a player."

It was a quippy line that hid the truth: Getting a boyfriend would be pushing my independent streak much too far. In Pashtun culture, dating doesn't exist. Most men in my community forbid their wives, daughters, and sisters to have any contact with the opposite sex. If a girl was seen talking to a boy, she disgraced her family and put her own life at risk. Even looking could cause trouble. People liked to remind young women of the rules with old sayings like "The most honorable girl will always keep her eyes on the ground, even when her village is on fire." And if a man ogled

54

her? That was also her fault, as she must have done something to draw attention to herself.

Most Pashtun fathers decide when their daughters will marry, often around fourteen or fifteen years old. Marriages are arranged and negotiated, a routine transfer of property between men. Defying their authority—and following your heart—can be dangerous. Growing up, I knew of several young women who were poisoned by their families for crimes of "dishonor"—from looking too long at a boy in the street to having a secret cell phone to exchange messages with their crush. The parents always claimed it was suicide, but everyone knew the truth.

I was now living five thousand miles away in a place with much different social norms, but people in my home country were still monitoring me. On a flight home from a trip to New York, I saw David Beckham on the plane, and we took a quick photo together. When a Pakistani newspaper published the image, friends and family called my dad to say the Pashtun community was outraged that I had stood so close to a man. "Did you tell them it was *David Beckham* and that he smells amazing?" I wanted to say to my parents, but I knew better and held my tongue.

On another occasion, Prince Harry and I were invited to speak at the same event. When he put his arm around my shoulders for a photo, my mom stepped in front of the cameras and swatted his hand away, to the dismay of everyone in the room. "No touch!" she boomed, wagging her finger in his face. Harry apologized profusely, and I was mortified. But my mom couldn't concern herself with royal protocol or publicly embarrassing her daughter in front of a prince; she was much more worried about what would happen if her neighbors in Mingora saw the picture.

Wearing jeans was one thing, but a college romance would make me a pariah in the eyes of my people. If I had explained all this to my friends, I knew what they would say: *Those views are archaic and antifeminist! You are an adult woman in a free country with the power to make your own decisions!* They would be right—but that didn't mean I could live as I pleased. Dating wasn't worth the potential damage to me, my family, and my work.

Besides, boys were a huge distraction. How else to explain my brilliant, accomplished friends making such poor decisions in their love lives? Not me, I was above all of that. I would have some fun at college, graduate, and then go straight back to work, dedicating the rest of my life to the good cause of girls' education. *I'll be like a nun*, I thought. *But Muslim.*

At least, that's the story I told myself. Sometimes late at night when I couldn't sleep and took to writing in my journal, another truth emerged: I didn't believe that anyone would want me. No matter how much confidence I projected onstage and in speeches, I felt too ugly to love.

It was a harsh truth, and one I hated admitting to myself because it felt so vain and trivial. Once upon a time, I would spend hours in the bathroom styling my hair, imagining myself in a Bollywood movie with Shah Rukh Khan. That teenage girl was puckishly pretty, quick to smile. But ever since the shooting, I was something different—my face and body were now meant for service, not romance. *You don't need to be attractive to be an activist*, I told myself.

When I was in the hospital, doctors said that my facial paralysis would decrease and the ability to move my face would return over time. After five years, the improvements were minor at best. My left eye still drooped. When I smiled, my mouth only moved on one side. Online trolls created memes comparing my laughing face to a braying donkey. I started covering my mouth with both hands whenever someone told a joke.

Every few months I saw a nurse for Botox injections; they

froze the muscles on the working side of my face to make the paralysis less noticeable. It seemed the best I could hope for was a flattening of all expression, a face locked in permanent solemnity like a statue in a cemetery.

Between the strict social norms I grew up with and the damage to my face, it was easier to tell myself that dating wasn't an option and put it out of my mind. Why spend time being sad about things you can't change?

Instead, I channeled all my energy into my friends' love lives, living vicariously through their dating dramas and laughing at their aspirational swooning. It seemed like every girl I knew was obsessed with Timothée Chalamet that winter, and could spend a full hour discussing his hair or playing clips of him speaking in French. I didn't get the infatuation, as I'd always been immune to the appeal of pretty boys. The man of my dreams was brown-skinned, rough, and hairy. My knees went weak at the sight of a dark beard, wooly forearms, and tufts of chest hair poking out of a shirt. Telling myself that I'd never have a boyfriend wasn't enough to stop me from secretly wanting one.

But that was all a fantasy, something to smile about as I fell asleep at night. Even if I woke up with a normal face and no cultural baggage, I wouldn't find a guy like that among the gawky Oxford undergrads.

And then I met Tarik.

10.

The first time I saw him, I was sitting on a bench outside my dorm, enjoying a fleeting moment of January sunshine. I looked across the quad to see a tall, broad-shouldered stranger walking toward me. As he got closer, I could make out his loose black curls and broody eyes.

He sat down on the opposite end of my bench; I froze. He didn't speak or even look at me, just curved his perfect lips around a cigarette, took out a book, and started to read.

"Um, hi," I said. My voice sounded like someone was squeezing it out of a tube. "I don't mind at all, but I think you're not allowed to smoke here?" I pointed to the space between us where a brass NO SMOKING sign was tacked to the back of the bench.

"Can't read that," he replied, still looking at his book. "Dyslexic."

"Oh, of course, I'm sorry. Well . . . enjoy!"

I hopped off the bench and scurried back to my room. "Of course" you're dyslexic? "Enjoy" smoking? Was there a type of dyslexia that meant you could read books but not signs? Had he made a joke and I missed it? For all the advice I gave to other people, I was disastrously bad at talking to boys.

The cold weather was back when I saw him again. Yasmin and I were standing in a hallway outside the library, warming our legs on the radiators and drinking low-grade hot chocolate from the vending machine. He walked past me and mumbled, "All right, mate."

As soon as he was gone, Yasmin grabbed my arm. "How do you know Tarik?"

"I don't even know his name! I've only seen him once before. Though I wouldn't mind seeing him again. . . ."

"Eh, I don't know, Malz," she said. "Gorgeous for sure, but he hasn't got the best reputation."

She told me Tarik's family had immigrated from Morocco to a rough neighborhood in North London. In high school, he'd been an academic sensation, earning some of the best scores in the country on his college entrance exams. When he enrolled in the business course at Lady Margaret Hall, he was one of the brightest students in his year. "But that was three years ago," Yasmin continued.

Since then, the college had put Tarik on academic probation multiple times for plagiarizing essays, skipping tutorials, and starting fistfights. "And everyone knows he sells drugs," she said. I assumed Yasmin was exaggerating. And if she wasn't, then all the more reason to befriend this mystery man. *I could help him get back on the right path. . . .*

Tarik was twenty-four and starting from scratch in first-year classes. Oxford was giving him one last chance to deliver on his academic promise. "So he'll graduate with us?" I asked.

"Don't hold your breath," she replied.

A week later, he drifted past the library around 11 p.m., looking so mysterious with the collar of his black coat pulled up around his ears to block the wind. I was on my way to pick up a book I needed for an essay due the next morning. I thought he might walk right by me, but he stopped about a foot away, looked at his phone, and said, "Ah, I guess I missed dinner."

"Yes, by about . . . four hours?"

"Shit, I'm so hungry now."

I saw my opening and took it. "I have some snacks in my room if you want to come up."

He shoved his hands deep in his pockets. "Sure."

We crossed the quad to my dorm. "You're in my building. That's me. Room 205," he said, pointing to a second-floor window.

"Really? How are you one floor below me and I've never seen you on the stairs?" I asked. Tarik shrugged.

"Would you like some tea?" I offered when we reached my room. He nodded.

"There's a bowl of fruit and some snacks on the bookshelf," I said. He took a banana. When he finished that, he ate an orange. Then he polished off a whole sleeve of biscuits and two oat bars with his tea. Neither of us said a word until he was finished.

"Well, thanks for that," he said, standing up to leave. "Appreciate it."

"Stop by anytime!"

He was gone, but my room still smelled like him. As long as I can remember, I've been attracted to strong scents. Petrol. Fresh paint and felt-tip pens. Chlorine fumes at an indoor pool. Tarik's sharp mix of cigarettes and cheap cologne made me collapse on my bed and laugh into my pillow.

⌒

IN ANTICIPATION OF another encounter, I restocked my snacks, adding Pot Noodles and heartier fare I thought Tarik might enjoy. He stopped by again and didn't ask for food but ate everything I offered him. Given his background, I assumed he was on scholarship and receiving a living expenses stipend from the university. Most of my friends got financial assistance, so I knew it was enough to cover books, meals, and more. But I had never seen him at the dining hall, the halal cart, or any of the restaurants in town. It seemed like the only time he ate was in my room.

"Maybe his family needs help, and he gives them his stipend to make ends meet," I suggested to Yasmin.

"Or maybe you just want to see the best in him," she replied. "Yeah, he's had a hard life, but honestly, if he doesn't have money, he's the world's worst drug dealer because I saw him selling pills in University Park literally yesterday." My shoulders slightly tensed at the thought that she was now the sensible one and I was the fantasist. I shook it off.

It must have been my snack selection, because Tarik certainly wasn't in it for the conversation. I tried my best to seem interesting and bright, but our chats usually went like this:

Me: "Are you going to the bop this week?"
Him: "Nah, I hate that stuff."
Me: "Do you like studying business?"
Him: "It's all right."
Me: "Well, it must be harder than my courses because you can't make things up like we do in politics and philosophy! Ha-ha!"
Him: "Ha. Yeah."

After a few lackluster visits, I had an idea to liven things up. "Do you want to see my favorite place in the whole college?" I asked. He

61

looked mildly intrigued. "But it has to be our secret," I said mysteri-ously. "You can't tell anyone."

"I'll take it to my grave," he replied.

Climbing up to the bell tower, I was thrilled by how many rules I was breaking: Oxford's restrictions against night climbing, my parents' prohibition on boys, the law of gravity. Tarik might've been the bad boy of Lady Margaret Hall, but tonight we were partners in crime.

When we reached the top, I looked up and saw a canopy of stars. Usually I preferred looking down at the campus—but tonight it felt like I was floating in the sky, like I could reach out and touch things that were light-years away. Tarik sat with his legs stretched out, looking more relaxed than I'd ever seen him.

"If you could go anywhere right now, where would it be?" he asked.

I put a hand to my mouth to hide a smile. It was the first real question he'd ever asked me—and the same thought I'd had the first time I stood in the bell tower. My answer hadn't changed: I wanted to stay here forever.

"I would go and find my dad and bring him home," he contin-ued. "He's in Marrakesh or maybe Algiers. I don't know where, but I think I could find him."

"When was the last time you saw him?" I asked.

"Years ago," he replied.

I understood what it was like to miss someone you hadn't seen in a long time. You worry that the other person might change in your absence, that you won't be able to connect in the same way when you see them again. As time goes on, you think of them less and feel guilty when you do. *I should call Moniba soon*, I thought. Tarik looked back up at the sky and we sat in silence for a while.

On the descent, I went ahead of him, deftly maneuvering over the balustrade and down the roof tiles. As Tarik made the big jump onto the ledge, one of his shoes came loose. I heard a loud *thwack* as it hit the ground and then watched with mounting panic as a campus security guard appeared on the ground below, shining his flashlight into the space between the buildings. Tarik and I scrambled through the window and then ran out of the prayer room in opposite directions.

My heart was still pumping when I reached the dorm and bumped into Cora. "Where were you?" she asked.

"On the roof. With Tarik."

"Yikes." Her face became a human emoji, mouth pulled into an exaggerated grimace.

She doesn't understand him like I do, I thought.

Tarik was always away on the weekends, and I lay in bed wondering where he went. To see his family? Or maybe Yasmin was right and he was wherever drug dealers go—I imagined a shadowy lair filled with men counting money and fixing motorcycles.

He turned up again after midnight on a Wednesday. I was still awake, sitting at my desk and working on an essay. "Hey! Where have you been?" I asked.

"Had to take care of some business. And see some friends."

"Am I your friend?" I said. My heart thumped hard in my chest, caught off guard by the flirtation in my voice.

"Of course you are," he replied without smiling.

I sat down on the floor next to him and tried to subtly play detective. "So you were . . . in London?"

"Yeah, and it made me wish I'd never left."

"Why is that?"

"'Cause there's real people in London, right? These college kids act like we're all in it together, but they only think about themselves. Everyone says they love Oxford, but they secretly hate it and hate each other. I'm just honest enough to admit it."

Everything in me wanted to shout, *That's not true!* and tell him all the reasons he was wrong—how amazing it was to make friends at college, how it felt to explore the world with them, how they could bring out the best in you. But I felt like I was finally making progress in getting him to open up, so I nodded coolly, like I understood what he meant.

He went silent again and I stared at the array of large silver rings he wore on his fingers. Before I could stop myself, I took his right hand and brought it up to my face. "Can I try this on?" I asked, pointing to a giant ring with a black stone in the middle and skulls engraved on either side.

"Sure," he said.

I slid it down my index finger and held out my hand to examine it. "I think it suits me. Can I keep it?" I asked, my stomach full of butterflies.

"Yeah," Tarik replied.

When he was gone, I felt relieved, like I could finally exhale. Flirting was a rush, but also terrifying, like it could career out of control at any moment and take you in a direction you weren't ready to go.

Tarik's ring was too big for me, but I wore it all the time, turning it over and over around my finger. Sometimes I took it off, placed it in the center of my palm, closed my hand around it, and then opened it again like a present. My friends didn't ask where I got the ring. They all knew about Tarik by now, and had made their uneasy peace with it.

It felt like we'd seen each other enough times now for me to invite him out. Not on a date, but something more interesting than tea in my room. Having already played my night climbing card, I needed another idea. The opportunity came a few days later when Hen texted Cora and me:

Dinner out tonight? Then back to campus and hang out in the bar?

I'm in. Do you mind if I invite Tarik?

Hen replied ☺. Then 👍.

As I walked down the stairs to his floor, I clutched a note in my hand. I assumed he'd be out and planned to slip the invite under his door, then scurry back up to my room. When I arrived, though, the door was open and he was sitting in his desk chair, facing the hall. Too late to run. I shoved the note in my pocket and looked around the room, trying to take it all in. A toothbrush and a couple of bath products sat on the edge of his sink. His bed had a thin blanket that didn't look warm enough for winter. Next to the door, an open dresser drawer held six or seven identical flip phones, but no clothes. There were no snacks or school supplies, no fairy lights or family photos. It felt more like a safe house than a dorm room.

After a few moments, I realized he was waiting for me to speak. "I thought I'd stop by your place for a change," I said, hoping he remembered telling me his room number a few weeks prior. "I'm going out with some friends for dinner tonight. Care to join us?"

He rubbed the back of his neck and looked at the floor. "Yeah, uh, thanks. It's just . . . my professors are being mental about my essays. And there's stuff outside Oxford I need to do. . . . " He paused for a moment. When he spoke again, it was more to himself than to me. "If I could undo it, I would. But it's too late now."

I tried to lighten the mood. "Maybe getting out of your room would help?"

"You're a good one, Malala. Sure, I'll stop by if I can." We exchanged numbers and I dropped a pin from the restaurant. Throughout dinner, my eyes darted to the door every time it opened. The evening came and went without him. I wasn't surprised, but it still hurt.

When nearly two weeks passed with no word from Tarik, I started to worry. If he missed this many days at Oxford, he could get put on academic probation again—or worse. My mind played out excuses: Maybe he was hurt somewhere and needed help. Maybe he wasn't texting me back because he'd lost his phone. I made myself frantic thinking of potential scenarios. I needed to know he was all right, and I wanted to be the one to rescue him if he wasn't.

One afternoon I went to Yasmin's room to ask if she knew anything. "You're not the only one looking for him," she said. "This girl was ranting in the laundry room a couple nights ago. Apparently she let him borrow her textbooks for a few hours and he never brought them back. She's tried calling and he doesn't pick up."

Another weekend went by with no sight of him, but on Monday evening I found him pacing outside the dining hall. "Hey, you're here! Is everything all right? I was worried."

"Hey," he replied without looking at me. Then he started pacing again. "I went to tutorial and the professor threw my essay in the trash without even looking at it!"

"Why would he do that?"

"He says I'm two essays behind. The one I turned in today was from last week, when I wasn't on campus. So now he refuses to read it. He gave me until tomorrow morning to turn in the current one. I missed the lectures, and no one will let me borrow their notes. The business course is full of assholes."

"Okay, but you have all night. I've started essays at three a.m. and still made it by the deadline! You're so clever, you can do this."

"Nah, 'cause it's useless, right? They promised I could stay in college as long as I pass collections every term. But my professor said today I might as well leave now and save everyone the trouble. Like they've already decided."

"Don't leave! If your professor won't help you get back on track, we can take your case to the student welfare advisor. Just get started on your essay. Come to my room and work on it. I'll make some tea."

He stopped pacing and looked at the ground. When he spoke, his voice was calm and quiet. "No. No, thanks. I'll be all right. See ya around."

I wasn't ready to accept defeat, but the best person to help Tarik was the last person I wanted to ask. When I got to Anisa's room, she was sitting at her desk, deep in a problem set.

"Sorry to bother you, but I really need a favor. You know Tarik in your course? He's about to get kicked out of college."

"Worse things happen at sea," she replied, turning away from me and flipping open her textbook.

"It's just that . . . you really helped me with econ when I got behind. I was wondering if you might share your last essay with him, just so he can get some ideas for his. It's due in the morning and he hasn't started yet."

"I help you because you're my friend, not some druggy git with no interest in college. If he rips off my essay, I could get in trouble too. Think about what you're asking here."

"Please, Ani, he might lose his place."

"Malala! Chicks before dicks!"

"I don't know what that means."

"It means you're obsessed with this guy, and you need to pull yourself together."

Walking away from her room, I felt strange, like the spell that had brought me there was broken. I'd failed in my mission to help Tarik, and Anisa thought I was a fool for trying. She was right—he had not asked for my help and didn't accept it when I offered. So why was I doing this?

Because I *enjoyed* crafting elaborate narratives around our brief interactions. I could have snapped myself out of the delusion at any time, but I didn't want to.

When Tarik disappeared for days, I would sit on my bed and listen to Bollywood duets, imagining the two of us embroiled in an epic love story. Then he'd show up again without explanation, eat my food, and leave. He didn't want to be close to me, didn't ask about my friends or weekend plans. And that never bothered me because I preferred the fantasy in my head, where everything was both thrilling and safe.

Obsessing over an unapproachable boy was just another way of avoiding rejection and staying single, filling my need for connection with a one-sided romance. When I realized I'd tricked myself into thinking it was real, I wanted to stamp out both the infatuation and the longing that created it.

A few days later, I walked to the pharmacy on a mission to buy a bottle of Axe Body Spray like the one I'd spotted in Tarik's room. I purchased a fragrance called Anarchy XL, went back to the dorm, and sprayed it all over my body.

When Yasmin came over that night, she stopped dead in her tracks at the door. "Ugh, why does your room smell like the patriarchy?" I showed her the can.

"I'm using it on myself, so I won't get distracted by Tarik or any other guy," I explained. "I know I am attracted to this smell, and now I have removed the temptation and claimed the power for myself." I looked at her smugly, satisfied by my genius solution.

"Well, I guess you solved it, Malz. There's nothing left that could attract you to a man," she said with a smirk.

The last time Tarik stopped by my room, I was at badminton practice. He sent a text saying he was sorry he missed me, and he'd come back later, but I never saw him again. My friends spotted him in town a few times after that. Eventually he disappeared altogether. I don't know if Oxford kicked him out or if he just gave up. Maybe he was far away, looking for his father.

Over the next year, I sent occasional texts to check on him. One night I sat in my room alone, listening to thunder rattle the old windowpanes.

Do you like storms? I wrote. I want to go outside right now and dance in the rain. He never replied.

11.

People often associate the scent of pine trees with winter, but it's actually strongest in the spring. I know this because, in Mingora, blue and longleaf pines grow on both sides of the Swat River; our valley smells like a Christmas candle when the temperatures rise and the snow melts.

One sunny afternoon at Oxford, I opened my window to find the air smelled like home. In a rush of nostalgia, I grabbed my laptop and opened Google Maps. A few clicks and I was there again, on the streets where I grew up.

Starting at my old house, I traced the route I used to walk to school. *There's the mulberry tree in our neighbor's yard.* When it dropped its fruit on the street in the summer, I would mash it until the soles of my shoes turned purple, leaving a trail of inky footprints behind me. I clicked past the ruins of a two-thousand-year-old Buddhist monastery where my brothers and I liked to play hide-and-seek. Turning the corner, I zoomed in to read a banner hanging on a restaurant: *Ramadan Iftar Dinner for Orphan Children.*

The porch light was on at Moniba's house. I stared at the image on the screen and then closed my eyes, picturing myself standing on her street, my hand on the garden gate, a moment away from seeing my oldest friend again.

Suddenly I missed everything at once—mangoes that tasted like butterscotch, the way the sun made the river sparkle, sleeping outside under the stars with my grandmother. The stillness of my dorm room began to agitate me. In Mingora, there was always noise—cars honking, people shouting out of windows, the crack of cricket bats, the local mosque's call to prayer. Instead of soothing my homesickness, taking a digital walk through my hometown had dredged up a dormant bitterness in me, grief at being ripped away from my old life.

When you haven't seen your home in years, it can become a mythical place in your mind. For days after I arrived at the hospital in Birmingham, I gazed out the window expecting to see the mountains that greeted me every morning when I woke up in Mingora, only to be startled by skyscrapers and traffic lights. In the years since, I'd traveled the world, seen the Colorado Rockies and the Sierra Nevada, flown over Qurnat as Sawdā' and Mount Kenya. And I always said the same thing: "The mountains in Swat Valley are taller than these." I felt honor-bound to defend the place where I grew up, to never be impressed by another mountain range as long as I lived.

When I realized my family would be staying in the UK, I promised myself that I wouldn't change—I'd be the same Pakistani girl I'd always been. But as the years went by, I felt like I was splitting into two different people. The new Malala understood the basics of soccer, the difference between Harry Potter and Harry Styles, what Brexit was and why everyone had an opinion about it. At the same time, the old Malala was still inside me, compiling years of thoughts on Pakistan's cricket team, TV shows, politics, even little things like why chicken biryani didn't taste the same in Birmingham. I kept all of these reflections in my head because I had no one to share them with. It made me feel like I could never be true to myself, like I didn't belong anywhere.

With eighty-five Pakistani students enrolled at Oxford in my first year, college should have been the perfect place to finally connect with people from my homeland. Instead, I kept my distance, sitting in the back row at Pakistan Society meetings and skipping their social events. If I walked past people having a conversation in Urdu, my ears perked up, but I didn't stop. Being alone, I decided, was better than being rejected or, worse, attacked.

LESS THAN A week after I was shot, people in Pakistan started claiming that the attack was staged. When I eventually heard about the conspiracy theories, I thought they were silly and pathetic, that no one would actually believe such a thing. Then thousands of people—even some politicians and journalists—began saying that my family had faked the whole thing for money and British passports. The Taliban issued a statement claiming credit for the attack. Doctors who'd treated me in Pakistan and the UK were interviewed on TV. But none of that evidence made a dent in the growing masses who believed it was all a setup. When my mom heard the lies people were spreading, she would cry and say, "I wish they were right. I wish it never happened."

The constant, widespread denial of what had happened to me was a second assault, leaving wounds that wouldn't heal. In one of my first interviews after being released from the hospital, the journalist asked me what I would say to the man who attacked me. I said that I forgave him—and that was true. But what I wrote in my diary that night, at fifteen years old, was also true: *What would I say to him? I only ask that next time you aim for the middle of my forehead. Make sure everyone sees it. Then they won't say I wasn't shot.*

While the conspiracy theorists maintained the shooting was staged, other people believed the attack was real, but loathed the attention I received after it. "Why does the world love Malala so much?" they asked over and over in comments on news sites and social media. Western countries had colonized our land, used our people as pawns in decades-long proxy wars, killed children and civilians in drone strikes. After all this, many Pakistanis resented that the United States and Europe now wanted to heap praise on a teenage girl from a mountain town. If the West loved me, that was reason enough for my fellow citizens to hate me. It felt like I had to live my life as if I were on trial, trying to prove myself to people who had already judged me guilty.

One afternoon, during a high school free period, I was scrolling on my phone and saw a picture of myself that a Pakistani news outlet had posted on Instagram. I paused to read the comments; as usual, they were full of words like "bitch," "whore," "traitor." Then I read: *I want to kill her.* I gasped and shrank down in my chair, feeling exposed and vulnerable. *Is he really planning to attack me? Is he part of the Taliban?* I clicked on his profile, but it didn't give any clues about who he was. Just some grainy pictures and stupid memes on his grid. If that was actually him in the photos, he wasn't much older than me.

I needed to understand why he hated me so much. *Did I say something in an interview that made him feel this way? Could I talk to him and change his mind?* Before I had time to think it over,

I was creating an Instagram profile with a fake name and filling it with pictures of male bodybuilders, virtual bodyguards for me to hide behind. Then I messaged the man who'd written that he wanted to murder me.

Why? I don't understand. Why do people from her own country think this way?

He replied quickly: Where you from?

I'm Pakistani. But I live in England, I answered truthfully.

Then you can't understand, he wrote. Those of us in Pakistan know she is a liar and a traitor. Don't worry, we will send her to hell.

My hands were still shaking when I found Alice in the student common room. "Malala! What were you thinking? Block him right now and don't ever do that again," she said, her eyes flashing with alarm. I promised her, and myself, that I wouldn't talk to trolls anymore.

For my own survival, I had to become immune to seeing hundreds of hateful comments about me every time I opened my phone, try to numb the pain and build a wall around my heart. But it always hurt when people said I had done nothing to help girls in Pakistan. It wasn't only that they ignored the physical price I'd paid for standing up to the Taliban, or the years of my life I'd spent advocating for education—what upset me was the implication that I didn't care, that I had voluntarily walked away from my home, forgetting about the millions of girls still fighting to go to school. That couldn't have been further from the truth.

No matter how many times people claimed that I'd done nothing to help, I kept quiet about my biggest project in Pakistan— it was so close to my heart that I couldn't bear to see it torn apart by my critics. When I won the Nobel at seventeen, I used the prize money to purchase land in Shangla, a remote cluster of villages high in the mountains, where my parents grew up. As a child, I spent every Eid holiday there, at my grandmother's house. And when my family fled the Taliban in Mingora, we took refuge in Shangla's rocky hills.

83% of the women from these villages, including my mom and aunts, were illiterate. Most parents took their daughters out of school in second grade, when they were old enough to help with cooking, cleaning, and caring for younger children. There wasn't a single high school for girls in the entire region—so I decided to build one.

Getting the school up and running was urgent to me: I had many cousins in Shangla; some were almost thirteen and fourteen, the age when fathers start to negotiate marriages for their daughters. If we opened a school, I thought, we could buy them some time, convince my relatives and other parents in the community that girls should finish their education before becoming wives. At the very least, they wouldn't grow up like their mothers and grandmothers, unable to read or write. I dreamed that some might even go to college.

For years, people claimed it was impossible to start a school in Shangla. They said it was too difficult to build anything on the craggy shoulders of the Hindu Kush mountain range. Most homes in the area consist of one or two rooms, are made of mud and stones, and can't be reached by car. Even if you somehow managed to construct a building, the parents would never allow their daughters to go to school, people warned. Tilting at windmills. Fool's errand. Lost cause, they said. But I was determined to pull it off. *If I can make this school successful*, I thought, *it will prove that girls' education is possible anywhere in the world.*

By the time I started college, construction was nearly complete—a four-story feat of engineering and determination. Soon we would throw open the doors and welcome the first students, from kindergarten through middle school. Our plan was to add a grade level every year until the oldest girls graduated. I pored over every scrap of information that came in from the architects, building foreman, and school administrators in Shangla—budgets, blueprints, photos, text messages—impatiently dreaming of the day when I could see it for myself.

If I didn't care about girls in Pakistan, I would have chosen a quieter life, one away from cameras, spotlights, and endless criticism. But I wanted to see my community thrive, so I ignored the haters and kept working. At night before I went to sleep, I told myself that someday this torment would end. Someday I would be able to speak freely about my homeland without laboring over every word, trying not to say anything that could be used against me. Someday there would be a place for me in Pakistan again.

All of this ran through my mind one winter afternoon when I received a message from Parveen, a computer science student at Oxford:

> Hey hey Malala! Hope your first year at college has been great so far! A group of Pak students will be hanging out and ordering food at my friend Raja's house tonight. We'd all love to meet you, so I was wondering if you want to join?? It's a really good group of people, a safe place to have fun and relax. The address is 24 Observatory Street.

I read the invite again and again, searching for subtext. Did Parveen and her friends have a good opinion of me? It was one thing to be mocked online, where I knew a good portion of the posts came from trolls who found it fun to start fights and spread misinformation; I didn't know how to handle someone saying those things to my face. Did "safe" mean I could trust them? Would our conversations stay between us? Would they post a picture of me standing too close to a boy or not wearing my headscarf? The last thing I wanted was another angry call from my mom saying that people were up in arms over something they'd seen on WhatsApp.

I could stay in my room and think about these questions all night, telling myself there would be another chance, another party, another invitation. But I wanted people from my country to believe the best about me and thought I owed them the same.

I typed Thanks, Parveen, I'd love to come, and hit send before I had time to change my mind.

12.

As the car turned down Observatory Street, I told my security officers that it wouldn't be a late night—just a quick hello, then back to campus. My stomach fluttered with a mix of anticipation and dread. I'd never even been to a birthday party in high school, and now I was going to a college house party where I didn't know a single person.

Thoughts tumbled over each other in my mind: *Will they think I'm less Pakistani than they are? Will they be conservative or open-minded? If they're open-minded, will there be dancing? And if I dance, will it end up on social media and cause a scandal? Be careful with everything you say and do, Malala. . . .*

I stood on the sidewalk and smoothed down the creases in my carefully chosen outfit. Back at the dorm, almost every item of clothing I owned was on the floor, as I'd changed ten times before leaving my room. I still wasn't sure if I'd gotten it right, but it was too late now. I took a deep breath and knocked on the door.

"Come in!" someone shouted from the other side. As soon as I stepped over the threshold, Parveen jumped off the couch to greet me. "Malala! You came! I'll give you a tour," she said. I tried to take it all in as she showed me around, stealthily clocking every person's face to see if they were smiling or scowling at me. A few glanced up and nodded warmly, but most were too wrapped up in their own conversations.

In the kitchen, Parveen introduced me to Raja, our host. "Great place," I said. The living and dining spaces were small, but much nicer than my dingy dorm room.

"Welcome to 24 Obs! And thanks. I lived on campus my first year and then my parents rented this house for me. I told them it would help me study, but it's turned into a bit of a party spot." As he was speaking, the front door swung open and five more people arrived. All the guests seemed to know each other, greeting one another by name and fetching food and drinks for the new arrivals.

As the house filled up with people, everyone was talking loudly in a mix of Urdu and English, huddled around biryani and shish kebabs on the dining room table. They all seemed nice, but whenever one of them spoke to me, I braced myself, wondering if this was the person who was going to ask me if I'd really been shot or why I no longer lived in Pakistan.

I'm going backward, I thought. Since coming to college, I'd had no trouble making friends. I had not lurked on the edges of the Diwali Ball or pub outings. *These people seem fun. Why can't I just be myself?*

I gathered up my courage and walked over to the dining room where Raja was hanging out. "So, if you weren't here tonight, what would you be doing?" he asked. "Let me guess . . . studying?" He had confident, happy eyes and a black pompadour that bobbled when he talked.

I chuckled. "Uh, less than you might expect."

"Same," Raja replied. "I'm in the engineering graduate program and I get by, but just barely. Technical reports, simulations, lab work . . . who has the time? Too easy to get sidetracked by all the great people at Oxford."

As we talked, I learned that his first love was cricket. After attending high school in Dubai, he'd gone back to Pakistan for a year to try to make it as a professional athlete. "I'm obsessed with cricket!" I said, proceeding to pepper him with questions about up-and-coming players, the advantages of left-handed bowlers, and recent ball tampering scandals.

"Do you play, Malala?"

"I did when I was little and I *loved* it. I joined the cricket club here, but I haven't been to any of their events yet. I'm a bit too rusty, I guess."

"How about next weekend I get out my gear and we'll have a practice session in University Park? You'll be back in shape in no time." I smiled, feeling looser and more at ease.

Parveen walked over with a few friends she wanted me to meet. One of the girls handed me a little red box. "Cocomos!" I squealed. The cookies were a staple of Pakistani childhood. In Mingora, I used to buy them from street vendors after school. "I haven't had these in so long."

"My mom sent them in a care package," the girl replied. "She sends the same thing every month—Cocomos and two bottles of Fair & Lovely." All of us doubled over with laughter and joked about the aunties we knew who swore by the popular skin-lightening cream. "Light skin opens doors!" Parveen shrilled, repeating a saying we'd all heard over and over growing up.

Around 10 p.m., the party guests stacked the dining chairs in a corner and wedged the coffee table into the foyer to make room for dancing. I noticed Zayan right away. Unlike the other guys, he didn't have a beard or hi-top haircut, instead sporting a shoulder-length style with feathered layers. And he *owned* the dance floor. I watched in baffled amazement as he effortlessly transitioned from a bhangra step to a pop-and-lock, all while carrying on a conversation with the person next to him.

We bumped into each other in the kitchen when he took a break. "You're here!" Zayan roared, tossing a sweaty arm around my shoulders. "I'm glad you came 'cause there's something I've always wanted to ask you. . . ."

I mentally prepared myself for whatever he was about to say. *Here it comes. . . .*

"What name do you give the barista when you go to Starbucks?" he asked.

I made a loud honking sound, a mixture of laughter and relief. "Sorry to disappoint you," I said, "but I don't drink coffee. So that's never happened."

"Ugh, lame. Okay, what about restaurant reservations then?"

I leaned against the kitchen cabinets and smirked at him, not sure if I wanted to give up my alias. But I was having too much fun so I decided to go for it. "*Jane Lewis*," I whispered.

"Shut up! Whaaaat?"

"Yep, it's the name on my college ID too."

"I mean, why? Like, no offense, but you don't really look like a Jane."

"Because my security team wanted me to pick a pseudonym to make it harder for people to find me on campus. They gave me a month to decide, but I couldn't choose one. So at the last minute, I looked around my room and saw this shopping bag from John Lewis, the department store. Changed John to Jane and now I'm stuck being Ms. Lewis for three years. On paper, at least."

We moved to a settee in the alcove under the stairs to keep chatting—that's when I learned that Zayan gossiped as well as he danced. Though only a fresher like me, he seemed to know everything about everyone. "There's a guy who just walked in, light-blue shirt. No, don't look! Okay, so he's *in love* with Parveen, seriously crazy for her. Like he's studying law, right? But *for some reason*, he does all his reading in the science library where she hangs out. And Parveen keeps getting mystery gifts from a secret admirer in her mailbox! She's really into calligraphy, so, like, a nice set of pens or whatever, stuff like that."

"Does she know they're from him?"

"No! She can't figure it out!"

"Shouldn't you tell her?"

"Well, it seems obvious to me, but I don't know *for sure*. And anyway, I want to see where this goes! Philosophical question: Do you think this is stalker behavior or is it sweet?"

"I think it's sweet," I said, and then paused, reconsidering. "I *hope* it's sweet. Tonight I'm choosing to believe in the good in people."

A moment later, the first notes of "Billo De Ghar," a Punjabi hit from 1995, erupted from the speakers and the room went electric. People abandoned their conversations mid-sentence and leapt off the couch. "I love this song!" I shouted.

"Come dance with us!" Zayan shouted back.

I motioned for him to go on without me and took it all in from my perch on the settee, nodding along as the crowd sang and jumped around Raja's living room. I couldn't stop smiling, amazed that I could be feeling the same unfiltered joy as everyone else at the party.

Around midnight, as I stood at the front door putting on my jacket to leave, Raja dropped his voice low and said, "Look, I know you deal with a lot of criticism. I've seen what's out there on the internet and heard what people say. But please believe that you're welcome here. Ask anyone and they will tell you I've always been a Malala fan."

I put a hand to my chin and cocked my head. "Malala?" I repeated. "Never heard of her."

⁓

SOON I WAS stopping by 24 Obs two or three times a week. It was our shared clubhouse, the place I wanted to go for everyday activities and special occasions. My new friends and I piled in front of the TV to watch Bollywood movies or cricket matches. During Ramadan, we gathered for iftar dinners and predawn donuts. We threw surprise birthday parties so often that the guest of honor was rarely caught off guard but played along anyway. Around Raja's dining table one night, I picked up a new hobby when a couple of grad students introduced me to poker. An enthusiastic and reckless beginner, I hated to fold and sometimes went all-in without even glancing at my cards. I was intrigued with the game as a way to test how well people could read my face and body language. At first the more experienced players felt bad taking ten pounds off me, but I kept showing up and they got over it.

My new friends were very different from anyone I knew growing up in Mingora. They were city dwellers born in Karachi, Lahore, or Islamabad; some had homes there but had grown up in Dubai, Kuala Lumpur, or London. Worldly and well traveled, they knew how to shoot pool and find their shoe size in multiple countries. They would visit family and friends in Pakistan once or twice a year, and come back with the latest news, fashions, and music. I slightly envied their sophistication, the way they moved through different cultures yet never felt scared of breaking some invisible rules. Wherever they roamed in the world, they seemed like themselves—comfortable and free.

The 24 Obs crew also represented a range of religious and cultural practices. About half only ate in halal restaurants; the rest were fine with any food except pork. The more devout students never missed morning prayers. Others drank whiskey and smoked weed. A few split the difference and partied until it was time to pray.

I was fascinated by their varied approaches to relationships as well. Some observed the "halal gap," standing a foot away from members of the opposite sex and keeping their hands in front of their bodies where everyone could see them. Others gave indiscriminate bear hugs to everyone in their path. There were guys with white American girlfriends, women who wanted to stay single forever, and those who planned to let their parents arrange a marriage after college. There were gay students too—though even in this liberal-by-Pakistani-standards group, no one talked about that. What I loved most was that none of these differences kept us apart—everyone was welcome and treated like family, no matter their background or beliefs.

That heaviness inside me, the fear of engaging with people from my home country, started to fade away. I began to think of the last five years not as a lonely era of my life, but as a time when I stored up friendship and love, waiting to bestow it on these exact people. It was nothing like the Pakistan where I grew up, but inside the walls of 24 Obs, every version of myself felt at home.

THAT SPRING, PARVEEN and I, along with a few other friends, decided to go to the Pakistan Society's *qawwali* concert, a celebration of Sufi devotional music popular across South Asia held in a small park on campus. On my way to the event, I remembered that I'd promised to bring mango juice to share and hurried to the nearest grocery store. I arrived late to find eight musicians sitting on a Persian rug in the grass, already playing their first song.

Qawwali is often described as "mystical" but it's far from the soothing, ambient sound popular at spas and health food shops. The frenetic, maximalist music combines percussion from a tabla and handclaps, the atonal drone of a harmonium, and a lead vocalist who sings or chants religious poems while the other musicians form a dissonant chorus in the background. A single song can run from fifteen minutes to an hour. The music is intended to induce a trancelike state, bringing listeners and performers closer to God.

From the edge of the park, I noticed the other students sitting still and silent, politely observing the artists at work. But qawwali should be a communal fever dream, not a performance. The musicians and audience should provoke each other, escalating the volume of their voices, while the tabla mimics a heart attack. Across South Asia, it's not unusual to see people dancing wildly or spinning in circles with their arms above their heads. The best qawwali sessions feel like getting caught outside in a sudden storm. You surrender to the rain, shivering and shaking, damp and delirious long after the sun returns.

In the back of the crowd, I noticed a group of elderly men from the local mosque, crowded together on a blanket. They sang along and clapped, their limbs flailing as they rocked and lurched to the music. The old men understood the art in a way that my peers did not. As I watched them, I wondered how ancient traditions could be lost over one generation or a few thousand miles.

My friends at 24 Obs helped me feel closer to my culture, but homesickness still gripped me in unexpected moments. It had been five years since I'd had to leave Pakistan. How long would it be before I could see my country again? What would I lose in the meantime?

To me, leaving home felt like entering a hedge maze. At the

start, you believe you can always find your way back. You hold tight to memories, retrace each step—take a right, another right, then a left at the birdbath, and you've returned to your original self. But the deeper inside the labyrinth you travel, the more you change. You forget the scent of your best friend's hair and the Urdu word for "rain." You develop a taste for expensive cheese and an ear for English irony.

When we emerge at the end of the maze, our best hope is to find people like the old men at the qawwali, those who remember who we were at home. At least we are together in this new place. At least someone here knows the songs we used to sing.

13.

When I arrived in Birmingham for spring break, I told my dad we needed to go to Pakistan. If my college friends could visit the country on their holidays, I should have that right as well. It felt like if it didn't happen now, it never would. I had waited long enough.

"Let's put it off until summer," he said.

"If you want to wait, that's fine. I'll go on my own," I shot back, with a dare in my voice. "I will book my own flight, leave this house in a cab, and call Moniba when I land to pick me up." Deep down, I knew I wasn't that bold, but I wasn't sure my dad knew it—and that might give me some leverage.

We'd had this conversation dozens of times over the years. Whenever I asked my dad to book the trip, he reached out to the Pakistani government, who had to give their permission for me to visit. They wanted to be sure they could protect me—and that my presence wouldn't disrupt the country or stir up controversy.

Every time, the same answer came back to us: "It's not the right moment for Malala's return." My dad had heard it so often that I worried he was giving up. "It will *never* be the 'right' moment!" I railed, trying to infect him with my indignation. "I am a Pakistani citizen with a valid passport. I have committed no crime. And they have no grounds to stop me."

I sounded angry, but inside, my heart was breaking. At 24 Obs, I'd had more experiences that reminded me of home—food, music, sports, language—in a few weeks than I'd had in the past five years. And now that reawakening felt painful, like blood rushing back into numbed limbs. I was done with stalking my old friends on Facebook, done with walking the streets on Google Maps. I couldn't keep dreaming of home at night and waking up disoriented every morning.

I don't know what my dad said, or if he channeled the righteous outrage that I felt, but the prime minister and the army chief agreed to a visit. Their approval came with some conditions: The trip would last four days, and they would oversee the itinerary. But we were going home.

I could barely believe it. My heart, so accustomed to yearning, struggled to catch up. I tried to temper my excitement in case the trip got canceled, filling pages of my diary with *Let's see what happens! Stay positive! Fingers crossed!*

My parents threw themselves into preparations—Mom selected my clothes for the trip, and Dad made plans to see his many friends and family members. My seventeen-year-old brother Khushal was apprehensive, though. In the two weeks leading up to our trip, he had terrible dreams. Some nights he didn't sleep at all, just paced around the house, checking and rechecking the locks on the ground-floor doors and windows. "I already have bodyguards," I told him gently. "Just be my brother, that's enough."

On the flight, my excitement unexpectedly curdled into anxiety. I fell asleep and dreamed of standing on the side of a dusty road, waving as my family boarded a bus and rode away. Then I watched the bus speed into a turn and careen over the side of a cliff. One nightmare rolled into another. I was in a wheelchair, surrounded by men in dark suits. They pushed me onto a stage and told me to make a speech. A man in the audience stood up, took out a gun, and shot me. My subconscious was scrambling my worst fears—losing my family, being attacked, never feeling safe in the world.

I woke up sweating as the plane descended into Islamabad. In the seat across the aisle, my dad closed his eyes and cupped his hands in front of his face in prayer. Was he thanking God for returning him to his homeland or asking for protection? Probably both.

In the airport, I didn't feel the exhilaration I had imagined I would. Instead, I examined every face for signs of trouble—the woman who inspected our passports, the men pushing carts of luggage, families of the other passengers waiting in the lobby. *What do they think of me? Have they seen the conspiracy theories on the internet? Are they happy I'm here or wishing I'd stayed away?* My legs were unsteady as we walked through the airport, like they wanted to break free and run.

Military personnel showed us to our cars, one for me and my parents, another for my brothers. As I sat in the backseat, waiting for the convoy to pull away, a dark thought overcame me: *If someone tries to kill me again, am I going to freeze? Will I know how to save myself?* My fears were not unfounded: As he started the car, our driver turned around and said, "If we suddenly stop, duck down as low as you can." I texted his instructions to Khushal and told him to look out for Atal. *Duck down*, I whispered to myself over and over.

The sky turned from black to pale blue on the thirty-minute drive. We reached the hotel just before dawn. As news of my arrival was already spreading across TV and social media, the hotel managers wanted to hurry us into our rooms. They worried about journalists swarming the lobby, disturbing the guests and creating a security risk.

As they whisked us toward the elevator, I caught a glimpse of the hotel's walled garden. "I'd like to go out there for a moment," I said. My parents started to protest, but I held up my hands. "Please," I said. "I promise not to wander too far or stay too long. I just want to watch the sunrise on my own."

Outside, I stepped onto a stone path lined with Madagascar periwinkles. Thick clusters of jasmine sat atop the garden walls, spilling their vines toward the ground below. There were apple blossom trees, spiky silver palms, and shades of green I had not seen in years. I took off my shoes, sat down, and sank my hands into the grass. *You are one of us*, the flowers and trees seemed to whisper. *Your skin was made to sit under this sun, your lungs were made to breathe the warm air.* As the sky changed from pink to gold, I felt at peace, grateful. When I stood up, my legs were strong again. I was determined not to waste another moment of the trip in fear.

That afternoon we piled back in the cars for a visit to the prime minister's office. My mom wore a dusty-rose shalwar kameez in a traditional print, like her grandmothers and great-grandmothers before her wore. Mine was more modern: a solid column of canary yellow topped with a color-blocked headscarf in purple, hot pink, green, and orange. Alarmingly bright in person, but perfect for television.

I was mortified by Khushal's and Atal's outfits—both wearing jeans, both a complete mess. Khushal's long-sleeved button-down shirt was wrinkled and untucked. But that was nothing compared to Atal, who had dressed to meet the leader of our country in an Air Jordan T-shirt and sneakers. "What is wrong with you?" I hissed. We sent him to change, and he came back in a tie-dye hoodie, the only other shirt he'd packed.

I could barely contain my annoyance. To prepare for the trip, my mom had spent two full days buying and tailoring outfits for herself and me. No one had bothered to think at all about my brothers' clothes. My outfit, my hair, my shoes, my scarf would all be described and dissected in newspapers and Facebook posts across Pakistan. But they were boys—it didn't matter what they wore because their bodies would never be a cause for scandal or shame.

We met Prime Minister Shahid Khaqan Abbasi in his office and took a few photos. I thanked him for providing security for me and my family and told him how happy we were to be back in Pakistan. Not one to waste an advocacy opportunity, I asked about initiatives aimed at promoting school enrollment for girls and pressed the prime minister to increase the budget for education.

After the meeting, we walked to an auditorium packed with scores of dignitaries and about as many TV news cameras. I had not been expecting to give a speech and had nothing prepared. *You only need to speak from your heart*, I told myself.

I stepped to the podium and began by thanking the government, the army, and everyone who made the trip possible. With the pleasantries out of the way, I took a breath and continued: "For more than five years, I have dreamed of being able to set foot in my country. I traveled around the world and, on every plane, I looked down to catch a glimpse of the city below. I always told myself, 'It is not New York, it is not Dubai or Rio or London.

When I land, I will be in Karachi, in Lahore, in Islamabad.' But it was never true."

My voice cracked. I covered my face with my hands and wiped away the tears. "I don't cry often. But I am only twenty years old, and I have seen so much in my life. When I was attacked, everything was out of my control. It wasn't my choice to leave Pakistan, but it was always my dream to return. Today, I am so happy to be home." Walking back to my seat in the auditorium, I felt the same contented buzz that I experienced when I climbed the roof at Oxford. Yes, I was scared and nervous; there were certainly risks for me in traveling to Pakistan. But I was becoming a person who was willing to take chances to have the life I wanted, and that included being able to visit my home country.

We left the prime minister's residence and went straight to a ballroom back at the hotel, where my dad had arranged a lunch for our extended family. He had ordered flowers, table settings, and a buffet for 150 people. When we arrived to greet the guests, we quickly realized there weren't enough seats. More than 300 people had made the five-hour drive from Khyber Pakhtunkhwa province to the capital.

The hotel staff scrambled to bring in more chairs and prepare more food. Wide-eyed children watched as waiters paraded through the hall with platters of chicken, saffron rice, and roti. I smiled at the women sitting and enjoying their meal without having to worry about cooking, serving, and cleaning up like they did at home. Familiar and unfamiliar voices layered on top of one another—an uncle's booming laugh, a baby's cry, my brothers yelling back and forth to their cousins across the room. It was overwhelming to see generations of my family reunited, to be surrounded by faces I remembered from my childhood.

As the guests took their plates and settled in their seats, I walked from table to table, taking care to speak to each person and pose for as many pictures as they liked. My favorite cousin, Nazneen, rushed up to hug me, and a dozen girls followed in her wake, swarming me and touching my hands and my hair.

"Hold on, hold on!" I said. "Not all at once, let me hug each of you individually."

They looked shocked at hearing my voice. "You remember Pashto?" one of them asked.

"Of course I do," I replied. *What a strange question*, I thought. Did they think I'd been away for so long that I'd forgotten my first language, or that the attack had injured my brain so badly that my life before it was erased?

Then they all took a shot at testing my memory. "Do you remember the time we ducked down in a field and hid from a farmer because we picked some fruit from his orchard?"

"Yes!" I said, laughing. "And then we ran all the way to the river with our stolen plums."

"Do you remember when we used to take our moms' jewelry and pretend we were getting married?"

"Yes, and you were always the bride because you're so pretty."

"Do you remember when you were mean to me?"

"Hmmm, I might have forgotten that one."

While we talked, I kept one eye on the door for my personal guest of honor, my grandmother Abai. About an hour after the gathering began, I saw my dad push her wheelchair into the room. Her head bent forward a bit and her frail hands trembled as she clutched a bouquet of flowers in her lap.

Abai was as beautiful as I remembered her. In a photo of her when she was about my age, she is pretty, but not remarkable. By the time I was born, though, age had revealed her exquisite features— bright eyes, high cheekbones, a playful smile. Almost all the women I knew as a child avoided the outdoors, careful to keep their complexions as pale as possible. But Abai's love of sitting in the sun gave her deep-brown skin and aristocratic creases around her eyes and mouth. Now in her seventies, she was the most stunning woman in the room.

After my grandfather's death, Abai lived with my uncle in Shangla and came to visit us in Mingora several times a year when I was young. I loved to sit in her lap and hear all the news from my cousins. She often spoke in Pashto proverbs or *tappa*, couplets of folk poetry passed down through oral tradition. When I felt slighted by some minor quarrel at school or left out of my brothers' games, she was ready with one of her favorites: "I have ridden on horses, so I cannot be jealous of your donkey." If I whined when she told me to stop watching cartoons and turn off the TV, she said, "Malala, you are playing the flute to a buffalo." Usually I resented our nonstop stream of houseguests, having to share my food and getting less time in the bathroom to style my hair. But I always wanted Abai to sleep in my room, to have her all to myself and spend the evening hours showing her my drawings and papers from school. When she had to leave, I begged her to stay. Every time, she would pat my head and whisper, "Love grows by coming and going."

Abai prayed all the time, raising her hands to Allah to ask for happiness and good health for her family and friends. If a stranger passed her on the street, she would pray for him too. The day I was shot, she was visiting my family. I had eaten a few bites of breakfast and rushed through my good-byes, excited to get to school. Abai told me to stop, then put her hand on my head and said, "May God give her a long life." For years, I wished I hadn't been so impatient to leave the house that day, that I'd spent another moment with her. Once we were in Birmingham, I worried that it would be my last memory of her, that she might pass away before I saw her again.

Now, in the ballroom, she looked just the same as she had that day. I walked over and knelt in front of her wheelchair. "Abai, I'm so happy to see you," I said. She looked down at me, then up at the women around her as if to ask them who I was. I took one of her hands in mine and she started to cry. Through her tears, she began to pray, like I'd watched her do so many times when I was young. When she opened her eyes, she asked, "What are you doing here?"

My parents had known for a while something was wrong with Abai. When they called to speak with her, she said strange things. Sometimes she was like a child again, talking about her mother and father as if they were still alive. At other moments, she couldn't remember what she'd done that day. Shangla had no hospital or doctors who could diagnose her with dementia or Alzheimer's disease. Everyone just called it "old age." I sat on my knees in front of her wheelchair for a long time, trying to memorize her face. She didn't speak, but never let go of my hand. I hoped she knew that I loved her, even if she didn't know me.

A few hours into the gathering, my dad stood on a small platform at one end of the room and asked me to join him. *Time for more speeches*, I thought. Pakistanis love to talk in front of a crowd. In the old days, people sat around sharing wild folktales and poetry. Now every school holds oratory competitions and every event features competing monologues. A gathering of almost any size will usually include a few men taking turns to gesture and pontificate for twenty or thirty minutes each, sometimes more.

After my dad spoke about what an honor it was to have so many guests, he handed the microphone to me. I tried not to glare at him. I gave speeches for a living—why did I have to perform for our family and friends, especially when I'd already given individual greetings to all three hundred people? I thanked everyone for coming, said how happy I was to be reunited with them and especially to see Abai and meet all the new babies. When I finished, one of my many uncles stepped up to the platform.

"We are happy to welcome our family back to their country,"

he said, "and hope it will not be too long before they are living among us again. We are grateful that the daughter has survived, though she will never be the same. Look at her face—she has sacrificed her beauty to give a good image to Pashtuns and Pakistan."

He continued with this particular point for the next few minutes, as I shrank to the back of the stage, embarrassed that hundreds of people I hadn't seen in years were now staring at me. Before the event, I had been nervous about how our friends and family would react to my facial paralysis. I knew they had a different picture of me in their minds. But my cousins hadn't seemed to notice at all; they only wanted to reminisce and be together again. The one reference they'd made to my appearance was gloating that I hadn't grown any taller. Now I felt exposed and reduced, as I had been so many times before, to my injuries and scars.

My uncle's comments also implied a worldview I could not endorse—that a woman's beauty was worth more than her mind or spirit, and that martyrdom was something to celebrate. I did not endure multiple surgeries and years of pain for "the glory of Pakistan." I didn't "sacrifice" my hearing, the ability to move the left side of my face, or the large piece of my skull that had to be removed. Those things and more were taken from me by men who didn't believe I had the right to go to school, who thought killing a child would make them stronger. I was seething by the time he finally finished and another man reached for the mic. But my dad stepped in and said we were done with speeches for the day.

Most of the guests left the hotel before dark, departing for their long journeys home. A few families stayed overnight, and I spent the evening playing with my little nieces and nephews, talking with their mothers, and shaking off any lingering annoyance from my uncle's speech. By the time I went to bed, I was full of excitement again—when I woke up the next morning, I would finally see the mountains.

14.

The helicopter ride from Islamabad to Mingora was one of the most thrilling hours of my life. My heart soared as we flew out of the city, over farmland and forests, between the peaks of the Hindu Kush mountain range. On the approach to Mingora, we glided over the Swat River, following the path the water cut through the mountains thousands of years ago.

I pressed my face against the window and stared down at the valley, trying to spot the landmarks I remembered from my childhood. The icy-blue waters of Saifullah Danda, an alpine glacial lake where people catch trout and build campfires on the shore, frying their fresh fish in mustard oil and chili flakes. The dense Ushu Forest, home to Himalayan black bears, golden eagles, and a three-hundred-foot waterfall. I looked for all the unnamed places too—wildflower meadows, hidden ravines, mountain caves—the rambling beauty and splendor of Swat Valley.

As we hovered over the helipad and prepared to disembark, my mom and dad looked at each other, then at me, and started to cry. It had not occurred to any of us that we would be landing in the exact same spot where another helicopter had taken me away five years ago. On that flight, I lay on a stretcher, semiconscious and vomiting blood, as the pilot prayed I would live long enough to reach the hospital. I could see the grief on my parents' ashen faces, how that moment had marked them forever—but I didn't want them to dwell on it. Today was sunny and gorgeous. I was alive and strong, in no mood for tears. When we stepped outside, I inhaled the mountain air, trying to fill up every inch of my lungs. "Come on," I said, grinning back at them. "Let's go home."

On the short drive to our old house, I expected to see the narrow streets crowded and bustling with activity as I remembered them. Instead, they were quiet and empty, no children playing, no fruit vendors jockeying for the best position, no brightly colored buses chugging along. The driver said the roads were closed for our arrival. I missed the noisy street life and imagined little kids stuck in their homes, grumbling that I had ruined their day.

The family who now lived in our house ushered us straight to my childhood bedroom, proud to show me how they kept everything exactly as I had left it: My trophy case, stuffed with academic awards and textbooks. The spot on the wall where I used to measure myself every morning, making a pencil mark to see if I'd grown overnight, stubbornly stuck at five feet since I was twelve years old. The scratchy bedspread my mom had bought at the bazaar. In the nightstand, I found drawings of ducks and kittens, and a small stuffed animal with a hidden zipper where I used to keep all the notes my friends and I passed during school. The scraps of paper were still inside, scrawled with petty feuds and rumors of field trips.

I put the fragments of my former life back where I'd found them and went to sit on the bed with my mom. "I never set foot in this room again after the helicopter took you away," she said. "I could have brought more of your things, you could have had them with you all this time, but . . ." She stared down at her hands and began to cry again.

"Mom, I want you to be happy today," I said, placing my arm around her shoulders. "Be *glad* you didn't bring anything—because I never got to take a last look at this room. And now everything is here just as I left it and I can say a proper good-bye."

We left the room to find my dad and Khushal speeding through the house, giddy with nostalgia. "Do you remember . . . ?" one of them would say; the other would finish his sentence and then they both laughed. Atal followed with an artificial light in his eyes. When we left Mingora, he was only seven years old. He was a British boy now, unable to share our memories or match our enthusiasm.

We'd been in Mingora for less than an hour when we were herded back into the cars. There was so much to see; we needed more time. Maybe a trip to the bazaar would put a smile on my mom's face. Khushal might want to chat with his friends who lived down the street. If I could persuade the pilot, it would take less than thirty minutes by helicopter to get to Shangla. The school I'd built had just opened its doors to the first two hundred girls— I could meet the students!

But I knew the security officials would never agree to that, nor would they turn my family loose in Mingora for our individual nostalgia tours. If I wanted to stay a little longer, I needed to ask for something simple, a nearby place that we could all enjoy.

My mind immediately went to the river, where I'd spent my happiest afternoons as a child. When Abai came to visit, we would load a rickshaw with pots of chicken and rice and enjoy a picnic on its banks. My dad would dunk a bag of mangoes in the water until they were cold, then scoop them out like ice cream for us kids. Khushal and Atal would dig up worms to tie to the ends of sticks with string, trying to catch a fish without a hook, as my mom sat in the shadow of the pine trees, watching me run back and forth through the wildflowers.

I only wanted a moment to feel the water run over my feet, to hear the river rumble through the valley and echo off the mountains. "Not possible," the security officials said when I asked. "It is too public and open a space to ensure your protection." My heart sank. I thanked them for doing their job, even as I silently mourned that I might never be able to roam freely along the riverbank again.

Everyone was quiet on the flight back to Islamabad. My mind drifted to a bit of philosophy I'd recently read, attributed to the ancient Greek thinker Heraclitus: "No man can step in the same river twice, for it is not the same river and he is not the same man." The idea, as I understood it, is that people and places are always changing, and that these changes are vital to our existence. Without the constant flow of water, the river cannot survive.

As a child, I was impatient for change—to be older, to grow taller, for the snow to melt, for the guests to leave. Then suddenly the changes would not stop: Thousands of girls kicked out of school. Millions of people afraid of the Taliban and fleeing their homes. And me waking up in a faraway land, not yet realizing I had left my world behind. I needed to see Mingora again, even if I knew things would never be the same. My life had changed forever, but the river in my heart would always flow toward home.

〰️

WE ARRIVED BACK in Islamabad just after lunchtime, in time to receive one final guest—my best friend, Moniba. Her mom had agreed to bring her to the hotel for an hour or so, as long as we could meet in private. Her father and brothers didn't want her to be photographed with me.

I paced around the hotel room waiting for her to arrive. Growing up, I couldn't have imagined a life without Moniba. Even though I am half a year older, she always felt like my confident, slightly bossy big sister. In primary school, I wanted to emulate her, coveting her straight, silky hair and elegant penmanship. As we got older, we competed for top grades and awards. I signed up for every contest—public speaking, drawing, essay writing, whatever gave me a shot at adding to my trophy case. Moniba tried to get me to focus my efforts. "Don't stretch your feet beyond the sheet, Malala," she said. My mischief-making and rivalries went too far on occasion, and she could be a bit of a wet blanket sometimes—but together, we found our center.

I hoped things would be the same between us. *Will I still be able to make her laugh? Will her memories be the same as mine? What if she thinks I've changed too much?* Finally I heard a soft knock on the door; I ran over and threw it open. As soon as she stepped inside, we fell into each other's arms and Moniba started to cry. I felt like crying too, but I wanted her to see me smiling and happy, the fun-loving girl she remembered.

"Until this moment, I don't think I really believed you were alive," Moniba said through her tears. We had talked on the phone often over the past five years. She'd seen pictures of me traveling around the world. But I understood what she meant. When an ordinary day is ripped apart by violence, your sense of certainty is shaken. For the rest of your life, it can be hard to know what's real and what's not.

The last thing I remembered on the day I was shot was sitting in the back of the school bus, chatting with my best friend. After that, everything was blank until I woke up in the hospital in Birmingham. Over the last five years, when Moniba and I talked, I'd sometimes asked her to tell me what had happened, what she saw that day. I trusted her—and no one else—to fill in the gaps for me.

Moniba always said the same thing: *The gunman asked, "Who is Malala?" You stared straight ahead and didn't speak. As he came closer, you gripped my hand so tight it hurt for days afterward. Then the gun went off and you slumped into my lap. I screamed when I saw the blood. The bus driver raced to the local medical center. Your injuries were too severe, so they flew you to a better hospital in a bigger city. I didn't get a chance to say good-bye.*

In the hotel room, I asked her to tell me again. She ran through the familiar beats, but then she said something I hadn't heard before: "When I got home that evening, I saw myself in the mirror. There was blood all over my school uniform, and I thought I'd been shot too. For days after that, I kept checking my body for bullets. Sometimes, even now, I wake up in the middle of the night and think that I've heard gunshots."

In that moment, I realized that Moniba was not the girl I remembered. How could she be? The attack on my life had changed everyone who witnessed it, everyone who loved me. So many people had talked about the pain I went through, the severity of my injuries, my difficult recovery. But they rarely asked about the other girls on that bus or the trauma they suffered from seeing blood run down the walls and hearing each other scream. Talking with Moniba, I came to believe that we were equally affected, just in different ways. My body carried the scars, but I had no memory of that day. Five years later, my best friend still had nightmares.

The hotel room was dark and heavy, and I couldn't stay there any longer. "Could we go outside to the garden?" I asked her mother. "All the journalists know I'm leaving tomorrow, and they've gone home now. Do you think we could walk around for just a few minutes?" She reluctantly agreed to my plan. We could go outside for a moment, then they would leave.

In the garden, Moniba and I made several laps around the perimeter, happy to stretch our legs and feel the sun on our faces. "You look amazing," I said to her. She was as beautiful and glamorous as always—shiny hair, perfect complexion, stud earrings, and a trendy handbag slung over her shoulder. When we were young, she dreamed of becoming a fashion designer. Even then, she knew her family would never allow it; now she studied medicine.

"Thanks," she replied. "So do you."

"Stop lying, Moniba!" I laughed. "I am like a middle-aged auntie, always trying to figure out what's cool to wear and never getting it right."

I told her about my attempts to put together a new wardrobe last summer and the rowing club controversy. "Oh, I wish I could have seen your mom's face when she found out about the jeans," she snickered.

"How are you enjoying college?" I asked.

"I love it, but my brothers are making it difficult," she sighed. They insisted on accompanying her to campus to make sure she didn't speak to men. If she became a doctor, they would only allow her to treat women. "It considerably narrows my options."

Moniba had never been interested in marriage, but now she was considering it. "If I happened to get a husband who was a nice man, maybe he would interfere less in my education and let me have a job in a hospital someday."

I took her hand, and she changed the subject. "Do you remember, when we were in primary school, you used to say that the only way we would ever get married was to a man who was willing to take both of us? You said we would marry as a set and that way we would always stay together!"

She broke into cascading giggles, each burst of laughter lasting until another one rose to take its place. I joined in and soon we were both struggling to compose ourselves. Everyone in the garden turned their heads to see what was so funny, but I didn't care. *Look if you like*, I thought. *We're just two girls, two best friends, reunited.*

Moniba's mom hurried to catch up with us and told her it was time to go. As I watched them walk away, I was glad that my last memory of this trip would be with her, just as it was five years ago.

15.

The trip helped to heal the disorientation that I had experienced over the previous five years. Pakistan was not "before" and England was not "after," but parts of an ongoing story. My country, family, and friends were no longer memories that I had to look backward to see; now they were the future too—people and places I could return to again and again.

When I got back to campus, I felt unstoppable, like my life could finally move forward. I wanted to have fun and push the boundaries of my independence—and it started with College Club Night.

As long as I can remember, I've loved to dance. In Mingora, dancing was forbidden for girls and women—"It's a sin," my mom would say. But at school, my friends and I would wait until the teacher left the classroom, race over to the tape player, and put on a mix of our favorite Bollywood hits. We didn't know any formal steps or technique; we just let our bodies find the rhythm and tried to outdo each other with increasingly dramatic moves. In those moments I felt weightless and free, like nothing outside those walls mattered.

When we moved to Birmingham, I would dance alone in my room and watch tutorials to try to improve my skills, even picking up a few hip-hop routines. By the time I got to college, I thought I was pretty good and wanted to show off my moves. "Damn, girl! Where did you learn to body-roll like that?" Hen asked one night while we were blasting Cardi B's "Bodak Yellow" in my room. I loved our dorm dance sessions, but now I was ready to go public.

The invite popped up in my Instagram feed: CLUB NIGHT // 1980s AEROBICS THEME // AT FEVER ON MAY 17. I had no idea what any of it meant, but I immediately sent it to Cora and Hen and wrote, Guyzzz, I think I want to go! Come with me! No excuses!

I wasn't sure what to wear, so I put on a chic gray sweater, black pants, and high-heeled patent leather boots. When my friends arrived to pick me up, they were not impressed. "No, no, this is all wrong," Hen said, pointing at my outfit and then throwing open the doors of my wardrobe.

Cora was dressed in what appeared to be a bright-orange bathing suit over pink and yellow nylon leggings. "What's up with your headband?" I asked, gesturing at her forehead.

"It's a sweatband! For workouts. In the eighties?" When she saw I wasn't getting it, she pulled up a video on her phone of women with big hair doing some sort of choreographed dance in a gym. I'd never seen moves like these, a mix of exaggerated marching, jumping jacks, and hip thrusts. The woman in the front of the group yelled, "Feel the burn! Feel the burn!"

"Oh, I can't do this. I've changed my mind," I said, backing away from both of them.

"*Relax*," Hen replied. "One step at a time, let's get your look sorted first." She pulled out a neon-yellow silk shirt from my closet. The price tag was still dangling off a sleeve.

"I don't even know why I bought that," I said. "It's too low-cut—it would get me in trouble."

But my friends were not having it and fired off a raft of instructions: "Add a black tank top underneath for coverage. Put the yellow shirt on over it, but leave the last few buttons undone and tie it at the waist. You can keep the black pants but swap out the boots for heels."

Cora ran to get her makeup kit and painted a lightning bolt in gold glitter on my right cheek. Hen found a pair of oversize hoop earrings in my dresser and handed them to me. They spun me around to face the mirror. I looked unrecognizable. *But maybe cool?* I thought. In a last-minute surge of caution, I added a baseball cap and sunglasses for anonymity.

Having only seen clubs on TV shows and social media, I assumed we would arrive to long lines, velvet ropes, and paparazzi jostling for position. I was relieved, if a little confused, when the car stopped in front of what looked like an office building. The club entrance was sandwiched between a dermatology clinic and a vacuum repair shop, and the only people outside were a few students smoking cigarettes.

We walked through the door, downstairs to the basement, and into a sea of undergrads dressed in neon and spandex. A few people were buying drinks at the bar, but most were on the dance floor—a giant chessboard with lights under each square that changed color in time with the song. There were overhead lights as well, spinning blues, reds, and yellows. I'd never seen a disco ball in real life and marveled at the fleet of glittering fireflies it sent whirling around the room.

A synth-y beat dropped and Cora pulled me onto the dance

floor. I didn't know the song, but I liked the soaring vocals and how everything sounded happy, even when the words were sad. In the packed crowd of college students, dancing seemed the same as it had with my school friends in Mingora—everyone doing their own thing, making it up as they went along. Except that, back then, I couldn't have imagined how electric it would feel to be encompassed in sound, light, and the collective energy of dozens of people losing themselves in the music. I loved it.

A few mutual acquaintances came over to talk and dance with Cora and Hen. At first I wondered why they were ignoring me, then realized they didn't recognize me in my clubbing disguise. "Hey, guys," I shouted, taking off my sunglasses. "It's me—Malz!" Their eyes widened dramatically and they looked at each other to make sure they were all seeing the same thing. "Malala Yousafzai at Club Night," one of them said. "I'm literally deceased right now."

Around 4 a.m., we tumbled through the LMH gates. "Ugh, these shoes are trying to take me out," Hen groaned. Cora looked pale and exhausted.

"What's wrong?" I asked. "You two go clubbing all the time."

They looked at each other, then back at me. "Malala, you're a legend," Hen explained, "but no one who isn't doing heavy drugs stays until the *very end* of Club Night. Like, they were packing up the bar by the time we dragged you out!"

"Usually we dance for an hour or two and then head to a pub to wind down," Cora added. "And, you know, *eat something*. God, I'm starving."

The corners of my mouth twitched as I tried not to laugh, then burst into giggles and snorts. It might be a long time before they went dancing with me again, but that was fine. I couldn't imagine a more magical night anyway.

108

IN HIGH SCHOOL, I would have prepared for weeks and stayed up all night reviewing my notes before a big test, but I wasn't worried going into my first-year prelims. They don't count toward your degree; as long as you pass, you get to stay at Oxford for two more years. Lara, though, remained concerned about my grasp of economics, and recommended I attend a couple of pre-exam study sessions with the tutor. I missed them both, too tired to make the 9 a.m. start time after late nights at 24 Obs.

Lara's job was to make sure I maximized my academic potential and performed at the highest possible level. I didn't want to disappoint her, but I had been a hardworking student at the top of the class since childhood—and now my goals had changed. I wanted to learn the fundamentals: how to seek knowledge, evaluate it, use it to make decisions. If I actually read the hundreds of pages my professors assigned every week, though, I'd never leave my desk. At any point in the rest of my life, I could go to the library, check out the same books, and pick up the finer points of price elasticity. But dancing all night with my friends? Hanging out at 24 Obs? Those moments were more precious to me than academic honors.

On the morning of my econ prelim, Cora and Hen barged into my room to wake me up and make sure I made it to the Examination Halls on time. I took my seat and waited for the test to begin, said a little prayer, and hoped I wouldn't bomb too badly. Whatever marks I received at the end of the term didn't matter, I told myself. I had already passed my own test, the one I'd set at the start of the year: to find a group of friends who understood me.

At Oxford, I could be myself, free from the expectations of the outside world. My friends didn't care about my thoughts on global events or what I wore. They accepted my quirks and contradictions, my bad days and chronic tardiness. Sometimes when they saved me a seat at dinner or laughed at my jokes, I tried to hide the swell of gratitude in my heart. I knew it wasn't normal to show so much intensity or say out loud how much I loved them. Though I never told them, their friendship made me feel that I'd finally come back to life. I couldn't imagine wanting anything more than what I had right now.

16.

I was loading my bags in the car when I got a text from Sofia, a music student I knew from 24 Obs: Hey you still around? Feel like going to the track to race go-karts?

I didn't think twice, happy to stay at college a little longer and delay my return to Birmingham, to work and the real world. In the parking lot outside the race track, I waved to Sofia, who was standing with two guys. I recognized Jamal, a part-time MBA with a good sense of humor and a trendy haircut. The other man was tall and seemed younger than Jamal, wearing a cherry-red spring jacket that looked out of place amid Oxford's ubiquitous olive-toned Barbour coats. I was curious why I'd never bumped into him before.

"Hi, I'm Asser," he said, sticking out his hand to shake mine.

"Thanks for coming out today," Jamal chimed in. "My friend

just arrived from Lahore and doesn't know anyone, so we have to show him a good time."

"What brings you here, Asser?" I asked.

"Just visiting," he replied. "I run an amateur cricket franchise back home and our team is playing in an international tournament in August. Until then, I'm visiting my sister, seeing some friends, and hopefully enjoying a warm English summer."

I laughed. "Well, good luck with that."

We went inside and the staff at the raceway said it didn't matter that Sofia and I didn't know how to drive a car, that go-karts were easy. A group of eleven-year-old birthday party guests were speeding around the track—how hard could it be?

On my first lap, I took a turn too fast, slammed on the brakes, and skidded into a nearby wall. The impact of it shocked me, and I immediately felt dizzy. Asser pulled up behind me and I asked him to get my security team, who took me inside to lie down on a couch in the manager's office.

One of the guards checked my vital signs, and asked me to follow his finger with my eyes and wiggle my fingers and toes. He said I was fine, but advised me to rest for a bit and let them know if anything changed. As they stepped out of the office, Asser poked his head in and said, "Feeling better? Want to get back out there?"

"In a minute," I replied, keeping my eyes closed, annoyed by his presence. *Is this grown man so excited by go-karts that he can't wait to see if I develop a concussion? What is he doing here? Where is Sofia?*

Asser sat down on the arm of the couch, unfazed by my grumpy tone. After a few moments, I propped myself up on my elbows. "All right, I think I'm okay now."

"That's good," he said. "I'm sure it was just a shock. I mean, you hit a bank of rubber tires at less than twenty miles an hour. Not exactly Formula One–level damage, is it?"

He smiled at me, and we both started to laugh. We'd only just met, but I liked that he didn't regard me as a breakable object, someone who couldn't cope with a minor accident or joke at her expense.

For the first time that day, I noticed how handsome he was. His hair was just ruffled enough to make you want to run your hands through it and change its shapes. A deep scar above his left eyebrow suggested competitive sports or youthful misadventure— an active, unpredictable life. His smile wasn't flashy or overly charming, but warm and sincere. Even under the fluorescent office lights, I thought he was gorgeous. For the rest of the afternoon, I found myself sitting up straight and posing anytime I felt he might be watching me.

By the time we got to dinner, my body felt possessed—an instinct to flirt with this good-looking stranger took over and I was powerless to stop it. I fidgeted, twirled my hair, and laughed too loudly at everything he said. When he asked me how I liked college, I tried to make myself sound cool and rebellious. "My favorite thing is climbing on the rooftop of this four-story building," I said. "I'd definitely get thrown out of college if anyone knew, but I only go late at night and I'm too good at it now to get caught. And I also go clubbing."

Sofia, who knew I'd only been out dancing once in my life, kicked me under the table. When I looked at her, her eyebrows shot up. *Okay, cool it*, I told myself. I kept it together for a few minutes until, while trying to maintain eye contact with Asser as he told a story, I reached for my glass and spilled water all over the table.

At the end of the night, Jamal suggested we take a group photo. He handed the waiter his phone and we all huddled together. As we were moving into position, Asser's arm brushed mine and a shiver raced through my entire body. *I'm dead*, I thought.

As soon as my car pulled out of the parking lot, I got a text from Sofia.

WHAT WAS THAT?!? You were flipping your hair so hard, it fell in your food a couple times.

Do you think he's single? Do you think he liked me?

I have no idea, but the entire restaurant absolutely knows that you like him.

On the drive back to Birmingham that night, I scanned his social media profiles. It felt a little subversive checking out a grown man, one with lines around his eyes that crinkled when he laughed, and who probably did a lot of things I hadn't tried yet like yoga or skincare. Everything I could find on him seemed nice and normal. And, most importantly, I saw no sign of a girlfriend. *Don't lose your head*, a voice in the back of my mind said, but I ignored it.

When I arrived home that night, I asked my mom to book laser hair removal for my unibrow. She had been badgering me to do it for over a year, and I was relieved she didn't ask why I'd changed my mind. I knew shapely eyebrows wouldn't fix all the flaws I saw in my face. But maybe, I thought, I should put a little more effort into my appearance —brush my hair, a dab of lip gloss, some concealer. Just in case I ever saw him again.

Two weeks later I had to travel to Brazil for Malala Fund work, and found myself with a free afternoon and evening in London before the early-morning flight to Rio. I pulled out my phone and composed a message to Jamal, asking if he and Asser wanted to meet up. As my finger hovered above the send button, I felt like I was standing on the edge of a cliff, nervous that I might actually jump.

We met for tea at the Ham Yard Hotel, where Jamal was staying for a few weeks. Asser looked better than I remembered—his long arms a deeper shade of brown than before, his face ruddy from days in the sun. He had just returned from visiting a friend in Scotland, where they went hiking and ate fish and chips by the sea. I had been to Scotland once myself, but only saw the inside of SUVs and conference rooms, the sterile cocoon of my working life.

"And the friend you were visiting . . . a man? A woman? Someone from college?" I asked.

"A man, a friend from high school," he replied.

"Asser has sworn off women," Jamal interjected. "He's been cursed by . . ."

" . . . the circumstances!" they shouted in unison, and laughed.

"Sorry for the inside joke," Asser said. "Please ignore us."

"Unfortunately for you, I have a couple of free hours and enjoy nothing more than prying into other people's love lives. So I will require an explanation."

"Oh, I'm happy to bore you with my stories, as long as you remember that you asked for this."

He began in high school, at age sixteen, when he met his first girlfriend. "She was a punk girl, black clothes, black leather boots—not something you see a lot in Lahore and that's why I liked her. We would talk online every night, and she would send me songs by the Ramones and the Sex Pistols."

They went on their first—and last—date at Pizza Hut. "I could claim it 'fizzled out,' but the truth is, I wasn't cool enough for her."

It always made my head spin to hear stories like these from

people who grew up around the same time as me, in the same country. When I was a child in Mingora, there were no Pizza Hut dates or punk records or online chats. I'd never imagined that the teenage world was so different just a few hundred miles away in Lahore.

Asser met his second girlfriend in college. "She was sweet and very smart. I could listen to her talk for hours. And I loved her parents and her siblings."

They had been dating almost a year when she was accepted to an exchange program at a prestigious university in the United States. He was proud and happy for her—and crushed that the relationship was over. He told her she should be free, to focus on her studies and enjoy her new surroundings without being tied to him.

"But she wouldn't accept it. She kept saying, 'It's only a year. Then I'll come back, and everything will be exactly as it is now.' I still felt uneasy about staying together, but I wanted to make her happy." While she was away, he worked odd jobs, texted her every day, and called most nights. He kept in touch with her family, visiting them for occasional dinners and delivering gifts on Eid.

As the academic year was coming to an end, the woman called Asser to say that an investment firm had offered her a great job. "I see my future in America," she told him. "And I don't think this will work anymore."

"I'm so sorry," I said, feeling genuinely bad for him.

"Thank you, it's really fine now. She's a good person and we're still friends. And I know how hard things are for women in Pakistan, so I couldn't blame her for taking the opportunity to build the life that she wanted."

Once he'd recovered from the heartbreak, he started dating again and found many women who were interested in seeing him. For a while, at least. "Everyone loved me in December," he said. "That's wedding season in Lahore—the best weather, the best parties, it's magical." Asser was a popular date for the festivities; his mom and older sisters had taught him to be punctual, respectful, and a good conversationalist.

"But things would always change by January, February at the latest. Girls who seemed really into me suddenly broke it off. It's like one of those signs for canceled events, businesses closing, the internet going down, whatever it is. And they always say, 'Due to the circumstances, we can no longer provide service.' But you never find out what the circumstances are! You're just supposed to accept that unseen forces will wreck your plans. That was my love life, essentially."

"So girls just broke up with you . . . for no reason?" I asked, skeptical.

"I had my suspicions," he answered. "Then finally one of the women spelled it out . . . and I really wished she hadn't."

He decided he was done with casual relationships, done with feeling like an accessory tossed in a closet after the party. That's when he met his third girlfriend. At first he thought it wasn't that serious. When he told her he was looking for a long-term relationship, he thought she'd move on. But she surprised him by saying she wanted the same thing.

Asser knew her parents were status-conscious, high-society types. He'd gone to a fancy private high school on scholarship and worked his way through college. Would her mom and dad approve of a mid-level cricket manager without a family fortune?

They spent the next few months eating street food, taking long walks, and watching movies. "She was going for it, trying to prove how down-to-earth she could be, sitting on the floor of my friends' living rooms, rolling joints and cracking jokes."

Asser thought things were going well when she asked him to lunch one day and said she couldn't see him anymore. "It's just that . . . my sister got engaged last week. Her fiancé's family is quite wealthy. As you know, I've never cared about any of that, but . . ." She hesitated and then looked up at him with big tears in her eyes. "What if my sister's husband buys her a designer bag and you can't afford one? It's not about the money—it just wouldn't be fair to me."

My mouth dropped open, and I covered my face with my hands.

"Yeah, that was my reaction too," Asser said with a laugh. "I was kind of disgusted with the Lahore scene after that, and have been really looking forward to these summer months out of the city. And now you know my story."

I sat staring into my tea, considering what advice I should give him.

"The worst is when everyone tries to give you advice," he said. "A friend who thinks he's a therapist told me, 'Maybe deep down you really want to be alone—that's why you're always chasing un-available women.' That wasn't true, though. I don't *want* to be alone.

"And then some other friends took me to a psychic—a big, burly man named Kitty—who stared into my eyes and said, 'Buy a journal and start writing every day because when you find true love, your romance will be remembered for ages.'"

"Did you do it?" I asked.

"No. I don't believe in palm reading, divination, any of that stuff. I'd be happy to be wrong, though!"

When I got back to my room that night, I sank into the bank of pillows on the hotel bed, pulled out my phone, and sent him a message.

> I think I should help you find a girlfriend. What are your requirements?

> Hahaha

118

How do you have time to
care about my love life??

I'm sure you have waaaaaay
more important things to do

I care about a lot of
things.

My heart is so big that the
entire city of London could
live inside it.

This was a lie. In what I believed to be the most clever and subtle way possible, I was doing reconnaissance for myself—trying to determine if I had a shot with this handsome and charming man. If Asser said he was hoping for a statuesque girl with a perfect face who played tennis and wanted to bear him seven children, then I could put him out of my mind and move on without embarrassment.

My "requirements"
(your word) are pretty
simple

–Honesty

–Sense of humor

–Not obsessed with money
and status

Okay, what about
nationality, religion,
profession, etc?

None of those are
deal-breakers to me.
I'm open to anyone.

Age range?

No preference

Height? Eye color?
Straight hair or wavy hair?
Athletic or curvy?

The world is full of beauties.
I am looking for a friend.

17.

I spent my twenty-first birthday in Rio, talking with teenage
street artists who used graffiti to bring attention to violence
against women. Over lunch, the young women told me about fre-
quent school closings due to clashes between police and gangs, discrimination against Afro-Brazilian students, the different styles of
their art, and their individual passions for chemistry, rap music, and
soccer. They even gave me a can of spray paint and let me contrib-
ute a small doodle to one of their walls.

Back at the hotel that evening, I opened my messages to a
flood of birthday texts from friends and family. I skipped past all
of them to read two from Asser:

> Happy Birthday! Hope you have
> fun plans today. Inshallah this
> will be your best year yet!

Also—I'm staying with my sister in Birmingham, starting next week. Don't have any friends there. Will you show me around the city?

My stomach did backflips as I fumbled to open my calendar app. On Tuesday, I would arrive back in London, head straight to a breakfast meeting, then make the two-hour drive back to Birmingham to toss my dirty clothes in the laundry and pack for Wednesday's flight to Dubai. I didn't want to miss my chance to see him again—so we made plans to meet for dinner on Tuesday night and I promised to give him a tour of the city later in the month when I had more time.

I booked a table at a quiet neighborhood pub called the High Field. The food was organic and the atmosphere was cozy, but the best thing about it was that I'd never seen anyone from Birmingham's sizable Pakistani community there. I didn't want to be spotted alone with a handsome young man on anything resembling a date.

But was it a date? I had no way to know. Maybe he was just being friendly or thought I was a good contact to cultivate. I hoped he wouldn't ask me if I'd made any progress in finding him a girlfriend.

"So last time," I began as soon as we sat down, "you told me about your recent past, but nothing about your family—"

"No, no, absolutely not. Tonight it's your turn."

"Nah, my life is boring."

Asser rolled his eyes. "I know for a fact that's not true."

"Come on, start at the beginning," I pressed on. "You were born in . . . what, the eighties?"

He feigned offense and then laughed. "For an Oxford student, your math is pretty bad. I was born in 1990."

"Close enough. What happened next?"

He rubbed his trim black beard and smirked at me. "If I tell you all my remaining secrets tonight, you'd have no reason to see me when you're back from Dubai."

I felt the heat rise in my cheeks and hid my face behind the menu. "Fine. You win," I said.

Over dinner, I told him about Oxford—my friends, parties at 24 Obs, the parks and sunrise walks—and how it felt strange to be back at home after months living on my own. My family had changed a bit, particularly Khushal. Last year he couldn't wait for his chance to go to college. Now he woke up at 2 p.m. every day and played video games until late at night. My parents kept pushing me to give him a motivational speech, to try to get him to do his summer reading in the hopes he could bring up his grades next year, but I didn't know what to say.

"That's pretty normal behavior for teenage boys in the UK, right?" Asser said.

"It makes me feel like I've failed. I'm supposed to be an advocate for education, and I can't even convince my own brother to care about school."

"It's not you. As a former adolescent boy myself, I can say they are often terrible, truly some of the worst people on the planet. And then they grow up!" He spread his palms and flashed a wide, reassuring smile.

When he asked about my work, I chatted excitedly about the Shangla school. "Right now, it's open to girls from kindergarten to sixth grade. Because they've never had a high school for girls in the area, we are adding a grade every year until we get to twelfth grade. It's so exciting to know that tomorrow morning a child is going to wake up, put on her uniform, and go to class.

And in a few years, she will be the very first girl ever to graduate from a high school in these villages. Can you imagine it?" I beamed, so proud to tell him about my work. If I accomplished nothing else in my life except helping these girls to graduate from high school, I would be happy.

"That's amazing! I'm so thrilled for you and for the community. How many students do you have?"

"Two hundred at the moment, but we're building more space every day."

"And what about sports facilities for the girls?"

"There's a playground and a basketball court."

"No cricket? You have to have cricket!"

"I would *love* to build a cricket facility for girls, but it wouldn't be in this area. There isn't enough ground for a pitch."

"What do you mean?"

"Well, these villages are jammed into the space between mountains and so narrow that a car can't fit on most of the roads. People use motorbikes or donkeys for transport. Or they walk. An 'ambulance' is just four guys and a wooden stretcher! But being so isolated is part of what makes it beautiful."

Before I realized what I was saying, I added, "I'll take you there someday."

A WEEK LATER, we met for the tour of Birmingham that I'd promised him. Because I hadn't spent much time out in the city, even when I lived there, I had trouble planning a day's worth of sights to see. When I tried to think of my best days there, I kept picturing the time Alice took me to Victoria's Secret and helped me buy my first underwire bra. Not appropriate for Asser and likely not on the Birmingham Tourism and Hospitality Board's top ten either.

Then I remembered an afternoon while I was still in the hospital, when the nurses drove me to the Birmingham Botanical Gardens. It was my first time outdoors in months. As they pushed my wheelchair beneath a canopy of trees, I felt like I could finally breathe again.

I decided we'd meet there in the afternoon and then have dinner. When I arrived, Asser was waiting outside, looking handsome in a pale-pink button-down shirt, freshly ironed and tucked into jeans. We walked along the path past dogwood trees, Irish irises, and foxtail ferns while he filled me in on his cricket league and their upcoming tournament.

At the southern border of the gardens, we entered a small greenhouse with glass walls. Inside, hundreds of butterflies drifted and hovered around tropical flowers, a kaleidoscope of colors in motion. "Can we live here?" Asser whispered. I bit my lip and looked away, suddenly feeling very shy.

Just before sunset, we headed to a rooftop steakhouse with panoramic views of the city. "What are 'French beans'? Do you know?" Asser asked, browsing the menu.

"Maybe like chickpeas . . . but fancy?"

"Let's find out!" He ordered a small steak and two sides, and I got the roast chicken.

While we waited for the food, he kept his promise to tell me about his family and childhood. Asser's mom was forty years old when he was born; his sisters were nineteen and fifteen. "No one will admit that I was an accident, but it seems pretty obvious to me," he said.

The family lived in a nice Lahori neighborhood across the street from a public park. His father worked in a bank and wasn't around much. During the day, his mom packed curries, flatbread, and fruit into a sack and took him on picnics or to the zoo. In the evenings, Ambreena and Afsa, his sisters, spent hours on the living room floor playing his favorite game, casting tiny rods into a battery-powered pool of plastic fish. Before bed, they would read to him from Roald Dahl books. When he was old enough, his parents enrolled him in a private boys' academy, one of the best schools in the country.

"Sounds like a lovely childhood," I said.

"It was . . . until the afternoon when Mom and I came back from visiting my cousins and the house was empty." Asser was eight years old when everything they owned disappeared in a weekend— the car, the furniture, the TV, even the little radio that sang him to sleep every night. That's when he learned that his father was not just a banker, but a gambling addict and an alcoholic. "In some ways, it's impressive. You have to work hard to be a drunk in a dry country."

Growing up, I'd never even seen a bottle of beer and had no clue about the underground liquor trade in Pakistan or the rise in alcohol-related diseases and deaths. Gambling was also illegal. I was glad I had not mentioned my poker games to Asser.

His father fled the country to escape his debtors and left the family with nothing. Like most women in Pakistan, Asser's mom, Farida, had never had a job. But she knew how to sew, so she went to work as a seamstress. His middle sister, Afsa, a graduate student in business, took a low-level position in a finance firm. Ambreena, now married and living in the UK, sent whatever money she could spare.

They rented out the bulk of their house to tenants while the family entered through the back door and kept to the small utility rooms behind the kitchen. For years, Asser slept on the floor in Farida's cramped workroom, surrounded by dress forms, poked by errant sewing needles in his sleep.

"My mom and sisters gave up a lot to make my life as normal as possible, but I could still feel the change. I was really young when I started to worry about where we would live if we lost the house and if we would be able to afford food the next day."

This revelation surprised me. When I first met Asser, I'd assumed he was like a lot of my Pakistani friends at Oxford—from a middle- or upper-class family, elite education, living an easy, urban lifestyle untouched by the struggles of the poor. I didn't blame these friends for their good fortune or for the decades of poverty, illiteracy, and conflict that people in my community suffered, but I couldn't fully relate to them either.

Now I realized Asser and I shared a deeper connection. Loss had shaped our childhoods, dislodged our sense of security, and changed the meaning of home. We both understood the damage that men could do, either through guns and bombs or through abandonment and neglect.

The waiter returned with a tray and dramatically raised each silver cloche to reveal our meals—my chicken, Asser's steak, roast potatoes, and . . . green beans. The same green beans that mothers all over the world force their children to eat. We looked at each other and burst out laughing.

"Well, that is the most disappointing thing the French have ever done," Asser said.

I let him eat for a few minutes, then asked, "So how was high school for you?"

He told me his classmates became obsessed with physical fights as they got older, brawling in the streets almost every afternoon. If the altercation escalated, their fathers or older brothers would rush in and break it up before anyone was seriously hurt.

Asser actively avoided conflict with the other boys. "I had no backup, no older man who could step in before things got bad," he said.

"So you were a pacifist out of necessity, not principle," I reasoned.

127

He laughed. "In a way, I guess."

One afternoon, a boy he thought was a friend led him to a park where a group of guys ambushed him, knocked him to the ground, and took turns kicking and punching him. "I remember this one kid yelling, 'He thinks he's such a pretty boy and I'm going to ruin his face!' And I lay there getting killed and thinking, 'But I'm not pretty! I'm skinny, my teeth are crooked, my facial hair is wispy and pathetic!'"

For the first time that evening, I wondered if he was telling the truth. I couldn't imagine that he'd ever been less than beautiful.

18.

Over the next few days, I felt a mixture of giddiness and confusion. The thrill of possibility, imagining waking up in the morning and seeing his face on the pillow next to mine, and the fear of rejection—*You don't even know if he feels the same way about you*, I reminded myself. Maybe this was a waste of time, a distraction from all the things I should be doing, like summer reading or working. Or maybe it was worse than that: I'd seen what happened to my friends when they staked their emotional equilibrium on someone else's moods and actions. But by that point, it didn't matter. I was too deep into my crush to pull back from the brink.

The following week, Asser and I met at a bowling alley. Halfway through the game, I had a thought: *If our combined score equals 150, then we're meant to be together.* Some part of me understood this was ridiculous, but I was desperate for a sign. I had no idea how to ask if he liked me. *What if I'm reading him all wrong?*

We chatted and shared french fries as I watched the numbers tick up—75, 91, 129. Asser got a spare, and then it was my turn to roll the last ball of the game. When it was over, I held my breath and looked up at the scoreboard: 148 points.

That night I lay awake in bed wondering how to interpret the number. I'd picked a random score, so it meant nothing. On the other hand, I'd asked the universe a question and it had returned the wrong answer. Unsatisfied, I grabbed my phone and texted Asser.

What's your birthday?

September 15

I wasn't sure how fully I believed in astrology, but it had to be better than bowling scores. According to Google, "Cancer [me] and Virgo [him] are highly compatible, making a relationship between the two destined for success." I fell asleep grateful for the good omen.

When I wasn't seeing Asser or working that summer, I hung out with my friends as much as possible: shopping with Alice, a weekend trip to the Lake District with Cora, lunch in London with Raja. I tried to keep doing normal things, tried to remind myself that Asser was just a new friend in my life and not the center of it. But no matter where I was or who I was with, his smile kept floating to the surface of my mind.

I started to have new worries as well. *If he actually does like me, then what?* Dating was forbidden, so would I have to keep our relationship a secret indefinitely? Was I falling in love? Or was I about to ruin my reputation? Both?

Since Sofia already knew about him and understood all the pressures on single young women in Pakistan, I decided to text her for advice. She was skeptical.

I can't believe you've seen him five times. Just feels like a lot of your summer to waste on a maindak.

Maindak means "frog" in Urdu. It's city kid slang for a guy who dates a lot, like a toad jumping from lily pad to lily pad.

That's really not Asser, though. He seems genuine.

I guess he didn't strike me as a serious person.

What do you mean?

Like shouldn't you be with someone more on your level, a guy who could become the head of the UN or IMF one day?

I couldn't think of anything I wanted less. I'd been in rooms with those types of men for years and never fancied any of them. And Asser *was* serious about his work in the sports world. I hadn't asked Sofia's opinion on whom I should date, but if I was dating at all.

How do I find out how he feels about me?

Want me to casually ask Jamal if he's heard anything?

I said yes and hoped for good news.

IN MID-AUGUST, I had to go to the US for six weeks, a combination of work travel and seeing a new doctor about my facial paralysis. When I returned, Asser would be back in Pakistan. He invited me for one last outing before I left—a visit to a cricket club in Chester where his amateur team from Pakistan was playing a match against New Zealand.

When I checked myself in the mirror before I left the house, I was surprised to find that I liked what I saw—two distinct and well-shaped eyebrows (thanks to my mom) and clear skin (thanks to my new skincare routine). Makeup still seemed too much for me, but I had started wearing tinted lip balm. I'd learned how to part and style my hair in a way that made the left side of my face less noticeable. Aiming for an outfit that was casual enough for cricket but sophisticated enough for a date, I settled on a gauzy white shirt, slim black jeans, and a chiffon headscarf. Pretty might be a stretch, but I thought I looked elegant and almost cool.

The afternoon sun cast long shadows on the pitch where the players were warming up. Pakistan threw out the first ball, and my eyes were fixed on the game. For the first time since we met, I wasn't taking every opportunity to steal glances at Asser.

"Bowl him out!" I yelled, gripping the handrail in the front row of the stands. "Did you catch that seam position? Perfection!"

Asser looked at me, eyes wide, mouth slightly open.

"What?" I said. "I told you I love cricket!"

"Yeah, you did," he replied, grinning and shaking his head. "I guess I just wasn't expecting so much fist-pumping and . . . growling!" I punched him on the arm and returned my focus to the pitch.

After the match, I posed for photos with the team. Normally I would have hung out with cricket players as long as they'd have me, but Asser and I only had ninety minutes left together, just as long as it took to get back to Birmingham. I said a silent prayer for heavy traffic.

When we got in the car, I gestured to the middle seat and asked, "Will you sit here, closer to me?" I spoke to Asser in Urdu so the security guards in the front couldn't eavesdrop. He smiled and slid toward me.

When the sun set and everything was dark, he pulled me closer and I laid my head on his shoulder. It was so quiet that I worried he would hear how fast my heart was beating.

The car stopped in front of his sister's house, and I sat straight up in a panic, unclear how to say good-bye or ask when I might see him again. He turned to me and said, "Will you keep in touch on your trip? Thank you for spending time with me this summer. I really loved getting to know you."

⌒

I WAS IN San Francisco when Sofia called. Anxious to hear what intel she'd gathered, I excused myself from a meeting and stepped into the hall to talk to her.

"Asser knows you like him," she said. "He had the best time with you, and he values your friendship, but . . . he thinks you're in different places in your life. I'm really sorry, Malala."

I felt the hot sting of shock and embarrassment spread across my face. Why had he kept asking me out if he knew it wasn't going to work? Did I say or do the wrong thing? I pulled up his number and almost called, but stopped myself. *He isn't your boyfriend and he doesn't owe you an explanation. Don't humiliate yourself.*

It was all my fault, in the end, for hoping he might fall in love with me.

Standing in the beige corridor of a California office block, I blinked back tears. *Pull yourself together. You're supposed to be working.* I wiped my eyes, walked back into the meeting, and tried to avoid speaking until I was sure my voice wouldn't break.

19.

More bad news was waiting for me back in Birmingham—
a letter from Lara:

*While I am pleased to share that you passed your
preliminary examinations, your marks correspond to a
Lower Second Class degree, near the bottom for Philosophy,
Politics, and Economics students in your year. For context,
in a typical year, approximately 22% of students attain
First Class, 73% attain Upper Second Class and 5% attain
Lower Second Class.*

*This is substantially below the level at which I believe you
are capable of performing. Given your passionate commitment
to education, I feel it would be a great pity if you do not fulfill
your academic potential while studying at Oxford.*

The letter continued, itemizing my sins: essays submitted after the deadline, failure to complete my weekly reading assignments, and skipped tutorial sessions meant to help struggling students catch up before exams. *You did not appear to be doing sufficient independent work.* I had passed my first year at university, but I wouldn't continue to scrape by as classes got more difficult, Lara warned.

I didn't care where I ranked among the other students, but Lara's line about my "passionate commitment to education" stung. Would people think I was a fraud or a hypocrite for giving speeches about the importance of girls going to school if they saw my prelim exam marks? My critics would love it: the world's most famous education advocate, the poster girl for bookish children and perennial teacher's pet, unmasked as a college delinquent.

When I received Lara's letter, I called her and asked if she could write another one for me—the same dire language about my academic performance, but in this version reiterating that she forbade me to travel during term time and that I needed to study over breaks as well. Then I put on a grave face and showed her letter to my dad, my speaking agent, and the staff at Malala Fund. If I didn't have the nerve to decline an important event or tell my family not to pack the house with guests while I was home, I knew Lara did. The plan worked: My team agreed not to schedule events while I was at Oxford, and my dad promised to try to contain his hospitality when I was at home.

This year will be different, I thought. I'd had a lot of fun as a fresher, but now it was time to hunker down and focus on my studies. I promised myself I'd spend more time in the library, do my reading, and turn in my essays on time. It was for the best that I wouldn't have a boyfriend to distract me.

But first: one last hurrah.

I didn't bother knocking at 24 Obs, where a welcome-back

party was in full swing on the eve of the new academic term. As soon as I stepped inside, I saw a sea of unfamiliar faces. If it weren't for the fact that most of them were speaking Urdu, I might have checked that I'd come through the right door.

I found Raja refilling drinks in the dining room. "Want to introduce me to your new friends?" I asked.

"I would if I knew who they were! First-years who somehow found their way here, I guess? I expect we'll get to know them by the end of the evening!"

The living room armchairs had been replaced by floor cushions and the coffee table removed to make way for a giant, four-hose hookah. Zayan was exhaling perfect rings of smoke and entertaining a crowd of newbies with his summer adventures in Karachi.

Parveen was not smoking, but continually shuffling coconut coals between the kitchen stove and the hookah. "Take a break," I told her. "Let the boys handle that and come chat with me."

We went out to the patio and commandeered chairs from two of Raja's mystery guests. Shortly after we sat down, her phone started pinging over and over. "Hmmm, something you want to tell me?" I pried. "Did you get a *boyfriend* since I saw you last?"

Parveen cackled and held the phone up for me to see a series of WhatsApp messages from her mom, recipes for aloo gosht, chicken jalfrezi, and kheer. "She does this at the start of every year. As if I have any time to cook in grad school."

I had planned to get to bed at a reasonable hour, but stayed longer than I intended—long enough to see the hookah cleared away, the 10 p.m. dance party kick up, and almost all of the guests depart. When the clock struck midnight, I was curled into a corner of the couch, deep in conversation with Zayan and two girls who had been strangers when the night began. *It's fine*, I told myself. *The term doesn't start until tomorrow.*

The next morning, I jolted awake and grabbed my phone to

check the time: 11:03 a.m. *No, no, no!* I'd missed the first lecture of the year. Lara's admonishments ran through my head, and I buried my face in the pillow in shame. This was more than a minor backslide—I hadn't managed to be a responsible student for *a single day.* Then, a week later, I was asking for an extension on my first essay. My complete inability to manage my time felt more like defeat than a setback. Why was my life such a mess?

Lara's letter had warned that the workload would be harder in my second year, and it was. Leonard, the professor for my Political Sociology course, assigned a weekly average of four hundred pages of reading from academic journal articles. I couldn't manage a fraction of it. After the sixth or seventh article, I was using my yellow highlighter not to mark important passages, but to keep my eyes focused on the page. I looked up information on how to speed-read, which suggested that humming while you read could help. It didn't.

Cora was my tutorial partner again, and at our Thursday meetings, Leonard assessed our analysis of the material in the Oxford tradition of "education through interrogation." Whenever he asked a question about one of the articles I'd failed to read, my eyes darted to Cora, and she jumped in to do the talking for both of us. Leonard wasn't fooled. "It seems that the empirical literature, of which there is a lot in this course, poses a challenge for you," he said to me with a smirk.

Determined to get on top of my work, I googled study tips. The suggestions included tidying your dorm room ("physical clutter leads to mental clutter"), ten minutes of meditation before studying ("calm your mind"), and drinking a full bottle of water ("brains need hydration too"). I tried all the suggestions except the ones I'd already mastered—"take breaks to see friends" or "reward yourself with ice cream or your favorite TV show."

I vowed to go to sleep early, get up by 6 a.m., and take an invigorating walk before beginning my studies. That strategy lasted forty-eight hours. Then I tried positive thinking. Before bed, I left motivational notes to myself for the following morning: *If you wake up late, that's fine. Don't worry, just go to the library and start your work.* These affirmations were worth less than the Post-its on which they were written. No matter what tricks and techniques I took up, my essays and tutorial contributions were mediocre at best.

This was all the more frustrating because, after slogging through political theory and economic models in my first year of college, I'd finally found a course that captivated me. In Ethics, we studied the forces that shape our personal morals and the practical applications of value systems. In tutorials, I participated with enthusiasm, debating various points with the professor, but I still couldn't articulate my thoughts in an essay.

Lara advised me, as she had several times in the previous year, to visit the Study Skills Center, where specially trained teachers. could help me improve my writing and analytical skills. Billed as a place for students to unlock their "latent potential," it sounded like remedial education to me.

I had never been embarrassed to ask for help. In high school, I would stay after class to get extra support from my teachers when I needed it. At Oxford, though, I didn't want the other students to know I was struggling. I worried that they suspected I wasn't as smart as them and didn't deserve to be there, having jumped the queue because I was famous.

At first I didn't believe that was true. I'd scored high marks on my A-levels, the tests that determine college placement. I didn't mention the Nobel or any of my awards in my application essay, against the advice of my guidance counselor. But now I was putting real effort into my work and still falling short. *Maybe I'm not cut out for Oxford*, I thought as I struggled to put words on the page for an essay or complete a problem set. When I couldn't grasp a concept or keep up with the reading, I thought about my dad, Malala Fund, and the Shangla school—how embarrassed everyone would be if I had to drop out, how it would hurt my work. I felt like I was standing in quicksand, scrambling to stay on top of my studies and only sinking farther and farther below the surface.

After the Ethics professor tactfully described my essay on Kant as "not so good, I'm afraid," I swallowed my pride and made an appointment at the Study Skills Center. My legs felt slow as I walked toward the building, defeated and sheepish. A woman named Valerie greeted me and showed me to her office. I expected to see a desk and a whiteboard, but this small, sunny space felt more like a Victorian drawing room. There were cookies and fruit on the coffee table, sunlight pouring through the window. She gestured for me to sit down on the sofa, then sat down next to me and asked how she could help.

"I have to ask for an essay extension almost every week. But extra time doesn't seem to help because my professors' comments aren't usually . . . complimentary."

"All right, we can work on time management and writing skills together. When are your essays due?"

"Ethics at nine a.m. on Monday, Political Sociology at nine a.m. on Thursday."

"And when do you start them?"

"I try to work on them over the weekends." I hesitated for a moment, and realized that wasn't entirely true. "It takes me *a lot* of time to get through the reading, so I usually don't start writing until the night before they're due. Like, sometimes I'll begin an essay at five a.m. and turn it in four hours later." As the words came out of my mouth, I started to wonder if maybe I needed the pressure, if my brain simply refused to engage until I was in crisis.

"That sounds quite stressful!" Valerie commented without judgment. "The good news is that there's a much easier way. What is missing from your writing process is the planning stage."

She told me to start my essay as soon as my professor assigned it. Before I dove into reading, I should analyze the question, think about my argument, and draft an outline. This would help me focus my reading on supporting my case, not on trying to form one. If something in the journal articles or philosophy texts changed my thinking, I would already have come up with the counterpoints.

I tried her approach and felt more confident in that week's essays, so I went back again and again, working with Valerie on how to structure my arguments and make a study plan that allowed me time to see my friends and fulfill my duties to the various clubs I had joined. The reading still took me a long time; I fell behind and sometimes missed deadlines, but the quality of my papers inched up. Over the eight weeks of the term, the feedback on my essays went from "a pile of unconnected thoughts" to "underdeveloped but improving."

One of the biggest things I learned was how to say no to my friends. In the past, I'd accepted every invitation, not wanting to miss a moment of social time. People still invited me out, but it quickly became a running joke that my reply to every offer was "Essay, mate." *Dinner in town? Poker tonight? Want to watch the world's sexiest Bollywood actors feeding ice cream to kittens on the quad?* Whatever the question, if my work wasn't finished, the answer was, "Can't. Essay, mate."

I wish I could say that the rest of the year ran like a movie montage—scenes of me clacking away on my laptop morning and night, professors beaming as they returned my near-perfect essays, sprinting through campus to tell Valerie the good news, the look of surprise on Lara's face when I moved up to First Class Honors. None of that happened. Studying was always a struggle for me at college. But I made progress and proved to myself that I deserved my place.

20.

G oing into the spring term, I felt self-assured and steady. As long as I stuck with my study plan, I could have it all—nights out with friends, extracurricular activities, and good academic standing. The weather was getting warmer and everything in my life was going well.

On Friday night before the official start of the term, Zayan and I went for an early dinner at 24 Obs. In eight weeks, so many of our friends from this group would be graduating and leaving Oxford to start their adult lives. Raja would complete his engineering degree and give up the lease. Next year, our clubhouse would belong to someone else.

I would particularly miss Raja, who had become like a big brother to me, giving me tips on everything from surviving the dreary Oxford winter to changing the settings on my phone so my parents couldn't read my texts from the lock screen. I wanted to spend as much time with him and Parveen as possible—and that meant sticking to a schedule, so that I wasn't constantly stressed about falling behind.

"What next?" Zayan asked as we left 24 Obs. "Ooh, let's climb on the roof!"

"I think I might get a jump on my econ reading for next week, actually."

"On a Friday night? Get this girl in some yoga pants because she is *balanced*!"

"Shut up," I said, laughing and rolling my eyes.

Back in my room, I opened a textbook, uncapped a highlighter, and reviewed the first essay question before beginning my reading, as Valerie had taught me to do.

Explain how the time inconsistency of optimal monetary policy can lead to a stabilization bias. How would the introduction of a price path target help to address it?

After reading the question three times, I still couldn't make sense of it. I groaned, went back to the textbook, tried to read, made a cup of tea, and tried again. Nothing improved my focus. Then my phone lit up with a message from Anisa: a picture of my name spelled out in Scrabble letters.

On my way. Stay there, I replied.

Perhaps a little break was what I needed. It was only 10:30 p.m., early by my standards. And maybe, if I asked nicely and she was in a good mood, Anisa would come back to my room and explain the essay question to me. I left the textbook on my desk and grabbed my coat.

Outside, the moon lit up rows of daffodils, and the fresh cut grass stuck to my shoes as I crossed the playing fields. At the farthermost edge of Lady Margaret Hall's gardens sat my destination—

an old potting shed that the college calls "the summerhouse" and students call "the shack." It had three walls clad in clapboard siding, small rectangular windows, and a wood-shingled roof covered in moss. The builders, whoever and whenever they were, had left the fourth wall open to nature. Sometimes I sat in the shack alone and listened to the rain splashing off the roof or watched otters play on the riverbank. It was one of my favorite places on campus, like something out of a storybook.

The interior was furnished with a wooden bench, chairs, and two small tables. On one wall, shelves held broken plates, green and blue glass bottles, and a bowl of old keys—treasures the gardeners dug up during their daily maintenance. On the opposite wall, three old mirrors hung above a bookshelf containing weather-beaten board games, pillar candles, and the occasional book. Dozens of loose Scrabble letters were scattered around the shack; students used them to spell out their names, an impermanent version of writing *X was here* on a bathroom wall.

Anisa was sitting with two boys I recognized from the business course, hovering around an unusual object on the table between them. The clear glass container had a smaller glass tube poking out at the base and looked like something nicked from the chemistry lab.

"Hi, guys," I said, nodding to the room. "What's that?"

Without answering, one of the boys picked it up and hovered a lighter over the smaller tube. I heard a bubbling sound and he disappeared behind a cloud of smoke. The smell answered my question.

It wasn't the first time I'd been around people smoking weed. I'd even tried it myself at 24 Obs; my friends shouted confusing instructions like "You have to inhale! Swallow and then breathe out at the same time! No, breathe with your mouth, not your nose!" As far as I knew, I'd never actually been high, but it felt cool and grown-up to blow smoke in the air and lazily pass the joint to the next person.

"Your turn," the boy said.

"Nah, I've done it before and it doesn't work on me," I replied. The beaker-thing looked complicated, plus I still had econ reading to do.

"Chalk and cheese," Anisa said. I gave her an exasperated look; she knew very well by now that I never understood her British-isms. "What I mean is," she continued, "a bong is totally different from a joint. Much more effective, fit for purpose."

I easily talked myself into it. *Fine, why not? I'm already out here, might as well have a new college experience.* The boy to my right held the lighter while I lifted the bong to my face. Then my face filled with smoke, and I doubled over, coughing. Anisa laughed. Everyone took a turn while we chatted about our holiday travels.

Eventually it came back around to me. "Okay, one more, but this is it," I said. I held the lighter myself this time, brought the mouthpiece slowly up to my face, and didn't cough. I sat back in my chair and zoned out while the others continued their conversation.

At some point, I looked at my phone and saw it was past 1 a.m., hours later than I expected. *How is that possible? I've only been here for a few minutes.* My mind tried to fill in the gaps, to find a logical explanation for where all the time went, but everything was blank. *How did I just erase two hours of my life without realizing it?* "I have to go," I said.

"I'll walk with you," Anisa offered.

The short path back to the dorms seemed to stretch out for miles. My legs felt heavy and rooted to the ground. *What's wrong with me?* I thought. Walking required a conscious effort, and it seemed like another hour had passed before I managed a single, stumbling step. "Sorry," I said to Anisa. "Just . . . feeling wobbly."

My leg muscles started to twitch and then my knees locked up. I couldn't move. *Just take a step. One foot in front of the other.* My brain was sending signals into a void. Again and again, no response, no movement. I balled up my fists, dug my nails into my palms, and tried again, more forcefully this time: *Keep walking, Malala!* When nothing happened, a cold, sharp fear climbed up from my stomach and settled in my shoulders.

Then everything went black. As I started to pass out, the truth hit me: I knew this feeling, the terror of being trapped inside my body. This had happened before.

SUDDENLY I WAS fifteen years old again, lying on my back under a white sheet; a tube running down my throat, eyes closed. For seven days, as doctors tended to my wounds, I was in a coma. From the outside, I looked to be in a deep sleep. But inside, my mind was awake, and it played a slideshow of recent events:

My school bus.

A man with a gun.

Blood everywhere.

My body carried through a crowded street.

Strangers hunched over me, yelling things I didn't understand.

My father rushing toward the stretcher to take my hand.

As the images repeated in the same sequence over and over, I raged against them, trying to beat them away. *This isn't true!* I told myself. *The real Malala is the one trapped in this nightmare, not the girl on the stretcher. Just wake up and it will stop. Wake up!*

I had tried to force my eyes open, to see something other than this carousel of horrors. Inside, I screamed; outside, my lips stayed closed, motionless. I was awake and buried alive in the coffin of my body.

And now, on a garden path in Oxford, it was happening again: my mind telling my body to move, my body turned to stone. "I can't walk!" I finally cried out to Anisa. "Please help me!"

"Shhhh, I'm here, you're okay," Anisa answered, her voice strained with alarm. Strong from years of competitive sports, she lifted me up and carried me back to her dorm. I crumpled to the floor, exhausted and dizzy, struggling to catch my breath.

Everything was still for a moment. I felt relieved to be inside, in the comfort of my friend's room. Then, out of nowhere, the images I had seen in the coma flashed before my eyes again: *Bus. Man. Gun. Blood.* It was like seeing it all for the first time, fresh waves of panic coursing through my body. I was not in a coma, but fully awake—and still, the memories found a way to reach me. There was no escape, no place to hide from my own mind.

"I need to go to a hospital," I gasped, barely able to get the words out.

Anisa sat down next to me. "You're having a bad reaction, but this will be over soon—thirty minutes, an hour at most. If you go to a doctor, they might run tests. It stays in your blood."

Seconds later I felt something caught in my throat, cutting off my air supply. I instantly remembered the pressure of the intubation tube, the sensation of choking every time I tried to swallow or speak. *Get it out now!* I thought, my memories of that time colliding into the present. Gathering all my strength, I lunged into Anisa's bathroom, leaned over the toilet, and vomited.

After a few minutes lying on the cold floor, I grabbed the sink and pulled myself up, catching sight of my pale, terrified face in the mirror. *What is happening to me?*

"Did that help?" Anisa asked. "Sit back down and let me get you some water."

I took a deep breath and tried to calm down. *It's over, lean back, just relax.* As soon as I closed my eyes, the slideshow began again. The images came faster now, relentlessly attacking me. My mind was free-falling deep inside my body. I opened my eyes and screamed.

"Malala, snap out of it!" Anisa yelled, shaking me by the shoulders. She ran down the hall and woke up a friend. They sat on either side of me, bracing my body upright. Anisa gave me a pillow to muffle the screams and wiped the sweat off my face with a damp washcloth.

We stayed on the floor for what seemed like hours, until the screaming and shaking had stopped. "Let's get some sleep," Anisa said. "You take the bed, I'll pass out here. In the morning you'll feel better, okay?"

I got in bed, but I didn't sleep. I could still see a familiar world around me—her books on the desk, polo mallet in the corner, the waning moon shining through the window. If I closed my eyes, it would all be gone forever. The nightmares would trap me, hold me hostage in an endless loop of terror. I drifted off only to jerk myself back to consciousness, jolting my body upright and slapping my own face. *Wake up, Malala! If you fall asleep, you will die!*

I was still awake in the morning when Anisa got up from the floor and stood over me. "I'm so relieved you're okay now," she said, tousling my hair. She stepped into the washroom and turned on the shower. I slipped out the door, hoping I wouldn't run into anyone on the walk to my dorm.

Attempting to wrest control of my thoughts made me seasick. I sat at my desk all morning, trying to distract myself—social media, news sites, Candy Crush—but the replay of the previous night, the helplessness I felt collapsed on Anisa's floor, kept creeping to the front of my mind and overwhelming me. I was nauseated, unable to stand up without feeling dizzy or sit down and be calm without shaking.

In the hospital, when I finally came out of the coma, I had no memory of what had happened to me or how I'd gotten there. Later I saw news footage of myself from the day of the shooting, bandaged and bleeding, carried through the street on a stretcher. In the video, the sun hits my face and my eyelashes flutter. Over the years, I'd seen that clip hundreds of times, but it never felt like part of my life. Those moments were a glitch in my timeline, the "and" in "before and after."

People always asked me what I remembered of the shooting. "My brain just erased it," I told them. "One moment I was at school and the next I woke up in Birmingham." I told myself that same story over and over—but now, I knew it wasn't true. I had seen it all, and the memories were still lurking in my brain, years later.

What had Anisa said?

It stays in your blood.

It stays in your blood.

It stays in your blood.

⌣⌐

I CALLED MY assistant and asked her to come to Oxford. Maria was nine years older than me, a Pakistani immigrant to the UK. She lived on her own as a single woman in London, and felt more like an older sister than an employee. She heard my shaky voice on the phone and left right away to make the two-hour drive from the city. When she got to my dorm, I told her everything. "Right," she said. "Take me to Anisa."

"Come to get your jacket?" Anisa asked. "You left it on the bed. Hey, Maria, what are you doing here?"

Maria closed the door behind us. "Tell me what happened last night." Anisa broke into nervous laughter, but Maria wasn't having it. "What did you give her?" she demanded. "Was it acid?

Mushrooms?" I steadied myself against the wall. I hadn't even thought of the questions Maria was asking.

"It was just weed!" Anisa shot back. "And then she started acting *insane*. She wouldn't stop screaming. It really freaked me out." I looked at the floor, Maria scowled, and Anisa's voice softened. "Look, I don't know what happened. She did a couple bong hits. It was honestly nothing."

"But my head is still spinning," I said. "It's been hours and I can barely breathe."

"Then it can't be the weed," Anisa replied. "It's something else."

From the look on Maria's face, I knew she was right.

21.

I staggered through the next few days, dragging myself to lectures and tutorials, but otherwise hiding out in my room. At night I was still afraid that when I closed my eyes I'd see those horrifying images on repeat, so I stayed awake and watched for the sun to rise. The best feeling I could manage was hollowness—a blank space was better than one filled with nightmares.

When Lara gave me the good news that I did well in collections—"Upper Second Class marks. I knew you could do it!"—I was ashamed instead of relieved. Since the night in Anisa's room, I hadn't done any of my reading. My first essays of the term would be late. After trying so hard to stay on top of my coursework, I felt lost. It wasn't a matter of will, priorities, or study skills anymore. I couldn't focus my mind long enough to read and write.

One of my courses that term focused on Plato's *Republic*. In the allegory of the cave, prisoners who have lived their whole lives in darkness believe that the shadows they see are the real world. When a prisoner is freed and walks into the sunlight, he realizes what he thought was reality was only an illusion. *Now I'm in the cave*, I thought. I desperately wanted to see things clearly again, to shake off the shadows and return to the light.

A week after that night in the shack, Lady Margaret Hall held its triennial Commemoration Ball, meant to be the social high-light of our college years. For months I had been beside myself with excitement for the big night—planning my outfit, checking every update from the ball committee on Instagram, making plans with my friends. Now I worried that it would be too much, too taxing for my fragile mental state.

On the afternoon before the ball, I went to the salon for an appointment I'd booked months earlier. The menacing rattle of the hair dryer frayed my nerves, and I couldn't wait to leave. Back at the dorm, everyone was getting ready in Cora's room, helping each other zip up their gowns and make last-minute decisions on jewelry and eyeliner. I wished I had another week to recover, or some sort of emotional decompression chamber that would help me switch from brutal flashbacks to this giggly, festive mood. But I didn't want to be the sad girl at the party, so I tried to mirror their energy and match the excitement in their voices.

We made the short walk to the gardens together, my friends' contagious laughter and exuberance pulling me along like a gentle current. By the time we arrived, I felt almost normal. Lady Marga-ret Hall had transformed into an elaborate dreamscape of music, revelry, and romance. Even the plants were putting on a show— the purple wisteria in full bloom, the magnolia tree bursting with giant, glossy leaves.

Throughout the evening, anxiety loosened its grip on me. I watched a troupe of drag queens warm up the crowd before the musical acts, ate churros, and marveled at the midnight fireworks. At 3 a.m., I sat on the ground in the corner of the silent disco tent, smiling as my friends donned headphones and danced to whatever beats were in their ears. At sunrise, we stood in line for breakfast sandwiches, then joined the crowd for the traditional "survivors' photo," a group picture of those who made it through the ball from start to finish.

It was the first time in days that I didn't have to stay vigilant all night, trying not to fall asleep. Everyone I loved was awake with me, filling the hours with laughter and movement. I wondered if the people who partied all the time, the ones I rarely saw sober, were also running away from nightmares.

The night after the ball, though, I went back to staying awake until dawn, afraid if I closed my eyes, the flashbacks would start again. During the day, I tried to rest, missing lectures and essay deadlines. I didn't want to alarm my friends, but Anisa and Cora saw me stumbling, ragged and bleary-eyed, and started to worry anyway. As Cora finished her reading for the week, she sent me her notes and outlines, hoping to kick-start me into doing my work. Anisa appointed herself the homework police, checking on my progress before she went to bed at night.

> Have you handed in your econ problem set?

no

> It was due at 9 pm! How much do you have left?

haven't started yet

> What about your philosophy essay?

Nothing

nothing is done

My friends were trying their best to help me stay on top of the academic work, but sleep deprivation made it impossible to study. Falling behind made me feel even more panicked and depressed, like I'd never be able to dig myself out of the hole. When I got overwhelmed, my heart would race. If I lay on my bed to try to slow it down, it felt like a stack of bricks was sitting on my chest. Standing up again made me dizzy. All of it made me want to scream and cry in frustration, but most days I was too tired to do more than sit and stare at the wall.

One evening, I asked Anisa if she would stay in my room for the night. If I tried to sleep and something went wrong, she could call for help. We set up her mattress on the floor next to my bed, changed into our pajamas, and talked for a while. At midnight, she turned out the light and dozed off. I lay awake and stared out the window for a long time. Eventually I took a deep breath, rolled over, closed my eyes, and prayed for rest.

And it worked—I slept through the whole night. I was so relieved that I got over my hesitation in telling my other friends about the flashbacks and asked them to sleep over in my room. Hen stayed the following night; Yasmin took the next shift. They seemed to know exactly what I needed—never pushing me to go into detail about my problems but merrily chatting about boys or showing me funny memes and videos. As much as their presence comforted me at night, I knew I couldn't keep doing this. My friends needed their space and time to study, and my problems were disrupting their schedules. I felt very old and way too young at the same time.

Could we maybe have
a phone call? If you're
busy, no worries.

Asser and I had continued to text each other, going from a few times a month at the start of the year to several times a week by the spring. At first it had been challenging. I felt a flicker of embarrassment and sadness when his name lit up my phone in our group chats with Jamal and Sofia; I would purposely respond to everyone but him. Eventually, though, Asser and I started texting on the side about cricket or music, and fell back into the easy banter we'd had over the summer. I knew it was a risk to ask for more, but he rang me as soon as he saw my message asking him to call.

I told him everything—the bong, the flashbacks, the sleepless nights. It all tumbled out of me, and I wasn't nervous or worried about what he would think. Like Maria, Asser was older than me, and I felt like I could share my experience without judgment. From some of the stories he'd told me about his high school and college experiences, I knew he'd experimented with drugs himself; a bad trip wasn't going to shock him. We were friends, I was a mess, and he might have good advice.

"Have you been to the doctor?" he asked.

"I can't. They could find the drugs in my blood and send me to jail."

On his end of the phone, I heard what was either a sigh or a muffled laugh. "Please, please listen to me: You are not going to jail. There is no law against smoking marijuana."

"Yes, there is, in the UK. You're thinking of America—"

"No, I'm not. The laws in the UK are against possession and only possession of large amounts. They are aimed at dealers, not people who touched a bong once in their life."

"Are you sure?"

"And if the doctor does a blood test, they will not be looking for drugs. Doctors and nurses don't report users, even for harder drugs like heroin."

"How do you know so much about this . . . possession and stuff?"

"Malala, I'm not a drug mule, if that's what you're wondering! It's just common knowledge. But I am worried about you. Please make an appointment and see a doctor."

I promised I would and thanked him for the advice. As soon as we said good-bye, I opened a message and wrote:

I miss you.

Go to the doctor.
I miss you too.

With time, the fear subsided, and I was able to sleep through the night on my own. I waited for the burst of energy that comes after you've been sick, when you wake up one morning and realize you're no longer vomiting or clammy, and you want to run out and greet the day, grateful to be alive and well. That feeling never came, but slowly I started to slip back into the routines of college life.

In May I went to my doctor's appointment and told her about my insomnia, exhaustion, and breathing difficulties. I left out the weed and flashbacks. She did a blood test and, a few days later, called to say I was anemic. "It's common for South Asian women and nothing to worry about. Take an iron supplement every day, and try to eat meat, leafy green vegetables, and fruit."

I knew anemia wasn't the source of my recent troubles, but I picked up the pills and informed Asser that I had completed the mission. A few days later, a package from him arrived in the mail.

Inside was an Iron Man toy and a note that said, *Put this on your desk to remind you to take your vitamins every morning.*

As spring turned to summer, I counted the days until I could leave Oxford; college wasn't a safe, happy place for me anymore. The flashbacks were gone, but I no longer felt free. Now I had to steady myself on an endless tightrope, worried that a loud noise or a sudden movement could knock me off-balance or shake loose a bad memory. The parties I'd once loved now made me unsteady and hypervigilant. I went to the 24 Obs graduation celebration but left before 10 p.m. Most nights I swapped dinners out for take-away and TV in my room. I was cautious with myself, careful not to disturb the enemy in my brain.

Every night I prayed, *Ya Allah, heal me quickly.*

22.

I looked to the summertime as a reset, a chance to put the nightmares behind me and start over—and Asser was a big part of that. When he told me he was coming back to the UK in July, I was delighted if not completely surprised. His niece was graduating from med school and England was hosting the Cricket World Cup, a great opportunity to broaden his professional network. But the main reason was me. He didn't need to say it—I knew I wasn't wrong about his feelings this time.

After that first phone call where I told him what I was going through, he called almost every day. At first he mostly checked on my health, making sure I took my iron pills and gently lecturing me when I admitted to eating nothing but french fries for two days in a row. Then our conversations got longer, stretching to include topics like celebrity crushes, our childhood dreams, the existence of God. Asser kept up with all the gossip about my friends' love lives; I learned that he loved to deejay in college but gave it up after he witnessed a murder at an illegal rave in Lahore. Like most people my age, I preferred texting over phone calls, but with Asser, I could talk for hours.

We had become more than friends and we both acknowledged it—he called me "babe" and said I looked beautiful in the pictures I sent him. My lack of dating experience sometimes meant I was trying to court a twenty-nine-year-old man with the romantic tool kit of a twelve-year-old girl. If he sent a text saying he had a busy day and couldn't call at our usual time, I sulked and replied, u don't even have time for me. must not be that important to u. Sometimes I picked fights just to get his attention. He laughed off these antics, calling me "president of the drama club" and promising that he missed me.

"How much time will we have together in your busy summer schedule?" he asked one night, a couple of weeks before he was set to arrive in London.

"Short trips to Ethiopia and France, a longer stay in the US in August. But my calendar has a lot of open spots and they're all yours! I'm actually more worried about . . ."

"Your parents?"

"Yeah. Last year they didn't pry too much, but the more we see each other, the more questions they'll ask. Could get tricky."

"Okay, what if I write your dad a letter? It will say, 'Dear Mr. Yousafzai, Hope you are doing well. As you are aware, you have a daughter who has grown up to be a wonderful and beautiful woman. And . . .'"

At this point, he broke into song, warbling, "*Le jayenge, Le jayenge, Dilwale Dulhania le jayenge!*" The song, "The Brave-Hearted Will Take the Bride," was an old Bollywood hit about a man making his case to the father of the woman he loved.

I had two thoughts at once:

I can't wait to see him again.
That is possibly the worst singing voice I've ever heard.

⌒⌒

FROM THE MOMENT Asser arrived in England, all our experiences—
last summer's fumbling around feelings and our recent four-hour
phone calls—blended to create the thrill of a new relationship
with the worn-in ease of an older one. We would spend all day
together, then call each other the minute we got home, staying on
the phone for hours. On long drives to London, we sat in comfortable silence, content to simply exist next to each other while
watching the countryside roll by and listening to my security
guards' nineties playlists.

One evening we went to a restaurant at an old manor in the
English countryside. "Excuse me for just one minute," I said to
Asser after the host showed us to a table by the window. I'd left my
parents' house in a shalwar kameez that met my mom's approval
but stuffed a change of clothes in my bag: a sleeveless, form-fitting
dress in pale pink lace and my highest heels.

When I returned to the table, Asser stood up and his mouth
broke into a smile I hadn't seen before. He pulled out my chair and
whispered, "You're a sex bomb!" in my ear. I hid my face behind my
dinner napkin, both delighted and bashful.

Asser's arrival vanquished the dark clouds that had hung over
my third term at Oxford, but it wasn't exactly the carefree summer
romance of rom-coms, as I worried a lot about getting caught.
When we were together, it was hard for me to turn off premoni-
tions of being publicly shamed in Pakistan for having a boyfriend. I agonized over what would happen to the Shangla girls,
imagining their parents pulling them out of our school over my
carelessness.

161

On a walk through London's Chiswick Gardens one afternoon, I was showing off for Asser, climbing up a tree and daring him to race me to the top. When I jumped down, I grabbed his hand and pulled him close to me. That's when I caught the eye of a woman on a park bench staring at us. She broke into a wide smile of recognition and pulled out her phone to take a picture. I freaked out and ran behind a hedge to hide, alarming both Asser and my security team. It was exhausting to constantly worry about being observed or photographed, to spend so much energy being aware of my surroundings that I could never fully be myself.

The next day I rode to the airport with my dad to catch a plane to Addis Ababa. I couldn't put it off anymore—I had to tell him about Asser. As he read the morning news on his phone, I stared out the window, rehearsing what I would say and bracing myself for his response. I wanted to stay in my secret world a little longer, free of people's opinions and reminders about what I was risking. But that couldn't last. My dad needed to hear it from me before someone snapped a picture of Asser and me together.

My dad and I loved to debate each other about politics, world events, feminism, anything at all. I would try to convince him to my side, and most of the time, I succeeded. My whole life, I felt like I could tell him anything—but I'd never been in love before.

"Dad, you know . . . it's hard to meet good people . . . like, people who have a good sense of humor but also find me funny," I began. He looked attentive, like he was trying to understand me. *Ugh, you're making this worse*, I thought. *Just spit it out!*

"It's just, like . . . when you meet someone and want to spend more time with them? Well, I guess . . . I guess, basically, I have met someone like that. He's, uh, twenty-nine . . . he lives in Lahore, but comes to England in the summer to see his sister. And he works in cricket, which is great for me."

My dad nodded slowly, as if everything I'd said up to this point was fine. "We . . . Asser and I . . ." I continued. "I like him, Dad. I like him . . . romantically." A wave of nausea rolled through me as I choked the word out, but my dad just stared back at me without even blinking.

"I wanted you to know," I continued, "but please, *please* don't tell Mom. I'm begging you—I am not ready to have this fight with her yet."

At first it seemed like he was about to ask a question. But he stopped himself, looked straight ahead, and said nothing. Then I watched in disbelief as my dad, my lifelong confidant, pulled out his phone and called home.

On the other end of the line, I heard my mom say, "Absolutely not! Does he even speak Pashto? She must marry a Pashtun man!"

"If he's here for the summer, we should meet him," my dad said crisply after he hung up. "But we won't announce the engagement until after your graduation." I glared out the window, fuming at myself for bringing it up, at my dad for calling my mom, at my mom for being so small-minded, and at them both for jumping to engagements and husbands.

Why are you even thinking about marriage? I wanted to scream. *Can I not just live my life like all the other twenty-one-year-olds at college?* But I knew the answer: While my parents wouldn't force me to get married against my will, they would never accept me having a boyfriend. No looking, no touching, no dating. Any conversations you had with a man before marriage had to be supervised by the parents. Those were the Pashtun rules, and I'd already broken all of them.

Asser, on the other hand, was thrilled that I'd told my dad. "What did he say? When can I meet your family? I am ready!" I hated the thought of him and my family in the same room, but I agreed to a visit, as I didn't want Asser or my parents to think I had something to hide.

It felt like things were moving too fast, like I'd been caught in the undertow and dragged out to sea against my will. The family introductions weren't Asser's idea; my dad was the first to suggest it. Still, I was irritable and withdrawn over the next few days, even feigning illness and canceling a lunch date with Asser.

Though we hadn't discussed it, I worried that someday he might want to get married—and I knew I didn't want that, with Asser or anyone else. In my culture, everything revolves around the man. After marriage, a woman is supposed to follow orders and do everything she can to please him. I would never submit to that sort of control, of course—but I wasn't keen on Western images of marriage either. The thought of meal planning on the weekend or loading the dishwasher together honestly gave me the ick. I even hated the word "wife." In my ideal world, my relationship with Asser could go on forever, free of expectations, existing without context or formal commitment.

I suppose some part of me considered falling in love not as a path to marriage, but simply part of my college experience—in the basket of risky behaviors like clubbing or night climbing. In my second summer with Asser, I was only beginning to understand that I could not control my feelings, or stop my dreams and desires from changing. Whatever fixed idea I had of myself, however rigid my future plans—to stay single and dedicate my life to my work— my humanity kept breaking through, kept leading me to connection, friendship, and love.

We waited until the day before my three-week trip to the United States for his visit with my family. I planned everything to the minute: Asser would arrive by train to Birmingham at 11:45 a.m., get to my parents' house for a 12:00 p.m. lunch, and leave by 1:00 p.m. to return to London. Not much could go wrong in an hour, I figured.

He turned up bearing flowers and seemed a little bit nervous. I was flustered too, and could barely look him in the eye as I showed him to the living room where Khushal and Atal were blaring drill rap and playing video games. My dad, who had double-booked by mistake and invited seven guests of his own, was in the garden trying to man the barbecue, serve tea, and carry on multiple conversations. My mom sat under a tree in a lawn chair, evaluating everyone, particularly Asser. She asked him if he knew any Pashto and he gamely stumbled through the few phrases he knew. My mom wasn't impressed, but she seemed at least to credit him for making an effort. The whole situation was making me increasingly anxious, while Asser loosened up, chatting with my dad and his guests about his grilling techniques, encouraging Khushal to keep up with his studies, and even beatboxing with Atal.

At 1 p.m. sharp, I called a car for him and whispered, "I'm sorry," as he left. When he was gone, a weight lifted from my shoulders. I was relieved to have my identities—the chaste Pashtun daughter my parents expected me to be, and the fun-loving girlfriend Asser knew—separated again, back in their own boxes. But the reprieve was short-lived, quickly replaced by the desire to run after his car, hop in, and escape together. I didn't know how I would survive the next few weeks without him.

23.

B efore sunrise the next day, my parents and I traveled to Heath-
row and boarded a plane for Boston. They were taking me to
Massachusetts Eye and Ear to see Dr. Tessa Hadlock, a Harvard
Medical School professor and pioneer in treating facial paralysis.

Under Dr. Hadlock's supervision, I was undergoing a complex
series of surgeries called a cross-facial nerve graft. If it worked, I
would have more movement on the left side of my face. A year
earlier, in the first procedure, doctors had removed a long nerve
from my left calf. Then they'd made a series of discreet cuts—
at my right ear, inside my right cheek, under my upper lip, inside
my left cheek—and positioned the nerve to run across my face. In
order to achieve "facial reanimation," both halves of the face had to
be "talking" to one another via the nerve.

The doctors had warned me I wouldn't see any improvement
after the first surgery—and I didn't. The left half of the nerve

166

couldn't connect to the facial muscles until they added fresh tissue. On our current visit, they would remove part of my upper left thigh and deposit it inside my cheek. With any luck, the nerve from my calf would attach to the tissue from my thigh and begin sending signals to the muscles in my face.

Initially I did not want to do the cross-facial nerve graft; it meant spending weeks of time in hospitals and recovery rooms for three consecutive summers. My parents, however, kept pushing for a cure. They wanted to erase the memory of seeing me for the first time in the Birmingham hospital with sunken eyes and a paralyzed mouth—to silence the comments, from relatives and online trolls, about how pretty I "used to be" before the shooting. My parents and the doctors had convinced me it would be worth the effort in the end, so off we went to Boston.

On the plane, I got a message from Asser: Have your mom and dad said anything about us? I told him the truth. They were worried. Someone could take a photo, they said, or word could get out through one of our friends. They anticipated a scandal and said I should stop seeing him. I wasn't going to do that, but I hated the tension my relationship created with my parents. Wasn't it their *job* to be happy for me? I normally would have sat next to my dad on the flight and chatted with him for hours. This time, I put a blanket over my head and went to sleep.

The morning of the surgery, Dr. Hadlock and her team stood over my hospital bed giving a matter-of-fact overview of the five-hour procedure, as if I were a car in the shop coming in for a routine tune-up. At this point, I'd had seven surgeries in my life and never felt scared of hospitals, doctors, the beeping machines, or bright lights. But now I was full of dread. What if something went wrong, and the doctors put me back in a coma? What if I didn't wake up this time? I would rather live the rest of my life with facial paralysis than be held hostage by the abyss in my brain.

I kept my fears to myself; it wasn't something I wanted to share with my parents or the doctors. Luckily, the procedure went as planned. When I woke up, I saw the sunshine coming through the hospital room window and my whole body relaxed. *You made it*, I thought. Even the overcooked oatmeal and Jell-O the nurse brought the next morning tasted good to me.

After two days in the recovery ward, I transferred to a nearby hotel. That evening I took oxycodone prescribed for the searing pain in my thigh and cheek. Half an hour later, my head was reeling. The dizziness and nausea transported me back to that night in Anisa's room, and I began to panic. What if it happened again? I stayed awake all night, praying that the flashbacks would stay away, making bargains with the universe: *I won't go to another party as long as I live; I'll study and turn in all my work on time as long as I never have to experience that again.* In the early-morning hours, I finally drifted off. When I woke up, I was resolute: no more pain pills. It wasn't worth the risk. Better to tough it out than open the door to my nightmares.

⌒

WHEN I GOT back to England, I met Asser at a Cantonese restaurant in London's Dorchester Hotel for one last dinner before he returned to Lahore. My face was still heavily swollen from the surgery, but he smiled at me the same way he had at the start of the summer when I wore my "sex bomb" dress.

For months we'd avoided defining our relationship, enjoying each other's company as if nothing would ever need to change. I had preferred it that way, but being away from him the past few weeks had intensified my feelings. Now I needed to know what he was thinking. Throughout dinner, I fumbled around the question, never quite asking it. But he must have known what I was after.

"I'm going to miss you a lot when I leave," he said. "I feel kind of . . . hollowed out at the thought of not seeing you every week. You know—because I told you the second time we saw each other—that I'm looking for a long-term relationship. . . ." He paused in thought and my heart sped up, unsure where the conversation was going next. Was he proposing or dumping me? They were both unfavorable outcomes in my mind.

"The truth is, I would marry you tomorrow, and I *hate* myself for saying that. It's not a fair thing to put on you. Because you're too young. You're still changing as a person, still trying to figure out what you want in life."

In the moment, his words seemed so condescending that I didn't pause long enough to admit to myself that they were true. "You think because I'm young I can't know how I feel? How do you, at the advanced age of twenty-nine, know if you love someone?"

"I ask myself questions. Do you have the best time with her? Enjoy talking to her for hours? Do you trust her? Do you want to kiss her in the cloakroom at the Dorchester Hotel?"

My face flushed and I tripped over my words. "What about . . . just for now . . . let's call it an open relationship . . . except that it's closed at your end," I ventured.

Asser laughed so loud that people at nearby tables turned to look at us. "Okay, that was funny . . . but it's also part of the problem. You won't even call me your boyfriend. Being someone's secret doesn't feel great, especially when I want to tell the world how amazing you are. I would love to go on beach vacations with you and have a phone full of pictures of us. And I don't know when, or if, that will happen."

"The secrecy is to keep my parents calm. They're scared of creating a scandal."

He leaned over and took my hand. "I will always protect your privacy. Always. But if I'm honest, Malala, I also think you're keeping it a secret because you're not sure what you want in life, or with me. And that's fine! But that feeling doesn't really change as you get older; there are no signs pointing us in the right direction. None of us are ever certain—there's always the possibility of making the wrong choice or getting your heart broken. It never goes away."

I pulled at the sleeve of my dress, suddenly nervous around him for the first time all summer. "Could we maybe pause our feelings for now, just until I finish my last year at Oxford? We can pick up right here next June and figure things out."

"I'm not sure feelings work that way," he said. "But, for you, I'm willing to try."

We found a low-lit corner of the hotel lobby to say good-bye. When he put his arms around me, I whispered, "I love you." Then he was gone, and the summer was over.

24.

I have heard of people snapping or breaking, seeming to shift in an instant from a sister or friend into a stranger. But I lost my mind in pieces.

My grasp on reality. Hope for the future. My faith in my friends. The sense of peace I felt watching the sun rise over the river or hearing Asser's voice on the phone. The ability to control my own body. That autumn, I lost them all.

⌇

IT WAS SUPPOSED to be my best year of college. Sure, there were exams at the end, but also balls, picnics, and graduation parties to look forward to. I felt like I'd shaken off the fear and anguish that the flashbacks had brought into my life. Asser and I had had a great time over the summer and left things in a good place. I was

171

ready to be the diligent student I knew I could be, and, of course, have some fun.

My friends and I had decided to leave the dormitories on the main quad and move to a smaller residence hall on the edge of campus. In the new building, we would have a kitchen, a little balcony, and the top floor of the dorm all to ourselves—me, Cora, Hen, Yasmin, and Anisa. As usual, my security team would take the room next to mine. There was one space left over, and the college assigned it to a sweet and, in terms of the housing lottery, unlucky guy named Alan.

On move-in day, we discovered the dorm was hardly the oasis we imagined. The building's elevator rarely worked and the walls between our rooms were as thin as hospital gowns. The kitchen was no bigger than a walk-in closet, so we had to maximize every inch of space. Most of us were, in theory, willing to share our stuff, but you couldn't put meat in a vegetarian's skillet, milk in a vegan's mug, or pork in a Muslim's pot. All of which added up to six kitchens' worth of cookware and pantry items crammed into four tiny cabinets.

Hen's neat-freakery and need for order meant she was often sending scolding messages to the rest of us. In previous years, our group chat had always been full of dinner plans, inside jokes, and requests to borrow clothes. Now it was: Someone forgot to turn off the stove. Be responsible! or Who left raw chicken on the worktop?? or If you use my dishes, wash them. It's common courtesy!

When you live with your friends, you see another side of them—and sometimes you don't like what you see. I thought our last year was going to be one big slumber party, but there were near-constant arguments instead. Someone was always forgetting it was her turn to replace the milk, borrowing things without asking, or sleeping through her morning alarm, leaving the rest of us to suffer through *beep! beep! beep!* until someone else finally got up and banged on the door.

The constant noise set everyone on edge. We couldn't have a conversation at normal volume without disturbing the adjacent rooms. When I had a few 24 Obs friends over or Yasmin hosted study group, it sounded like the entire college had gathered in the kitchen. In the past, we might have just rolled our eyes, put on our headphones, and ignored it, but this was our final year. In May and June, we would all go to the Examination Halls and spend hours writing essays and solving equations. Eight grueling exams over four weeks, designed to test everything we'd learned at Oxford. Underperform and you'd hurt your career prospects. Fail a test, and you left college without a degree, as if the last three years of your life had never happened. All the third-year students were stressed, shuffling quickly from the library to the lecture hall and back again—and in our case, shouting at each other to be quiet in the kitchen.

The collective stress level was higher than ever as my friends were all working toward ambitious post-college goals. Anisa already had a conditional offer from a top consulting firm, and Cora was interviewing for jobs in finance. Hen and Yasmin were applying for master's programs at Harvard and Cambridge. Yasmin wanted to study law at Cambridge. Unlike them, I pitched from plan to plan: I decided to go to grad school. Then I changed my mind, thinking I should take a job and learn about the working world. No, I resolved, I'd travel and get a better understanding of girls' education in other countries. Sometimes I daydreamed about running away to a sunny beach with Asser. Then I'd cycle back to grad school and repeat my thought processes again. The longer my indecisiveness wore on, the more nervous and insecure I felt about not having a road map for my future.

I was working hard, but the study skills I'd learned from Valerie had gotten rusty over the summer. My professors gave sobering comments on my first few essays of the term—*little mention of extant literature / empirical examples were weak / argument lacked structure*. My friends would drop by my room in the evenings, as they always had, but I no longer looked forward to their interruptions. When I asked them to come back later, after I'd finished with my reading, Hen and Anisa would make snide comments like "Wow, can't believe even *you* are feeling the pressure now" or "Well, well, the girl who advocates for education has finally picked up a book!" In the past, I'd laughed off these jokes; now my responses were clipped and annoyed.

Everywhere I went—tutorials, dorm, dining hall—felt stressful, and my equilibrium started sliding away. I stayed up all night writing essays, often missing the deadlines. The instructions the doctor had given me last spring—"eat meat, leafy green vegetables, and fruit"—were long forgotten, and my diet was reduced to digestive biscuits or cereal, if I bothered to eat at all. My friends snarked and sniped at each other. I felt disoriented, like all of Oxford was a video game and I was a coding error.

$\backsim$

ON MY WAY to a lecture one morning, I got a text message from a cousin in Pakistan: Please call. I rang him right away, but no one answered. When I hung up the phone, I had a terrible premonition: My grandmother Abai was dead.

The panic welled up inside me, and I tightened my throat, fighting off the urge to cry or vomit. I couldn't focus on the lecture, lost in dark thoughts, eyes fixed on my phone in case my cousin called back. The second the professor finished speaking, I raced out of the room. A girl from the PPE study group called my name, but

I pretended not to hear her. *Just get to the dorm. Just get to the dorm.* As soon as I closed the door, my eyes filled with tears. I always hated to cry, hated the way that it made me feel weak. But my body was acting without my permission now, throwing itself into grief.

Lying on my bed, I shut my swollen eyes and tried to remember everything I could about Abai: How she built a campfire in front of her house in the mountains every time I came to visit because she knew I'd be cold when I arrived. The way she smelled like woodsmoke and roses. How, unlike a lot of older women in Pakistan, she never treated her daughter-in-law like a servant, and always gave my mom the best cut of meat at dinnertime. The day I was attacked, when she put her hand on me and asked God to give me a long life. I cried over all the things I didn't know about her as well. Who was her best friend? What were her dreams when she was a child? Had she ever seen the ocean?

I should have realized that none of this made sense. If anything happened to Abai, our relatives in Pakistan would notify my father, not me. I would hear the news from him. But I was incapable of rational thought, disconnected from reality. *Who will pray for me now that Abai is gone?* The hours ticked by. I was supposed to be working on a problem set, but I couldn't focus on anything but my sorrow and fear.

My cousin finally called back that afternoon. I answered the phone breathlessly—"Hello, what happened? Why did you call?"—and steeled myself for the news I knew was coming.

"Wanted to tell you I stopped in at the girls' school in Shangla," he said. "Construction on the new building is going well and we should be able to double enrollment next year." He mentioned a few other things about plumbing and playground equipment, but I cut him off.

"Is Abai okay?"

"Yes, she's fine. Stopped by to see her this evening and she was sitting outside, watching the sunset, like always. She forgets a lot of things these days, but her health seems good."

Those words should have been a huge relief to me; they should have lifted the curse that had possessed my heart and mind all day. But I was still staggering, trying to understand what had just happened. Why wasn't I able to control my thoughts, calm myself, wait to find out why he was calling before falling apart? I didn't have an answer, and that frightened and unnerved me.

My friends' voices drifted down the hallway and I locked my door from the inside. I couldn't see them right now—though I felt scared to be alone too, like I couldn't trust myself. I splashed cold water on my face, and looked around my room, trying to find comfort in familiar things—family photos, my favorite scarf, the cricket bat Raja gave me when he graduated. But it felt like I was seeing it all through someone else's eyes.

A WEEK OR so later, I was working on an essay when Hen barged into my room. It was after 1 a.m., and she was a bit drunk. I needed to study and thought about telling her so; but it had been a while since we hung out, and I figured I could spare a few minutes.

"Where have you been?" I asked.

"Oh, just out with Brandon," she replied.

"Brandon who?"

"You know . . . the American one." She twirled her hair with her fingers and blinked slowly at me.

"Brandon from PPE? What were you doing with him?" I saw Hen every day and Brandon almost as often at lectures and study groups. In the last two years, I'd never seen them together.

"I mean . . . well, we've been seeing each other for a few months."

I rolled my eyes at her and turned back to my textbook. My friends had this annoying prank where they would make up stories and convince me to believe them—a rolling game of Two Truths and a Lie, except they were always fibbing, and I fell for it over and over. The joke had been played out long ago, and I wasn't in the mood for it tonight.

"No, I'm serious!" Hen said. I tapped my pen on my notebook, hoping she would get the hint and leave me alone.

"Really, I don't know how you haven't noticed," she continued. "Remember last term, the 'Dress Like a London Tube Station' bop at the college bar?"

"Yeah, what about it? Brandon wasn't there."

"He was, though. You even talked to him on your way to the loo! And then he came and sat by me and we were, like, making out in front of everyone. I can't believe you missed it!"

I whipped back around, studying her face for the truth. For the next twenty minutes, I grilled her on the details of their relationship and she told me everything—the initial spark between them, first kiss, late-night phone calls over the summer. "No," I protested at various points, "I don't believe any of this." How could one of my best friends have a boyfriend that I didn't know about? She mentioned specific events and places we'd been together; I had no recollection of Brandon being there. If this was reality, what world had I been living in? How could I trust my own memory if all this had been happening and I didn't realize or remember it?

My left eye started to pulse in time with my heartbeat. It seemed to speed up with every disorienting revelation. *How long have we been talking?* I asked myself, realizing I was no longer sure if it was morning or night. Sweat rolled down my back and my hands went numb.

"Hen, I don't feel well," I mumbled.

"What's wrong, babe? Did you forget to eat today?"

"I don't know, I just . . . please tell me the truth. Is this real?"

She looked hurt for a moment, then broke out laughing. "Of course not! I've never even talked to that guy. I *cannot believe* you thought I was serious."

If I'd had the strength, I might have thrown a book or a mug at her. "Get out!" I growled. She froze for a moment, then started apologizing, repeating that it was only a joke. "Please," I said, my voice deflated, "just leave."

When she was gone, a fever seemed to grip me; even the roots of my hair felt like they were on fire. The pulsing migrated from my eye to my ears, getting louder and louder with every second. It sounded like a stampede, like I had a thousand hearts, all running for their lives.

I flew out of the room and banged on my security team's door. Liam, one of the older bodyguards, answered, his gray hair sticking out at wild angles, eyes squinting at the hall lights. I'd never woken them up before and felt bad about it, but I was too scared to be polite.

"Something is wrong with me," I choked out, struggling for air. "I think I'm having a heart attack."

He quickly helped me to my bed and checked my vital signs. "Your heart rate is high," he said. "But you're conscious and breathing." His voice sounded like an announcement in a busy airport. I heard the sound and recognized some of the words, but I couldn't process their meaning.

For the next hour, Liam kept checking my temperature, pulse, respiratory rate. Eventually my heart went back to normal and he went back to bed. My body felt heavy with exhaustion, and I fell into a deep sleep.

When I woke up the next day, I was afraid to leave my room,

convinced that the real world—the one I recognized, the one where I felt safe—wouldn't be on the other side of my door when I opened it. Whatever I encountered out there might send me spiraling again, so I stayed inside, alone and afraid. *What is happening to me?*

25.

When you search my name, the word you see over and over is "brave." I always thought it was true, thought I had a strong heart and a tough chest, that I could handle anything. When I started breaking down in college, I felt powerless. It made me angry that I couldn't conquer my fears or control my thoughts. Being afraid made me feel like I'd lost an essential part of myself.

My isolation grew more severe every day. After that night on Anisa's floor, I'd told my close friends about the flashbacks, but this new reality—the constant state of fear, the physical reactions, the endless bottoming out—was too much to share. They had already helped out so much the year before, checking on me, sharing their lecture notes and essays, staying in my room at night. How could I lean on them again, especially when they were so stressed about exams and post-college life? I didn't want to be the needy friend. I had to handle this on my own.

Suspecting that I'd been having panic attacks, I consulted Google for advice. *Dissociation or derealization can be triggered by schizophrenia, temporal lobe epilepsy, migraines, sleep disorders, head injury* . . . The list went on and on, and reading it only made me more frantic. I put down my phone and shuddered.

Going about my daily life and having to be "on" felt excruciating. In tutorials, I told the professors I was sick, so they'd go easy on me. When my friends bickered over who made a mess in the kitchen, I quietly walked away. Every interaction with other people felt dangerous, like it might cause my mind to fracture even further. In my journal, I inventoried my mental state.

Something is wrong with me and I'm worried that I can't stop it from happening again.

My recent problems
- *flashbacks last spring*
- *final year of university and exams coming up*
- *trouble with friends*
- *relationship with Asser / uncertainty*

Feelings and physical issues
- *heart racing, hard to breathe*
- *fear of someone I love dying*
- *unable to sleep*
- *constantly thinking "What am I thinking?"*
- *head feels heavy and body feels weak*

Seeing it on paper, in my own handwriting, was jarring. *Normal people don't have lists like this,* I thought.

Malz, you've left me on
read so long i'm growing
gray hairs

u alive or what?

so we just don't talk
anymore or ???

I'd been ghosting Sofia for weeks, ignoring her texts and DMs. Finally I agreed to meet her in town for dessert one night in early November. On the walk over, I was already planning my exit—just say a quick hello, and then make an excuse and go back to the dorm. From across the street, I watched groups of friends filter in and out, smiling and laughing, hot chocolate in hand. *They don't even know how happy they are*, I thought. I had once been among these cheery students, and Oxford had been my favorite place in the world. But I couldn't make myself feel that way again, and I didn't think that feeling would ever return. The realization crushed me.

"Hey there," I said to Sofia as soon as I walked up. "Really sorry to do this, but I need to leave, not feeling well. You stay, though. I'll be okay." She heard the cracks in my voice and looked concerned.

"At least let me walk with you," she replied.

I wanted to be alone, but I didn't have the energy to argue with her. After a few blocks of silence, Sofia turned and faced me. "What's wrong, Malz?" she asked. "You haven't been yourself lately. Is it Asser?"

"I'm ... uh ..." I stammered. "It's not Asser." Sofia looked at me expectantly. "I don't know, Sof, I don't want to bother you with this."

"You don't have to pretend to be okay around me," she said. "I'm not going to push you, but I will worry about it whether you tell me or not."

"I mean . . . part of the problem is that I don't know what's wrong." I paused for a moment, still reluctant to say it out loud. "I think I'm having panic attacks. Really bad ones. For no reason, out of nowhere . . . It's scary."

She put her arm around my shoulders. "I'm so sorry, that sounds really intense. Have you thought about seeing a therapist?"

"No, not sure it would help."

"They can't solve every problem in your life, but you might get some answers, you know? You could at least make sure your self-diagnosis is correct."

"I feel like fixating on it won't really help," I said. "It will probably resolve on its own, right?" After all, the flashbacks had gone away on their own last spring, I reasoned. I just needed to wait this out, I told her.

Sofia looked at me cautiously and said, "I mean . . . maybe? But there's no harm in asking for help."

I wish I had listened to Sofia. Four days later, I was studying alone in the dorm kitchen on a gray, rainy morning. I tried to focus on my textbooks, hoping I could absorb enough to prevent another lecture from Lara. But I couldn't concentrate, no matter how hard I tried. *This is pointless,* I thought. *You're never going to make it through exams. Why can't you get it together?*

When I got up to rinse my mug and make a new cup of tea, my eyes settled on a large knife at the bottom of the sink. A cold dread spread over me, the same sensation as watching the sky turn a sickly, unnatural green before a cyclone. For a moment, you stand still, uneasy but awestruck by the sight of it. Then you remember to be afraid.

My hands trembled, and violent thoughts took over my brain.

What would happen if I picked up the knife? Would I hurt someone with it? Would I hurt myself? What if I leave the knife alone and someone comes into the room and uses it on me? Overwhelmed, I dropped my mug and sank to my knees, gasping wildly to catch my breath.

When I had the strength to stand, I went back to my room. *It's over, it's over*, I repeated. I was supposed to be strong, someone who looked fear in the eye and kept walking. But I could not make myself believe that everything was fine. I can't remember how long I sat there screaming into a pillow, pulling my hair, pounding my fists on the floor—only that, when it was over, I knew I needed help.

26.

I n Pashto, my mother tongue, we have no word for "anxiety."
Where I grew up, people didn't speak about their mental health—I hadn't heard the words or the concept before we came to England. In Pakistan, psychological concerns are often ignored or seen as "a curse from God." When I finally worked up the courage to ask Maria to book an appointment with a counselor for me, she understood why I asked her not to mention it to my parents. "I've been there too," she said. "When I had a long period of depression at seventeen, my mother said to make *duas* and ask Allah for forgiveness. According to her, I had strayed from God and the devil was controlling me."

In communities like Maria's and mine, mental illness leads to social isolation. It's better to suffer in silence, people believe, than to give your neighbors something to gossip about. The stigma against mental illness is so strong that, until 2022, suicide was considered a criminal act. If you attempted it and lived, you could be thrown in jail for a year or more. Those brave enough to ask for help are not likely to find it. The country has fewer than five hundred psychiatrists to serve a population of 235 million.

My only experience with therapy had been in the hospital in Birmingham. A month into my recovery, a counselor had started coming to my room every week and asking me questions: *How are you feeling about what happened to you? Do you feel afraid on a regular basis? What is causing you the most distress today?*

I hated these visits. At fifteen, I was learning how to walk and talk again, like a baby. Doctors had just put a metal plate in my head where a large piece of my skull used to be. Everyone had to stand on my right side to speak to me because the bullet had shattered my left eardrum. *What is causing me distress? Look around, ma'am!* My physical problems seemed so much bigger than my feelings.

When doctors suggested I continue to see a counselor after leaving the hospital, my dad declined. "Only a completely non-functioning person needs a therapist," he said. "Malala is fine." My parents were raised to ask "What will people say?" in every situation and choose the option least likely to embarrass or shame their families. He thought he was protecting me.

But was I a functioning person now? A kitchen knife had brought me to my knees.

MY DRIVER STOPPED in front of a small pebble dash house on the outskirts of Oxford. We were a few miles from campus, but I looked out the window before opening the car door, checking to make sure there were no students or photographers nearby. As I walked past the rows of cheery flowers that lined the path to the house, I wondered if I was making a bad choice.

I was considering turning around and going back to the car when the door opened. A tall, middle-aged woman with hair pulled into a tidy French braid said, "Hello, Malala. I'm Evelyn. Nice to meet you." She led me back to her office, a cozy space with a fireplace and lots of lamps—a much more welcoming environment than the hospital's clinical setting. "How can I help?" she asked with a smile.

Earlier that day, I'd done a little research online about what to expect at my first appointment. The main advice was: *Tell your therapist why you're there. Don't be vague.* Part of me was nervous to trust a complete stranger with things I kept secret from my family and friends. But I desperately wanted to get better, so I pushed my doubts aside and began.

"I'm worried about failing my exams," I said. That was definitely true, but far from the only reason I was sitting in Evelyn's office. *Okay*, I thought, *maybe not quite ready yet.*

"Anything else?" she asked in a gentle, even tone.

I took a deep breath and looked up. My eyes stayed on the ceiling as I spoke, as if not seeing the room I was sitting in, or the world around me, made my problems less real. For a moment, I wondered if Evelyn thought it was rude of me not to look at her while I was speaking. But focusing on the ceiling was working, so I kept going.

I started with what I considered the beginning—when I got high last spring. I described the flashbacks of the shooting and that night in Anisa's room. Then I told her about my relationship with Asser, that summer's surgery, the conflict with my parents. I moved on to the recent panic attacks—Abai and Hen, chest pains, intrusive thoughts, the overwhelming dread that hung over me most days. My list of worries was long: That I couldn't trust my friends. That Asser would move on with someone else. That I had no plan beyond college.

When I was finished, I lowered my eyes and looked at Evelyn, scared of what I would see. But she was calm and still, and did not seem overwhelmed or alarmed by my confessions. "Let's start with last spring," she said. "The flashbacks began after you took marijuana—do I have that right?"

"Yes, but those aren't happening anymore. Now it's something different," I replied.

"Can you describe a bit more about what you experienced during the flashbacks?" she asked.

I tugged at the sleeves of my sweater and looked back at Evelyn, hoping she'd see that I was uncomfortable and tell me I didn't have to answer. When she said nothing, I began softly, "It felt like I had nowhere to hide. Even if I closed my eyes, those images were there." I looked up at the ceiling again before continuing. "I always thought my brain had erased the shooting. That my mind just . . . shut off. But I had seen things. And now I want to forget again."

"Malala, I believe what you experienced was post-traumatic stress disorder."

It wasn't the first time I'd heard of PTSD or considered that I might have it. But I didn't like the term or how overused it was. People at college claimed they "got PTSD" from group projects or waiting in line too long for food. This experience was so awful and different that I couldn't imagine the same four letters capturing what I felt.

"Intrusive memories and flashbacks are common symptoms," Evelyn explained. "And stress can exacerbate PTSD. For instance, your concerns about your academic performance and the pressures of your work, your family, your relationship—they aren't directly related to the shooting, but they can trigger the same trauma response. Think of it like your body's alarm system getting stuck in the 'on' position."

"That's interesting," I said. "But, again, the flashbacks went away and haven't come back. The panic attacks happening now are different."

Evelyn nodded and leaned toward me a bit. "I understand. At some point, though, when you're ready, I'd like to talk about PTSD again, as we can't separate it from your overall mental health just because you're not having flashbacks at the moment."

I looked away. It was hard enough to show up for this first appointment. I didn't want to think about having to come back.

"Now, when it comes to your more recent experiences," Evelyn continued, "the first thing you should know is that feeling panicked or unable to control your thoughts can be very frightening, but it is not unusual. Many of your fellow students are going through similar struggles, especially in their last year of college. For you, this might be heightened by PTSD, and the fact that you're a well-known person who is always in the spotlight. There is no blood test for mental illness, but I believe most of what you are describing is anxiety. And we can work on strategies to help you manage these episodes."

"Anxiety" didn't sound so bad. I knew it was something a lot of people experienced, as common as allergies or paper cuts. Maybe I had a particularly bad case—but when Evelyn said she could teach me to control it, I started to relax. That was what I had hoped to find today: a way out.

She went on to explain the concept of "the window of tolerance." If a person is functioning day-to-day, navigating stressful situations, and regulating their emotions, they are "within their window." Some windows are wider and some smaller—but everyone can be pushed outside the frame if the stress piles up too high. Beyond the window lie all the things I had been experiencing—panic, fear, disorientation.

As Evelyn spoke, the patterns became clearer. With everything going on in my life, I had been constantly climbing in and out of my window. Sleepless nights, poor nutrition, and stress narrowed my margins, making my window smaller. Getting back to safety grew more difficult each time—and that was part of the reason I was having these extreme reactions.

It was helpful to get this context—how the pieces fit together, how the hard parts of my life sparked off each other and started a fire. I wouldn't say that I felt good, necessarily, but for the first time in weeks, I had hope that I might get better.

Evelyn ended our first session by asking me to keep a log of when I felt panicked, overwhelmed, "outside the window." The last thing I wanted was more homework, but if it would help, I was willing to try.

27.

I t didn't take me too long to start noticing the ups and downs. A visit from my parents raised my anxiety level, and listening to music lowered it. Throughout the week, I also identified a sensitivity to certain words—"killed," "murdered," "dead"—the violent words we reappropriate all the time, but that had never set me on edge before. The same thing happened when people touched me; hugs made me feel trapped. One day I was gripped with fear for no clear reason. I could hear my heartbeat ringing in my ears again. *Weird thoughts remain,* I wrote in my journal.

"Did you know we are the only species who can think about our thoughts?" Evelyn asked in our next session. She told me to look at unwanted thoughts like waves on a beach. They come and they go. You can observe them. You can be curious about them. But they are not, in themselves, something to fear. Everyone has thoughts that are strange, unnerving, unkind. We all have feelings that take us by surprise. But we are judged on our actions, not what creeps around our brains.

"When we're anxious, we sometimes generate 'what if' scenarios in our heads—the brain might show us its version of the worst that could happen to prepare and protect us. That may be why you felt you'd go back into a coma if you went to sleep or why you were afraid when you saw the kitchen knife."

It gave me comfort to think of my brain as overprotective instead of addled or broken. Next time it happened, I would tell myself, "That's just a thought. It's not something I am going to do." If that didn't work, if the feelings still triggered my body to respond, Evelyn taught me to "take manual control of my limbic system." When my heart sped up and I felt dizzy, I would try 7/11 breathing—breathe in for a count of seven and out for a count of eleven—for at least five minutes. The long exhale calms the body.

A few days after our session, I was tense and scared again, overwhelmed by exam prep. *It's coming back*, I thought, my pulse quickening. I sat on the edge of my bed and tried the breathing exercise Evelyn had taught me. After a few minutes, I realized I was feeling more lucid, my pulse steady and strong.

I was grateful that it hadn't turned into a full panic attack, but another part of me was frustrated that I had not conquered my anxiety yet. All of my health issues took so long to fix—months in recovery after the shooting, years of surgeries to restore my facial symmetry. This was my last year of college, and I wanted to feel better already, to return to my fun, independent life before the responsibilities of the real world took over.

A few sessions later, Evelyn and I talked about my inclination to divide the world into good and bad people, why Hen's joke had shocked and disoriented me. She told me that this binary way of thinking was causing me more anxiety and paranoia, narrowing my window of tolerance. Everyone is capable of kindness. Everyone, including me, has hurt people we love.

I had been avoiding Hen since the Brandon incident, declining her dinner invites and studying in the library instead of my room. I took Evelyn's words under consideration. Hen had a bad moment, but she wasn't a bad person. It felt like Evelyn was giving me permission to trust my friends again.

"That night, the prank about Brandon really messed me up, made me feel so disoriented," I told Hen the next time she stopped by my room.

"Aw, babe! Why didn't you tell me?" she said.

"I was *trying* to tell you."

She looked at the floor and I continued, "After you left, I had a panic attack. It was scary, Hen, like I thought I would die. But that wasn't the first time or the last. It's been happening a lot, so I finally decided to see a therapist."

"I'm so sorry, Malz. I had no idea."

"It's okay. Normally what you did would just *really* annoy me," I joked. "It's not your fault that I had such a bad reaction. I just wanted you to know I'm not upset. But also I'm still working on this, and I feel pretty delicate right now. So maybe don't try to test my gullibility for a while?"

"No more fake boyfriends—I promise!" she said. "The truth is, I haven't been on a date in forever. My love life is in its flop era. I'll open the apps and be like, 'Is this phone on airplane mode?' What is happening?! Just tumbleweeds in the DMs. . . ."

Hen went on and on, and I laughed for the first time in weeks, feeling happy that I could enjoy the simple pleasure of chatting with a friend again. Little by little, I was finding my way back to myself.

LATER THAT WEEK I had a long call with Asser. He knew I was going to therapy—and that I didn't want to talk about it every time we spoke. It was nice to hear his voice and catch up on his latest news. But after we hung up, I found myself thinking about the state of our relationship. The next day I wrote in my emotional log: *Preoccupied with thoughts about my boyfriend. How do I know whether my feelings for him are real or not? I am looking for an answer. . . .*

"What do I do about him?" I asked in my final therapy session before the Christmas break. "How can I be sure we're meant to be together? And if we can't be, how do I stop feeling in love with him?"

Evelyn smiled. "Well, Malala, you might be better off asking a poet or musician that question. Therapy can only go so far.

"I can tell you this, not just about relationships, but every big decision you face—there are different paths through this wonderful journey of life, and whichever one you pick will bring different problems and different rewards. When you make a choice, don't look back and imagine that there were other better options. Make the best decision you can with what you happen to know at the time and then explore, enjoy, meet the challenges."

That evening, I took a walk to the river and thought of Abai. Whenever she came to visit our home in Mingora, she would sleep in my room. As she grew older, she didn't like sleeping indoors, so my parents made up cots for us to sleep on the porch. Abai would fall asleep quickly, but I would stay awake looking up at the stars and imagining myself one day studying physics, even going to space. I pictured the many places on earth I wanted to see as well, imagining all the possibilities for my future, my own ever-expanding universe.

Tonight I thought of constellations closer to home—and how quickly they could change. At fifteen, I had almost died. Survival and recovery didn't mean reclaiming everything I had lost. Abai and I might never sleep under the stars together again. I would never know the person I could have been in Pakistan. And if the shooting hadn't happened, I would not have gone to Oxford and had wild adventures with my college friends. Girls in Shangla would not have a high school. *Different paths through life, each with its own challenges and joys.*

Who knew what would happen next? Maybe Asser and I would end up together, maybe not. I might pass my exams and come up with the perfect post-college plan, or move back home with my parents. Perhaps the panic attacks would never completely go away, and I would have to fight them off each time. But I felt stronger now, able to face all I had lost and all the uncertainties ahead.

28.

O n January 1, 2020, I sat on my bed in Birmingham making a
list of things I wanted to do before graduation. I hadn't had
a panic attack in weeks. The relief I experienced was not a manic
high, but that of a breaking fever—serene at first, then followed by
excitement and impatience to rejoin the world.

Now, going into the second term of my third and final year of
college, I was determined to make up for lost time. I wanted to
drink tea in my favorite café, spend lazy afternoons by the river,
and have all the classic Oxford adventures I'd yet to experience in
my first two years—crossing the Bridge of Sighs, taking in the
view from the top of Radcliffe Camera, watching horses roam
across Port Meadow. Instead of saying yes to every invitation, I
would guard my time and reserve it for my closest friends, the
people I missed when they weren't around. But I wouldn't let my
social life get so busy that I fell behind in my studies and stayed up

all night trying to catch up. I planned to keep writing in my journal and practicing the breathing exercises Evelyn had taught me. After three years of college, I finally felt like I had the tools to keep my life in balance.

When I returned to my dorm at the end of break, everyone on our floor seemed to be getting along better. There were no shouting matches, and about half as many kitchen and noise complaints on the group chat. I smiled when I heard them laughing in the kitchen together or when we all gathered for dinner. The initial growing pains of going from friends to roommates were behind us, and I was overjoyed to have my girl gang back together again.

I was also thankful we'd all made up in time for our annual Galentines' Day brunch, an event I looked forward to every February. The tradition had started in our first year, as an attempt to cheer up Cora after a breakup. From there it morphed into a general celebration and an excuse to bring everyone together.

I wouldn't get out of bed early for anything other than morning lectures, but on Galentines' Day, I was up with the sun. After sending a brunch reminder to the group chat, I popped into Yasmin's room to work on a playlist, adding a couple of songs from each of our friends' favorite artists—a peculiar jumble of Stevie Wonder, M83, Stormzy, Billie Eilish, and more.

Thump, thump. Back in my room getting dressed, I opened the door to find Cora gently kicking it, both her hands around a large flower arrangement. "For you," she said, winking. I opened the card—from Asser, of course. He never forgot a holiday or a special occasion. I sent him a thank-you message, then tucked his card in my desk. *A perfect centerpiece for brunch!* I thought. I appreciated Asser's thoughtful gesture, but today was for the girls.

In the kitchen, Hen blew up balloons, and I hung them on the wall alongside some multicolored bunting I'd bought. "What do you think?" I asked her halfway through.

"Well . . ." she said, trying to contain the giggle in her voice. "You've put everything at eye level. Like, *your* eye level. There's a lot of empty wall above your head, shorty. Let me help."

"Yeah, that's better," I said when she'd rehung the decorations. "It still looks a bit sad, though, and I don't have anything else to add. Unless . . ." I grabbed the tape and stuck a heart-shaped red paper plate on the wall.

Hen cracked up. "Nobody's gonna put it on Pinterest, but . . . sure, that works!"

I'd planned to serve heart-shaped waffles as well, but the novelty waffle maker I'd ordered had not arrived by the morning of the brunch. Anisa, who had volunteered to cook, found me standing in the kitchen, furiously scrolling my phone to order takeout. She riffled through my bag of supplies and said, "Okay, relax. We've got waffle mix, which is basically the same thing as pancake mix. Step aside, please." Then she pulled her hair into a ponytail, took out a skillet and cooking oil, and went to work churning out batches of perfectly fluffy pancakes.

After everyone arrived, we took our seats and clinked our mismatched mugs in a toast to friendship. "To our last Galentines' Day!" Hen said.

"Ugh, no, don't remind me," Yasmin grumbled. "That means it's only four months to exams."

"How about some rules of order for this brunch?" Anisa said. "No discussion of exams, essays, or tutorials."

"And no mention of love interests," Hen added. "Or lack of love interests."

When I turned on my playlist, Cora rolled her eyes. "Please tell me you've spared us that Future song that Hen played on repeat all of our first year!"

I laughed. "Oh, it's on here! It wouldn't be our last Galentines' Day if we didn't relive our questionable choices."

That set my friends off, listing all the embarrassing things they'd done: *Waking up alone at a desk in the library at 2 a.m. Trying to make a grilled cheese with a clothes iron. Getting mono from making out with too many people during Freshers' Week.*

"Jell-O shots," Hen volunteered.

"Oh, I remember Jell-O shots!" I said. "You and Cora busted into my room singing One Direction songs. Or slurring them, actually. I'd never seen a drunk person before!"

"Your face!" Cora snorted.

"Yeah, well, we had only just met a week earlier, and that night Hen kept telling me she loved me," I added. "It was extremely confusing! Like, should I say, 'I love you too'? Was it rude not to? I had no idea!"

"Not the first or last time she's put one of us to bed after a night out," Yasmin said.

Anisa covered her face with her hands and said, "I just remembered the time I sent her to get me bagels the next morning. Oof, sorry, Malz."

"A toast to our Hangover Helper!" Hen cheered.

The kitchen door swung open and a startled face stared back at us. "ALAN!" everyone roared.

"Sorry, guys, didn't mean to interrupt the party," he replied. "Just got back from the library and grabbing a snack before econometrics study group."

"Isn't that later this afternoon?" Anisa asked.

"Uh, it's two-thirty now, so in half an hour."

Everyone grabbed their phones to check the time, surprised to learn we'd been chatting for so long. "Wait, Alan," I said. "Can you take a picture of us before you go?" The photo he snapped that afternoon remains one of my favorites from college—half-eaten pancakes, plates on the wall, and all my friends smiling from ear to ear.

As I cleaned up the kitchen afterward, my brain ticked through the list of philosophy texts I needed to reread for exams. That night I opened Aristotle's *Nicomachean Ethics*, much of which is dedicated to his thoughts on friendship. Three years prior, when I'd read "The wish to be friends can come about quickly, but friendship cannot," it had made me sad. I didn't like the idea of waiting so long to feel close to someone, as if it was a skill you had to master over many years.

I understood it better now. It took effort to see past differences in someone's background, beliefs, or personality. It took courage to be vulnerable, to share the embarrassing and scary parts of yourself—the parts you don't even understand—with friends. It took humility to repair your connections, to forgive and be forgiven.

Friendship is the only type of love available to all of us, at any point in our lives; it is common, often overlooked, unmarked by major holidays. To me, friends should be embraced with the same magnitude of wonder and care that we feel for lovers and family members. When I started college, I just wanted to be less lonely. Three years later, I felt like I belonged—not simply included, but loved.

I kept my promise to myself to enjoy as much of Oxford as possible that term. My memories from those three months are some of the happiest of my college years—dancing with Zayan at the Bollywood Bop, binge-watching *Sex Education* with Hen, gossiping in the kitchen until 4 a.m. with Cora and Yasmin. At the Polo Club Ball, I stood outdoors under a space heater and laughed as Anisa arrived on her horse—a cowboy in an evening gown.

On the last night before spring break, Sofia threw herself a birthday party at a high-street bar. She and I sat side by side in a demilune booth like queens granting an audience to the public. A stream of friends drifted in and out, dropping by between stops on the end-of-term party circuit or on their way to catch a night train out of town. "Have a good holiday! See you in April!" we said.

The next day I loaded my bag into the car and settled in for the drive to Birmingham, ready to relax before exam season. As we pulled away, I looked back at Lady Margaret Hall, feeling grateful for the bounty of experiences I'd had that winter—completely unaware that they were a farewell tour, that my days as an Oxford student were already over.

29.

I sat on my bed reading and rereading the email: *All teaching and assessment next term will take place remotely.* Then I texted all my friends to make sure I wasn't misinterpreting the words. They confirmed the bad news: Oxford was closed for the spring term; tutorials, exams, and, likely, graduation would be online.

Covid was new and scary—they had no other choice. But I couldn't help but feel stunned and heartbroken at the loss. I would miss the warm weather months with my friends, walking down to the river in my pajamas at sunrise, climbing up to the bell tower at night, post-exam parties and tearful good-byes. For the third time in my twenty-two years, I'd been forced out of a place I loved and a life I was building for myself.

But graduation is months away, I thought. *Surely it will be over by then and we'll go back.* So many students had traveled to their home countries for the five-week break. Now we were all stuck as borders closed and flights were canceled. I didn't want to believe I might never see them again, so I told myself that wouldn't happen, that this would get sorted out and we'd be back after a few weeks, a month at most.

While I tried to maintain hope for a return to college, my mom couldn't hide her happiness at having all her children under the same roof again with nowhere to go and no one to see but each other. She spent the afternoons cooking—chicken pilau, curried okra, paratha—and insisted my brothers and I sit at the table and eat together every night.

I noticed my dad watching me at dinner. "You should have more chicken," he'd say, heaping food on my plate before I could protest. During the day, he barged into my room with bowls of fruit cut into neat squares. "Please eat it," he'd insist, then stand over me to make sure I did.

After a couple weeks of this, I was done. "Enough, Dad! You are not allowed to stare at my plate or monitor my diet. I eat what and when I want to. Sometimes I like to have extra chicken. Sometimes I don't. But the moment you interfere, I feel like a child who can't make a choice for herself. If your goal is to get me to eat more, then leave me alone."

He switched up his tactics. When I sat down in the living room, a bowl of fruit would magically appear on the coffee table. "I am not asking anyone to eat this," he'd announce, even though we were the only two in the room. "I'm just pointing out that it's here should someone want it." Or he would sit on the sofa by himself, peeling an orange: "Wow, this is the best orange I've ever had in my life! If you don't taste it, you're really missing out." Most of the time, I rolled my eyes and went about my business, but on occasion I sat down and ate the orange to keep him from backsliding into more aggressive fruit-marketing efforts.

My mom, on the other hand, kept trying to give me a makeover.

"Why do you have to wear these gray clothes, Malala?" she asked, pointing at my leggings and cozy jumper. "Go change into something more colorful. Put on some earrings for once."

"It makes no sense to dress up only to sit at home all day. No one is looking at me."

"I don't understand—you wear sad clothes, have no interest in fashion, never want to go shopping. You are too young to stop enjoying your life." If her favorite Pakistani dress shops weren't closed because of the lockdown, I had no doubt she would have taken me shopping and forced me to "enjoy my life" for hours a day. I thumped upstairs and came back in a pink shalwar kameez just so she would stop complaining.

Being at home felt like going in reverse. As soon as I stepped through their door, my parents saw me as a child again, a daughter in need of supervision and direction. Did they not realize I'd been managing my life for the last two and a half years? At Oxford, I'd overcome so much—nerves over making friends, poor study skills, heartbreak, mental health challenges—and I'd done it on my own. Part of me wanted to tell them everything, to show them I could handle myself, but a bigger part wanted to retain what little privacy I had at home.

While they still thought of me as a little girl, I noticed how much my parents had changed while I was at college. Since my dad no longer traveled with me for speaking engagements or advocacy work, they had settled into a new domestic routine: He picked up some chores and looked after my brothers, while my mom had more time for leisure and her English language classes. In years past, I rarely saw my dad in the kitchen; now he fried eggs for breakfast and vacuumed under the table after dinner. The entire house knew when he was doing dishes because he clanged the pots and pans around like a one-man marching band, leaving behind a trail of sudsy water on the floor and a shaky tower of cookware piled high on the drying mat. My mom found the transformation amusing. "When guests come over and see him standing at the sink in his apron, they say, 'How impressive, what a good man,'" she snickered. "I did these things my whole life and nobody gave me a parade!"

During lockdown, Dad did all the shopping as well. It gave him an excuse to get out of the house and talk to strangers, one of his favorite pastimes. He was bewildered and sad, at the start of the pandemic, when people crossed to the other side of the street to avoid coming too close to him. Social distancing was a concept he could never quite grasp.

My mother tried and failed to get him to stay at home. One afternoon she sat on the couch lamenting the gray hair cropping up around her temples and wishing she could go to the salon. "Toor Pekai, do you remember the Pashtun legend about the woman who had no food for dinner and the man who went on an epic hunt through the forest to prove his love?" my dad asked. "I will take up this quest for your hair dye!"

"You may bring the hunt, Ziauddin, but you will also bring coronavirus!" she yelled after him, but he was already halfway out the door. Three days later, he sequestered himself in the guest bedroom, suffering joint pains and a fever.

As the weeks wore on, both my irritation at being stuck at home and my hope that things would change blanded out into a spiritless monotony. Every time I left my room to make tea, it seemed smaller when I came back. I tried to break up the days with computer games like *Among Us*, Netflix binges, and awkward birthday parties on Zoom. When I ran out of ideas, I picked up a dull pair of desk scissors and gave myself bangs.

Right before the pandemic, Asser had taken a prestigious job as a performance manager for the Pakistan Cricket Board. Our country is so obsessed with cricket that his office never went remote during lockdowns and his team was among the first to get the vaccine. He worked all day and I tried to keep him on the phone all night. After a few hours of talking to me, he would yawn and say, "All right, I need to do my prayers and get to bed."

"Pray for my exams!" I said.

"I will, but maybe you should also study for them?"

"Pray that this will be over soon so we can see each other again."

"*Inshallah.*"

"And pray for all the people who are ill, of course."

"I always do. *Good night*, Malala."

My brothers might have provided some distraction were they not lost in their own worlds. Atal, the youngest, had always been able to turn my mood around. In my lonely high school years, he'd provided hours of entertainment. I cracked up at his rising exasperation as he tried to explain the foreign concept of a sleepover to my parents or teach them new words like "burrito."

But he was a teenager now, and I saw less and less of him. During the lockdown, he spent all day in his room, writing rap lyrics or computer code. More than once, he faked a cough to get out of Mom's mandatory dinners. And sometimes, when my parents went to sleep, he'd slip out the back door and vanish for hours. He became a hologram in the house, only a blurry version of himself appearing here, while the real Atal existed somewhere I couldn't see.

Meanwhile, my middle brother, Khushal, was having his own academic crisis. In high school, he'd spent more time playing video games and smoking weed than studying. To no one's surprise but his own, he had failed his A-levels and couldn't get into college.

When he made the decision to retake the tests during the pandemic, Khushal threw himself into his studies. He commandeered our living room, piling up books, flash cards, and practice essays on every available surface. My dad rejoiced, believing his wayward son had finally become a serious student. As the only one in the house who understood the level of concentration that A-levels required, I was more skeptical. But either way, Khushal was too preoccupied saving himself to spend time with me.

The group chat pinged less and less as the weeks went by. Maybe my Oxford friends were focused on exam prep or enjoying their time at home, having socially distanced get-togethers with their high school pals. Or maybe they were feeling the same as me—stripped of the life I'd created for myself in college and realizing that, without my friends, without our inside jokes and midnight snack runs, without our favorite restaurants and hidden corners of campus, without Club Nights and essay deadlines, I had little to say.

30.

In my parents' house, I turned nocturnal, drawing the curtains and climbing in bed at the first hint of daylight. *The days don't count if you can't see them*, I decided. I felt hollow and listless, a bit depressed. If I had been able to laugh, I would have found it funny that Evelyn and I had never covered this type of mental illness. My anxiety in college was unpredictable, explosive and violent. I had learned to interrupt a panic attack, but not how to stop this slow-creeping void.

From the day I came home, my mom and dad had been badgering me to join them on their nightly stroll through the neighborhood. After reading an article on "low mood" that suggested that exercise, particularly walking outside, could help, I relented and agreed to go with them. Just one time.

My mom ambled out of our house and down two blocks

where the sidewalk deposited us at the top of a steep concrete stairway. "Where are we going?" I asked.

"To the canals!" she replied. Though I'd lived here for four years of high school, I had not set foot alongside any part of Birmingham's extensive waterway system. Built during the Industrial Revolution to haul iron and coal to London, the canals were eventually repurposed for leisure activities like running and kayaking. My mom led us along the pebble footpath by the water, under tree canopies and old bridges. Why had I spent so much time cooped up in my room when this sanctuary existed two blocks from our house? I should have realized, by that point, that the outdoors always brightened my spirits.

We exited the canals via another long flight of stairs. When we reached the top, we were standing near a soccer pitch. My mom pointed to a brick building across the field. "See where the grass ends?" she asked. "That's my gym."

"Your . . . gym?" I was struggling to keep up with all this new information. The mom I knew had never shown a hint of interest in sports or fitness. I looked over at my dad, who was smiling proudly at her.

"I had just started weight lifting right before everything shut down," she sighed.

My eyes bugged out and I felt almost lightheaded for a moment. The mom I remembered was decidedly not a gym rat. Before we came to the UK, she had not traveled far beyond Mingora and never outside of Pakistan. At first, Birmingham's elevators and escalators terrified her. She startled at everything from street musicians to skyscrapers. After I was released from the hospital, she rarely left the house.

My dad, my brothers, and I could all speak in Pashto, Urdu, and English. Because my mom had not gone to school, she could only speak Pashto, the language she'd heard as a child. In Mingora, she chatted all day with neighbors as they cooked over wood fires and hung their laundry to dry in the yard. In Birmingham, she could not, as my father put it, "convey to anyone but us the thoughts in her head or the emotions in her heart." As her oldest child lay hovering between life and death in the hospital, she had no friend with whom she could pray.

For the first three years we lived in Birmingham, my mom cried every single day. She would call our relatives in Pakistan and talk for seven or eight hours at a time. The first phrase she learned in English was "top up" so she could refill the minutes on her mobile phone card at the corner store.

Eventually she started settling into her new home. She made a few friends. She learned the bus route to Ladypool Road, where you can find stores selling shalwar kameez and halal meat. When she didn't feel like cooking, she sent my dad to pick up roti and kebabs from a restaurant. She didn't cry as much, but I always had the sense that she was treading water, waiting for her "real life" to start again in Pakistan.

On our first evening walk, my mom revealed how much she had moved on. She talked about Janet, her former English teacher and now a close friend. "We have movie nights because she thinks that watching will help me learn the language," she said. "But her choices are so boring, I always fall asleep!" My mom preferred films featuring Mr. Bean, whose physical comedy needed no translation. I overheard her on the phone with Janet some nights while she made dinner and was shocked at how much her English had improved. My mom had clearly put more effort into her studies than I'd put into mine over the last three years.

The following night we walked in the opposite direction, toward Queen Elizabeth Hospital, where my mom had spent every day during the months of my recovery. Before the pandemic, she visited patients there a few times a week. My parents quietly helped cover the costs for other Pakistani children, victims of violence like me, to come to Birmingham for surgeries to repair their limbs, faces, and teeth. When their families couldn't accompany them, she brought them home-cooked meals and used the knowledge she'd gained from my time in the hospital to make sure they received the best care.

She was even planning to travel alone, to take her sisters on a girls' trip to Dubai once it was safe to fly again. In Mingora, she wouldn't leave the house without my dad or one of my brothers; few Pashtun women would face the scrutiny and shame of breaking our society's rules. I was happy to see her building a life for herself now. And, as she claimed her independence, I hoped she might extend some of it to me.

My mom and I had never enjoyed the easy, warm relationship I had with my dad. As a child, I was scared of drawing her ire, which I seemed to do every day. She was strict and didn't hesitate to punish me, often physically, when I fell short of her standards. I didn't feel like I could talk to her at all. When I got my first period at eleven years old, I told my dad and asked him to buy menstrual pads for me.

She refused to relax the social norms I'd known growing up when we moved to the UK. My brothers could do whatever they liked, but I was forbidden to wear Western clothes or go to high school parties. She shouted at me if I let my scarf slip off my head in public or stood too close to a man in a photo. I was an adult now, but her rebukes still stung, and I gave in to almost all her demands.

When I'd spent time with Asser the previous summer, she admonished me every time I left the house: We were not allowed to be alone, we were not to take photos together, we had to stay ten feet apart at all times. Of course, I broke all of these rules—but

I didn't feel great about deceiving my mom. I knew she was only trying to protect me.

She understood how dangerous a bad reputation could be to a Pashtun woman. My mom mourned women and girls we knew— a fifteen-year-old poisoned by her family for looking too long at a boy on the street, a woman strangled to death for running away from her abusive husband. She heard the news of a student hanged for speaking to a man at her college, a woman shot because her father saw a picture of her on Facebook, four women murdered for dancing at a wedding. We were thousands of miles away now, but my mom still lived in fear of me losing my "honor." I could trace each of her concerns back to those we had buried.

When I was thirteen years old, my mom brought a girl named Apana to live with us. She was my age, and her father had died when she was a baby, leaving her mother to clean homes for a few rupees a week to support the children. My mom decided that Apana would share my bedroom and go to my dad's school for free. He and I had no say in the matter.

Shortly after she arrived, I noticed Apana was sick all the time. She would go pale and run outside to vomit. "You're always ill, you must be pregnant!" I joked. The only thing I knew about how a girl got pregnant was what I'd seen on Indian soap operas. A man and a woman looked longingly at each other; in the next scene, she was throwing up. Then came a big belly and, finally, a baby.

One day my mom took Apana out of the house without mentioning where they were headed. When they returned, Apana slept for hours. After that day, she wasn't sick anymore. Years later I heard the story: the girl had been in a park on her own one afternoon when a man approached her. He said he was visiting from Dubai and seemed friendly, even inviting Apana to see his hotel room. She'd never been inside a hotel, so she said yes. As soon as the door closed, he raped her.

Abortion is illegal in Pakistan, except to save the life of the mother, and is punishable by three to ten years in prison, depending on how far the fetus has developed. If I had asked my mom whether she supported reproductive rights, she would have said no. She might have added that none of this would have happened if Apana had followed the rules, stayed inside her house, and never talked to men. But she knew the fate of an unmarried, pregnant thirteen-year-old in our society. And she risked what little freedom she had to save a girl's life.

My mom was a hero, brave and generous. She was also judgmental, unsparing, and strict, especially with me. I longed for a day when I could tell her all my secrets and call her my friend. In the meantime, I laced up my sneakers and joined her evening stroll every night.

31.

In the month before exams, I never needed to set an early-morning alarm; I woke up at dawn, my mind already racing with practice essays and problem sets. During the day, I combed through my notes and participated in Zoom study groups with Cora and the other PPE students. I was pleased to discover that I'd retained more than I had realized, and started to feel a bit of excitement about the approaching finish line.

"You're working so hard that I'm concerned about study burnout," Valerie said in one of our remote study skills sessions. "You don't have the same fun distractions as you did at college, but try to take a break and reward yourself once in a while."

As soon as she said that, I realized how much I missed takeaway dinner nights, the times when my friends and I would all order from a different place and then sit on the floor in my room sampling each other's meals. I told my mom to take the night off from cooking and ordered hamburgers from Five Guys and mango mochi from Kyoto Grill for dessert. The next night, I ordered us falafel and salads from Shawarma City. A few days later, we compared the spicy chicken dishes at Nando's and Pepe's Piri Piri.

Hen told me she and her sister liked a place called TGI Fridays. I had never heard of it, but when I scrolled through the menu, I saw that the barbecue ribs were the most popular item and had them delivered. My family was obsessed with the meal, and asked me to order the same exact thing almost every night for two weeks. The next time I spoke to Hen, I thanked her for the tip. "We can't get enough!"

"Um, before I say what I'm about to say, I want you to remember that I recommended the *restaurant*, not the *ribs*," she replied. "Malala . . . you've been eating pork!"

I gasped and immediately googled it to make sure she wasn't pranking me again. Pork is haram, forbidden to Muslims by multiple verses of scripture. It wasn't technically a sin if you did it unwittingly, but what God might forgive, I suspected my mom would not. When I confessed the mistake to my family, though, no one got mad or said I'd been careless. They were too caught up in the disappointment of learning that our rib-eating days were done.

Asser was my other "reward" at the end of every day. Around 1:30 a.m., when my brain was tired from studying, I would sit in the window seat in my room, look up at the stars, and call him. "I've been reading a little bit of astronomy at night to clear my head," I told him one night. "Supposedly Jupiter and Saturn are having some sort of big conjunction. They're the two brightest planets so I thought I'd be able to see them. But maybe you need a telescope for that because all I see is the moon."

For a couple of weeks, our calls included my nightly astronomy report. He listened to my bleary-eyed rambling about stars and planets, how I wished I could get a better view. Meanwhile, it was

5 a.m. in Lahore and he was just waking up before getting dressed and heading to his office at the Cricket Board. I suspected he was only half listening to me, and I couldn't blame him. Still, I loved that he was the last person I spoke to before going to bed.

ON THE MORNING of my first exam—macroeconomics, my most challenging subject—I woke up early and dressed in my black academic robes. The clothes weren't required at home, as they would have been if I were taking the test at Oxford, but I wanted to honor the tradition, to give the moment the weight it deserved.

My dad made me eggs and toast, but I was too nervous to eat more than a couple of bites. "Don't worry," he said. "I have every confidence that you will get the highest possible marks!" He had been exaggerating my academic abilities since the day I was born, but I didn't have time to manage his expectations this morning.

"Promise me you'll keep the house quiet. Don't let *anyone* knock on my door." He gave me a solemn nod, like a knight turning his horse toward the battle.

The exam began at 9:30 a.m. I had four hours to solve three complex math problems, write two essays, and upload my answers. I used up fifty minutes on the first question. As I was reading over the second problem, my bedroom door swung open. My dad stood there, wide-eyed and smiling with a cup of tea and a plate of biscuits in his hand. Before he could speak, I glared at him and went back to my work. He set the mug on my desk and tiptoed out of the room.

When it was over, I stomped downstairs. "What did I tell you? No interruptions! I don't have time for a single sip of tea during an exam."

"You said 'don't knock'!" he replied, bewildered.

There wasn't much time to feel relieved that I was done with macroeconomics for the rest of my life, as it was only the first of eight exams spread over three weeks. As soon as I finished a test, I would jump on a group call with the other PPE students for a debrief. I was glad when we all found the same questions difficult, as it meant I hadn't been the only one ill-prepared for a particular topic or problem. After we hung up, I'd dive into preparing for the next exam. I would study in five-hour blocks, take a short break to eat, and plunge back into my books.

In the middle of all this, people kept contacting me to participate in TV programs and online events meant to encourage other students who were missing their last month of high school or college because of Covid. I was exhausted and didn't want to do any of it. "Doesn't anyone realize that I'm also trying to graduate right now?" I snapped at Maria. But I still had not learned to say no, especially not when LeBron James, who was organizing a star-studded virtual graduation ceremony, made the request. In the middle of my second week of exams, producers and camera operators were lugging equipment through my parents' house and setting up in the backyard. I spent an afternoon shivering in the rain while they filmed me smiling and congratulating the class of 2020. The whole time I could only worry about how much exam prep I was missing. *Failing to graduate because I was busy doing virtual graduations for other people will be my villain origin story,* I thought.

When I remembered all the third-year traditions I was missing at Oxford, my sense of disappointment was intense. If I were still on campus, I would exit the Examination Halls after my last-ever exam, step into the sunshine, and participate in the hallowed Oxford tradition of "trashing," where friends gather around a newly liberated scholar and cover her in shaving foam, confetti, custard pies, canned beans—anything sticky and messy. The chaos ends with everyone jumping in the River Cherwell together to wash off the mess.

It was a trivial thing to obsess over, but I had been looking forward to that moment ever since I'd watched my first trashing two years ago. Determined to salvage what I could, I ordered all the typical trashing supplies and gave them to my dad to distribute on the big day. It wouldn't be the same without my friends, but any celebration was better than the anticlimax of closing my laptop and announcing "I'm done with college!" to an empty bedroom.

If my first exam was the hardest, my last, Politics in South Asia, was a breeze. When it was over, I bounced out of my chair and headed downstairs to find my family in the living room, holding cans of whipped cream and bags of glitter. They looked uneasily at each other, waiting for someone to make the first move.

"No, not here! You'll ruin the furniture!" I cried. "Go outside!"

My brothers unleashed their inner vandals in the backyard, emptying cans of Silly String directly into my hair. I covered my face with my hands to protect my eyes and alternated between screaming, laughing, and shouting curses in Pashto. *We should have warned the neighbors*, I thought. They chased me around the garden with packets of Holi powder and confetti until everything I'd bought was used up.

In a picture of that day, I look like something from a children's book—a more silly than scary monster with a patchy white foam beard and brightly colored paper feathers poking out of my head. The boys are in T-shirts, their forearms netted with Silly String and their hair sparkling like cartoon fairies. My mom, who was hit with a cloud of neon-yellow powder, looks like someone dragged a giant highlighter over her face. Somehow my dad, in his smart navy blazer and leather lace-ups, emerged unscathed.

In the years since I left Oxford and students returned to in-person classes, university officials have tried to crack down on trashing, claiming it's wasteful and expensive to clean up. But I think they're unlikely to kill the tradition. To me, it seemed that only something so ridiculous, something with no purpose other than to joyfully make the biggest possible mess, could carry us from the underworld of exams back to normal life. I was happy to join the long line of students who took one last moment to be carefree before stepping into adulthood.

⁓

EXAMS WERE OVER, but I couldn't fully relax until Oxford released my results and I was certain that I'd earned a degree. While I waited, my family learned that Atal had done well on his tenth-grade standardized tests. Even better, Khushal had brought his A-level marks up enough to get into college.

My dad was thrilled with the boys. I tried to manage his expectations and warn him that my results might be disappointing. Over the years, Lara had informed me several times that I was on track for Lower Second Class Honors—the stamp of mediocrity assigned to those whose work was, on the whole, without effort or excellence—and I wasn't confident that I had done enough in the past year to bring myself up a level.

"Look, I'm not a genius," I explained to my dad. He opened his mouth to argue, but I kept going. "I would have had to work really hard to get a First Class degree. You can't have a good life and good grades at Oxford. So even if I get a 2:2, wouldn't you rather I was happy in college?" He said, "Of course, Malala," and I hoped he meant it.

My friends in other disciplines started receiving their results— a First for Zayan! Upper Second for Sofia, Yasmin, and Hen! Since

Anisa already had a job lined up, she'd taken predicted marks and skipped exams.

Then I got a text from Cora: 2:1! Have you checked yet?

I typed my name and password into the portal, closed my eyes and hit enter. *All you need to do is pass*, I said to myself, as if I could change the result at this point. When I finally looked at the screen, I saw:

Malala Yousafzai
BA in Philosophy, Politics, and Economics
Final Award: Second Class, Division One

I blinked. It took me a minute to realize that I'd also scored a 2:1. Upon further inspection, I saw that I'd made the cutoff by a single percentage point. But who cares about that? I'd made it! I sprinted downstairs to tell my parents, then ran back upstairs to text my friends and call Asser.

After sharing the good news with everyone I knew, I collapsed backward on my bed, still buzzing with happiness. That's when I realized: I won. From the time I was a girl, I had carried this dream of graduating from university, even when I didn't know a single woman who had done it. *I won't be a teenage bride and spend my life wondering what I could have contributed to the world*, I had told myself. *I will go to college*. The Taliban had forced me out of school when I was eleven years old and tried to kill me when I was fifteen. With bombs and guns, they'd fought against little girls who only wanted to learn, to understand the world around them. There were long periods of my childhood and teen years when even finishing high school seemed impossible.

I am not someone who believes everyone should go to college; I know plenty of brilliant people who don't have a degree. But, for

me, education was my guiding light, the only way I could save myself from a life I didn't want.

Now, no matter where my life went next, I was a college graduate, and I always would be. It didn't mean the end of misogyny or
an enduring triumph for the right to education, of course. This
was a personal victory. Between me and the men who'd tried to
stop me, the fight was over. I had won.

32.

Two weeks after I received my exam results, the security team drove me back to Lady Margaret Hall to collect everything I'd left in my dorm room before spring break.

As I stood at the front gate waiting for the porter to buzz me in, the quiet unsettled me—no students calling to each other across the lawn, no music drifting from open windows or food delivery bikers ringing their bells at passing cars. The normally pristine hedges were overgrown, and weeds sprouted in the flower beds. It felt like someone had cast an evil spell on Lady Margaret Hall, stopping time and turning it into a haunted place.

It looked so different from the first time I saw this beautiful campus as a high school student on a prospective college tour. After visiting the library, dining hall, and dorms that day, I had hung back and let my guidance counselor chat with our guide; I was hoping for a quiet moment to get a sense of the place. We

followed a winding path past formal gardens, forests, and meadows full of wildflowers. The landscape felt so familiar to me, even
though I'd never been there. When the trail ended at a riverbank
dotted with daffodils, I stood watching the late-afternoon sun
glint off the surface of the River Cherwell. It was all so dreamy;
I envisioned myself spending hours in that very spot, sitting by
the water until the stars came out.

Some people assume that I chose Lady Margaret Hall because
it was the first women's college at Oxford. Or because Benazir
Bhutto, Pakistan's first female prime minister, studied PPE there.
They imagine I had some master plan to follow in her footsteps
and one day lead my country.

The truth is: The flowers on campus reminded me of Swat
Valley in the springtime, and the lazy swirls of the Cherwell
brought back memories of the streams and rivers in Mingora. For
the first time since moving to the UK, I had found a place that felt
like home.

And now it was time to say good-bye.

⟬⟬⟬

PACKING ANYTHING, EVEN an overnight bag, always makes me
melancholy. I tend to wait until the last possible minute, throw
some things into my luggage, and, without fail, arrive at my destination missing a toothbrush or socks. Lingering too long in the
dorm—to neatly fold my Diwali ball gown or consider why I'd
dog-eared the page of a book—would only dredge up memories of
all the homes and people I've had to leave behind.

As I entered my room, I found it precisely as I left it, albeit
dustier. I loaded my belongings as quickly as possible, not even
stopping to label the boxes. When I was finished, I drifted down
the long hall toward the common space, running my hands along

the door frames of each friend's empty room. The kitchen was dark, quiet, and cleaner than I'd ever seen it, scoured of the literal and emotional messes we'd made while learning to be adults.

I stepped out onto the little balcony off the kitchen and scanned the horizon, my eyes landing on the bell tower. I'd climbed it so many times, but I couldn't recall the very last one. *It must have been in February or March*, I thought. *Who was with me?* It bothered me that I couldn't remember—because I knew I'd never do it again, never be the person I was when I flew across the rooftops.

Something moved and caught my eye on the ground below— *Yasmin!* She was there, reading a book on the bench where I'd first met Tarik. My heart leapt, but I didn't call out to her—somewhere inside I knew that this must be some sort of waking dream, that she wasn't really there. Then I heard laughter and saw Hen rounding the corner, talking a mile a minute on her phone. In the distance, Cora and Anisa lugged their backpacks into University Park and toward the lecture halls.

The quad filled up with friends and acquaintances, professors and librarians. Raja, Parveen, and everyone from 24 Obs were playing music and dancing. Zayan bounced from foot to foot excitedly as Sofia laughed. I spotted Lara, Valerie, and the professor who always gave me a permissive smirk when he knew I hadn't done the reading. There was the guy who wore his pajamas to breakfast every morning and the girl who coached the rowing club. I saw faces I couldn't place too—groups of friends picnicking and chatting, people I'd never met. At some point, I realized that these strangers were our inheritors, the next batch of students who would fill this place with curiosity, laughter, and longing. My college would be theirs soon.

Some religions believe in the concept of the "astral plane," a space between heaven and earth where the souls of those who have passed away mingle with those yet to be born. That's the closest description I can find for what I experienced that day, seeing backward and forward, past and future, at the same time. It only lasted a few moments. The sun emerged from behind a cloud, I blinked, and everyone was gone.

I stepped off the balcony and back into the kitchen, my heart full of love and gratitude. I thought I understood what the vision was meant to teach me, the last lesson of Lady Margaret Hall: I wasn't here to grasp at ghosts, to stop time or even mourn its loss. In college, I was surrounded by friends, free to explore, happy. Of course, I never wanted it to end. But this was not another home I was forced to leave—it was a gate I passed through to become something new.

33.

Asser sent me a telescope for my birthday. *What an odd gift*, I thought, staring at the long, narrow box in the middle of the living room floor. Then I remembered my brief exam-season obsession with astronomy, how I'd mentioned in passing that I would like to have a telescope one day. Every night that month I'd called Asser and rambled, delirious from exam prep and half asleep. He had been listening after all. He'd collected my transient thoughts, the things I'd already forgotten I said, and held on to them.

I knew how much he loved me—and that felt heavy at times, like a countdown clock always ticking in my mind. I'd made him a promise almost a year ago, that we would figure out our future after I finished college. He wasn't pressuring me for an answer, but I felt a kind of fog between us, a distance that hadn't been there before.

I loved Asser, but I did not want to get married. When I told

226

him this in the month after exams, he said that was fine. He didn't care what we called it—marriage, partnership, cohabitation—as long as we were together. For a few weeks, I let myself live in that fantasy, looking up London apartments and researching visa options that would allow him to live in the UK. When my friends asked how things were going with him, I told them we were moving in together. They all seemed excited for me, but I could tell they knew it would never happen.

Asser knew it too, though I think he hoped I would find the courage to follow my heart. But I couldn't do it. If we lived together without getting married, my parents would stop speaking to me, at least for a while. People would inevitably find out about us, and all my work in Pakistan would go up in flames. It was too big of a risk.

There were only two options—get married or let him go. I hated them both.

⁓

I HAD ALWAYS known marriage was not for me. When I was nine years old, I made a vow never to learn to cook because I figured that no man in Mingora would take a wife who was useless in the kitchen. As I got older, I started saying, "I'll consider marriage when I'm thirty-five," but that was just a placeholder, something to placate my mom and keep her from launching into a lecture. "You will get married," she always said. "You must. Marriage is beautiful."

For my mom and most women in Pakistan, I suppose it was self-preservation to believe marriage was "beautiful," as it was also mandatory. Growing up, I spent hours in my aunts' kitchens as they prepared meal after meal, caring for eight or nine children at a time, waiting hand and foot on husbands they hadn't chosen and,

I suspected, would never love. Their sons, barely old enough to talk, would amble in and order their mothers to bring more tea for their fathers' guests. And marriage could be dangerous as well. I remembered walking down the street as a child, hearing a woman being beaten behind the walls of her home. None of it was beautiful to me.

As a girl, I believed that things would be different for me and my friends. We were an unstoppable force who would fight for our right to be educated, to have careers as airline pilots and engineers. My cousin Nazneen planned to be a doctor and also a poet. She and I would talk for hours about the changes we wanted to see in our community, how things would be better when we were adults. While I was in the hospital in Birmingham, she sent me a package containing page after page of handwritten poems. As I read them, I learned her father had forced her to marry. She was sixteen and devastated.

When we talk on the phone now, she tells me she's fine. Her husband is nice enough. She loves her children. But I can't forget the girl she was, the aspirations she had, and how she lost them all when she got married. I thought of her often at Oxford—how she would have thrived at university, how unfair it was that I was the only one living the life we both dreamed of when we were young.

My friends in college, of course, lived in a much different world, one where they would be allowed to choose their partners. Still, most of them weren't sure they wanted to marry. When they had a crush, they swooned like romance novel heroines. But they talked about marriage as an abstract, political concept, in terms of compromise and how much women stood to lose—the expectation to prioritize a husband's needs over your own, putting your professional life on hold to have children, the emotional labor and unequal division of domestic duties, the cost of divorce if it doesn't work out. It seemed to me that, in a society where you could choose whether to marry or not, a lot of women preferred to stay single.

The only argument for marrying Asser was how I felt inside. I loved him and loved the prospect of having his companionship for the rest of my life. I couldn't imagine him ever hurting me or imposing harsh rules after we were married, but I knew women who never expected it to happen to them either. If I was going to change my mind, I needed some guarantees.

"Would you try to tell me what I can and can't wear?" I asked Asser over FaceTime early in the summer. I was thinking of a Pakistani student at Oxford, who had gotten engaged to a supposedly educated and "feminist" man. He ended up barring her from attending parties and balls, and made her remove any photos from Instagram that he hadn't approved, including a perfectly normal picture of her in a tank top.

"Well, last summer when we planned to go hiking, you showed up in heels," Asser replied. "I would prefer you not do that again. Otherwise, dress however you like."

I swatted away his joke and moved on. "Fine, what about kids? I don't want any. I may change my mind in the future, but you should not assume that I will. Can you live with that?"

He was quiet for a moment. "To be honest, I haven't thought a lot about having children." In my mind, this was the heart of the problem. Women have to contemplate every aspect of a relationship, how it will affect them, what they might lose—while men can afford to consider only themselves and their desires.

"I guess not thinking about it is a kind of an answer in itself, though," Asser continued. "Kids aren't as important to me as being with the woman I love. When I picture my future, you are the person I see. And if you do change your mind at some point, we can talk about it then, right?"

That response seemed good enough for now, so I pressed on. "Would you ever want to take another wife?"

Some people interpret the Quran as allowing a man to have up to four wives, as long as he can care for them all equally. From my perspective, it's impossible to treat multiple partners with parity, and hard enough to have a happy marriage with only one spouse.

Asser rolled his eyes and said, "You are all four wives in one, Malala."

"This isn't a joke!" I shot back. "I need some assurances. I need to know your answers to all my questions before I could even think about getting married. Will you be faithful to me? Will you get angry and yell? Would you ever lie to me?"

"I can only tell you that I love you and would never intentionally hurt you," he replied. "There are no promises or magic words to take away all your doubts. No one can guarantee the future."

I ignored that nonanswer and kept plowing through my list of questions like an interrogator one query away from nailing the suspect. "You know my work for girls' education is the most important thing to me. It always will be. Would you try to stop me from working?"

"And you know I was raised by three women who work." His voice had changed from upbeat to annoyed. "If I'm honest, Malala, it feels like we've known each other too long for you to still wonder what kind of man I am. You're looking for certainty, a sign that will give you a definitive yes-or-no answer. But anything can be a sign if you want it to be. So my question to you is, what do you want?"

That night I wrote him a letter.

Asser,

I have a huge fear of marriage. I don't want a ceremony, and I don't want to sign legal papers. I don't want to take any man's last name (though I'll happily offer mine).

I just want a partner who I trust. I want to support your dreams and for you to support me in my work. I want a friend who will listen to my thoughts no matter how stupid or silly they are. I want a man who looks sexy playing cricket!

You should be sure about me too. There are things I have accepted about myself, but I understand if other people can't accept the asymmetry of my face and smile, my hearing problems, my scars. I would rather die alone than to think you took pity on me because no one else would have me.

My life hasn't been and won't be easy. I have already lived through the worst things, so gossip and lies, the cruel things people say online, and even the death threats don't bother me. But you might not want that in your life. Are you sure you can live like this?

I am trying to push myself to consider what it would mean to marry. Right now I feel like I'm still learning who I am. Our brains don't fully develop until twenty-five years old! I have to wonder if I can trust my own judgment at twenty-three. I need more time.

In all of this, I love you and don't want to lose you. But I don't want to hurt you either. Is it wrong to continue our relationship when there is so much uncertainty within me?

I didn't send the letter, but getting my thoughts out on paper brought some temporary solace. I stopped grilling Asser over the phone. These types of conversations were better in person, when I could look in his eyes and search for the truth. I hoped that could happen again soon, though it seemed like I might be waiting a long time. Asser had applied for a UK visitor's visa, but, five months into the pandemic, he was still waiting on approval to travel. I tried not to dwell on the fact that we hadn't seen each other in almost a year.

⌒

WHILE I WAS contemplating marriage with Asser, Sofia was going through her own relationship drama. We spent hours talking about our problems and getting nowhere. Then she came up with the idea that we should read our way to clarity—to consult the experts on matters of love and feminism. I joked that Oxford had taught us well how to analyze a text and form an argument, so it was worth a shot.

That summer we developed our reading list, everyone from bell hooks to Dolly Alderton, books by American psychologists, Lebanese poets, Victorian-era novelists. Soon we were talking about Amia Srinivasan's *The Right to Sex* as much as we talked about our boyfriends, and that alone felt like progress. The list kept growing—Chimamanda Ngozi Adichie, Virginia Woolf, magazine articles with titles like "The Five Red Flags to Look Out for in Men." As she was in Islamabad and I was in Birmingham, we mostly conducted our book club via text, both waking up in different time zones to messages full of quotes and pictures of highlighted passages.

Several books gave strong evidence for how marriage supports patriarchy. I filed away the stats and arguments, always eager to add more nuance to my understanding of gender and power dynamics. But I was also moved by stories of marriage that matched Adichie's description—"a source of joy and love and mutual support." The passage seemed to describe what I already had with Asser, though not what I'd seen in most married couples. And as much as I enjoyed the reading, I couldn't find an answer to my specific question: how to choose between an institution I didn't believe in and a life without the person I loved.

I decided to poll a few of my older married friends, on the assumption that people who knew my situation might be better able to guide me. The British and American women said things like "You *cannot* marry your first boyfriend!" and "Think of it as a corporate procurement policy: you need to review at least three quotes from vendors before you sign a contract." I wondered if Tarik or my teenage crushes on Bollywood stars and cricket players qualified as romantic experience. How did other women face going through this crucible—having a crush, flirting, worrying about your ambiguous relationship status, falling in love, deciding your future—multiple times?

When I spoke to married women from Pakistan, they were focused on certainty. One of them said I should take a long time to decide because "being single isn't good, but it's better than a bad marriage." I knew she was right about the last part at least.

These conversations made me think about my mom. When she got married, she knew a lot less about her future husband than I did about Asser. Though they came from neighboring villages in Shangla, my parents had never been alone together or exchanged more than a few words until their wedding day. I felt embarrassed that I'd never thought about my mom as a young woman, how scared she must have been, what dreams she might have given up after becoming a wife.

One night, while we were alone in the living room, I decided to ask her. "How did you know you could trust Dad? I mean, before you got married, were you scared to go and live with him?"

She let out a long sigh and closed her eyes. "Malala, listen, you *must* marry a Pashtun man, and he *must* speak Pashto and come from our culture. Your father and I will come up with a list of options and you can pick from those."

In the weary way she answered me, I glimpsed the exhaustion of a life spent trying to be a mother in a restrictive patriarchal society; the constant scrutiny and blame placed on you if your children, particularly daughters, stepped out of line. I wasn't sure if she really believed what she said or if she was only repeating the admonitions she would hear from extended family members if they learned about Asser. "Mom, can we just forget about my life right now?" I pleaded. "I really want to know how you felt when you got married. You've never told me."

She cocked an eyebrow at me as if to say, *I know exactly why you're asking these questions. But, fine, I'll play along.* "Your dad was one of the only men in the nearby villages who had been to college. I thought I was very fortunate to be marrying him. Because he was educated, I imagined we might go away someday. It was an opportunity to make my dream come true."

"What was your dream?" I asked, a bit shocked. My mom had never admitted to these sorts of things, and my mind ran through images of her as a scientist, a businesswoman, a diplomat.

"Well, as you know, there are hardly any roads or cars in Shangla. And no restaurants. So I hoped for a faster pace of life. My biggest wish was to sit in the backseat of a car as it drove through the rain, eating a takeaway kebab."

Hearing that was shocking, funny, and heartbreaking all at the same time. My mom deserved more than such a small, achievable dream. But she and the women she grew up with weren't allowed to have lofty aspirations. They looked at marriage as a bet, a gamble that their lives might slightly improve if they ended up with a decent man. My mom got lucky; many of her sisters and friends did not.

"If you ask me what's my biggest blessing," she added, "I will always say my husband." I was happy for my mom that she felt safe and content in her marriage; but it was deeply unjust and depressing that her life's fortunes had always been bound to men.

At that point, I'd asked dozens of people for advice; sought revelation everywhere from social science to astrology. And I still hadn't landed on a decision that felt right. Maybe what Asser said was true—no one can guarantee the future. But I still clung to the myth of certainty, to the idea that someday I would find a definitive answer.

The one person I wished I could talk to—my beloved grandmother, Abai—was no longer with me. She'd passed away on a quiet afternoon, early in the pandemic. My grief over her loss was much different from the uncontrollable sorrow I'd felt at Oxford, when I had convinced myself that she was dead. I was sad, of course, but spent more time reflecting on how grateful I was for the time we'd spent together and her influence on my life. My parents, brothers, and I sat around the kitchen table for hours and shared our favorite Abai stories. We mourned her with the gifts she gave us—family, laughter, and prayer.

In the weeks after she died, I kept coming back to one particular memory—a visit to Shangla when I was nine or ten years old. Abai called me in from playing with my cousins and led me to the backyard where she had built a fire under her clay oven. "Sit here and chop this tomato," she said. "Today I am going to teach you to make chicken karahi."

"I'll help," I replied. "But I'm not learning to cook."

Abai smirked. "Lots of girls your age can already prepare this dish on their own."

If she thought she could use my competitive nature against me, she was wrong. "That's why I'm not going to learn—because then I'll get stuck doing it all the time!"

"No, you learn because one day you'll want to get married."

"I will *never* want that," I vowed.

Abai looked at me appraisingly for a moment, smiled, and handed me another tomato. She didn't scold me for disrespecting my culture or try to tell me that marriage was beautiful—she didn't say anything at all. Thinking about this memory now, I wondered about that look she gave me. I'll never know exactly, but I believe what I saw in her eyes was a grandmother's knowledge that the dreams we have when we're young will reshape themselves as we grow. As I agonized over the decision to marry or not, I wished that Abai and I could talk again, that I could have one more chance to ask her everything she knew about love.

34.

The . . . what? Doesn't ring a bell for me, sorry. . . ."

"*The Cotswolds*, Malala! Storybook England? Charming villages? Rolling green hills?"

I knew exactly what Zayan was describing, but played dumb because I wanted to hear his over-the-top sales pitch for the weekend getaway he was planning.

"Look, I'm sending you the details," he said. "It's you, me, and Parveen. I've made a full itinerary—hiking, shopping, dinner in a fifteenth-century pub. All you have to do is show up next Thursday."

"I'll be there," I promised.

By midsummer, the UK had lifted lockdown restrictions, and I fled my parents' house to be with friends as often as possible—Yasmin's birthday party in London, sleepovers with Hen, spa days with Alice. It was overwhelming to see a face you knew so well, no longer trapped in a tiny digital square on Zoom but attached to a body and walking around in the real world. I loved hearing my friends' laughter again, so much more alive and contagious in person than over the phone. Typically I'm not much of a hugger, but I couldn't stop myself at these happy reunions.

When I arrived at the stone cottage Zayan had rented, he and Parveen tumbled out to meet me. "Hurry up!" he said. "We've been waiting till you got here to start movie night." I tossed my bag in the bedroom assigned to me and settled in on the couch to watch a nineties film called *The Bodyguard*.

"So, how accurate was it?" Zayan asked me as the credits rolled.

"Uh, let's see. . . . I've never been picked up and carried out of a crowd. Never fallen in love with anyone from the Met Police. But the scene where the bodyguard is annoyed because she wants to go shopping? That's definitely accurate in my experience."

After the movie, we stood around in the kitchen, snacking on chocolate and crisps. "We should do this for all our breaks," Parveen said to Zayan. "Maybe the Lake District or Scotland after fall term?" They were both headed back into academia soon— an MBA for him, a PhD for her.

"What about you, Malz? What's next?" she asked.

"I wish I knew," I said, biting a hangnail. "I need to get back to work. I feel so useless stuck in my parents' house while all these schools are closing because of Covid. Like I should be doing something about that. And I want to travel, but it's impossible right now with all the border closings."

"And what about . . ." I knew what was coming and shot her a look to say *Stop talking right now*. I'd told Parveen a bit about Asser, but Zayan was too much of a gossip to handle sensitive information. At least, that's what I thought at the time. I later learned that he knew all along, but somehow managed to keep the secret.

The next day, Zayan donned a bright-yellow raincoat and led Parveen and me on a soggy hike through the countryside. "English weather builds character!" he shouted over loudly bleating sheep.

"I'm standing in half a foot of mud, bro," Parveen snarked. "Please spare us your life lessons."

My phone buzzed and I tried to read a text from Asser through my rain-speckled screen.

> I got the visa!!!

After shrieking and nearly dropping my phone in a puddle, I told my friends to go ahead of me while I made a quick call. Asser picked up right away and gave me the details: He would visit for fifteen days in mid-September, and was bringing his mother, who wanted to see her daughter and grandchildren.

"Cannot wait to see you," he gushed. "I love you, Malala! And I love you too, Lahore Visa Office!"

I doubled over laughing. "Please tell me you're not standing in a government building and shouting my name."

"No, no, I'm in the car," he replied. "Sorry, I'm just really excited."

Later that evening, I sent him a message:

> I would love to meet your mother. Bring her to my parents' house for lunch.

I watched as Asser's text bubble appeared and disappeared several times.

> I don't know. She's 70 years old and I don't want to get her hopes up. With my last two girlfriends, she thought I would get married each time. I can't disappoint her again.

The next time he called, we talked it over and agreed to manage both our parents' expectations, firmly establishing that this was a meal between friends, nothing more. When I got home from the Cotswolds, I informed my parents of the plan. "*Don't* be awkward," I instructed them. "Don't ask any questions about marriage. Don't ask if Asser will move to the UK or what his mother's expectations are for a daughter-in-law. Don't ask . . . anything!" They seemed momentarily cowed by my hectoring, but I knew better than to assume that they would behave and reminded them several times in the days leading up to Asser's arrival.

FARIDA LOOKED LIKE a film star standing in my driveway—brown hair with golden highlights, big sunglasses, lip gloss. She wore a perfectly pressed shalwar and taupe kitten heels, waving hello to my family and me.

My mom and dad greeted her first. Then Farida gave me a hug and thanked us for inviting her. I hugged Asser's sister Ambreena next, and gave him a circumspect nod. He laughed.

By the time we got from the front door to the living room, my dad and Asser's mom were deep in conversation, discussing all the latest headlines from Pakistan. When my dad went off to fetch tea, Farida sat down next to my mom. English was the only language they had in common, and neither was fluent, but their shared interest in fashion carried them through. For an hour, Farida held court, the chat bouncing between Pakistani politics and shopping tips. To my relief, no one even glanced at Asser and me sitting quietly nearby.

We moved outside to the garden where my parents had prepared lunch. As everyone took a seat, my dad turned to Farida and said, "So what can you tell us about your son?"

My stomach lurched. *What is he doing?* This was supposed to be a visit among friends with no expectations or serious talk. I didn't want anyone, on Asser's side or mine, to think this gathering meant that a wedding was coming. To stay out of the spotlight, I assigned myself the job of sitting next to my mom and translating the conversation into Pashto.

"I was forty when Asser was born," Farida said. "He's much younger than his sisters, but I was so excited to have him. He was due in November, but he came two months early." I made a mental note: *Asser was supposed to be a Scorpio. Recheck astrological compatibility.*

"As soon as he was out, the nurses told me, 'This baby is not going to survive.' I refused to believe it and began handing out the box of pastries I'd brought to the hospital to celebrate his birth. He was so tiny and weak, and stayed in the incubator for many days. All I could do was to pray for him."

She looked at Asser and said, "He is very precious to me."

My mom quietly wiped away tears, and I wondered if she was remembering the baby she'd lost before I was born. Farida patted her hand and said, "You'd think, after all that, he could have at least become a doctor." Everyone laughed and she shot me a conspiratorial wink. I had not changed my mind on marriage, but if I were ever to have a mother-in-law, Farida would be my first choice.

ASSER AND I packed as much as we could into his fifteen-day trip. The evening after Farida's visit, we fled to the city for the weekend. We ate sushi and shopped for shoes; I made him ride the London Eye with me. In the remaining days, we watched a match at the Newbury Cricket Club, played badminton in the backyard with my dad and brothers, and went back to the botanical gardens for long walks. I didn't initiate discussions about our relationship as I had planned, preferring to enjoy his company without thinking of the future.

But two nights before he had to go back to Lahore, I felt so depressed that he was leaving, unable to hold in my sadness and confusion. "When we're together, I forget all the worries that I have about getting married," I told him. "I'm just so happy and want to be with you forever. And when you leave, I start over-thinking again."

"I want to make it easy for you to be with me," he said. "I hate to see you under so much pressure when my goal is to add joy to your life. I wish I had the resources to take a year off and stay here with you until we figure it out, but I can't do that."

He reached for my hand and added, "Sometimes it's stressful for me too. My job is full-on, all the time. Trying to keep my mom safe during a pandemic. Trying to impress your parents. Trying to figure out how to show you that I will make a good partner. I wouldn't put you or myself through this if I didn't think we were right for each other."

"You're already a good partner, Asser. Things are great between us, but I still don't know how I feel about being a wife."

"So . . . you're saying that I just need to find a way to reverse about five thousand years of patriarchy and social norms around marriage . . . and then we can be together?"

I rolled my eyes at him.

"For you, I'll try anything," he said.

35.

A sser didn't need to start an international debate about marriage. I did that all on my own.

In January 2021, *British Vogue* asked if I could do a photo shoot and interview for their July issue. I'd never done a fashion magazine cover before and didn't understand why they would want to feature someone who was five feet tall and couldn't form a proper smile. But my team said the interview was a chance to "reintroduce myself to the world," and that got my attention.

After Asser left in September, the UK government issued new lockdown orders. I was stuck in the house again, unable to travel or see friends, and wondering why my life seemed to be going in reverse. At age eleven, I was on TV, telling the world about life under Taliban control. By fifteen, I'd gained so much influence that the extremists tried to kill me. At seventeen, I won the Nobel Peace Prize. And now I was an adult living with my parents.

Even though I was still working as much as I could, I some-times felt like I was drifting from my purpose in life—to help girls who were denied their right to education. Schools around the world were closed because of Covid, and millions of students, mostly girls, might never return to the classroom. Some had been married off, some aged out. Others were working as street vendors and factory laborers to try to support their families.

The Shangla school provided all students with tablets so they could join online lessons and stay on top of their studies during the lockdowns. This caused a major issue with many of the parents, as giving girls access to technology went against their social norms. They wanted complete control and surveillance of their daughters' lives, and the internet made that impossible. The principal and school administrators stood their ground, saying that the girls were required to attend remote classes and do their home-work during the pandemic. Still, it wasn't a perfect option. Hardly any of the families had internet access and cellular service was often too spotty for the girls to get online. I hoped that the girls wouldn't give up and would try to keep learning from home how-ever they could.

I wanted to be out in the world, advocating for young women. Every night I lay awake wondering how to prove myself worthy of this calling. Maybe *British Vogue* wasn't the perfect match for my message, but it was definitely high-profile and a big microphone I could use to remind people what was at stake for millions of girls.

In early April, I traveled to London for the photo shoot and interview. The first day was fittings, making sure the clothes were precisely hemmed, gathered, and darted to my body. I woke up at 6 a.m. the following morning to make my call time at the studio. For the next ten hours, the creative team plucked my eyebrows, curled my hair, painted my nails, dressed me in multiple outfits, told me where to stand and what to do with my hands while the photographer's camera snapped away. Halfway through the shoot, the makeup artist suggested we try a bright-red lipstick. It was much more dramatic than the tinted lip balm I usually wore, but I was in the mood to try something new, so I said, "Let's do it!" When I got back to the hotel that night, I collapsed on the bed. Everyone at the shoot had treated me so well, but it was strangely exhausting to be photographed for an entire day.

The next morning I woke up, ate breakfast in my room, and walked down to the hotel lobby to meet Sirin Kale, the writer doing my interview. As it was a cover story, I expected to find a middle-aged journalist with stately streaks of gray hair, wearing a business suit. But Sirin wasn't that much older than me; she had a nose ring, dark wavy hair that fell to her waist, and black eyeliner drawn in an impressive cat-eye shape.

We left the hotel and went for a walk in St. James's Park, chatting easily about Oxford and my student life. She wanted to hear about my trip to Pakistan, and I told her how it felt to breathe the air of my home country again. We talked about online activism and how outrage so often gets in the way of real change.

She asked what I would do with my life now that I'd finished college. I said that was the question keeping me up at night, and that my biggest fear was failing girls like the one I used to be—girls who were full of dreams, but living at the mercy of a patriarchal society that doesn't value them. Millions of girls watch their brothers go to school in the morning, while they stay home to cook and clean. I talked about the girls I'd met who were married off to old men, and those in refugee camps who felt their aspirations and hopes slipping away day by day. "I care a lot about my work and I worry about how long it will take to reach the goals we have set," I said.

Sirin was so disarming that I sometimes forgot our talk was a magazine interview and not an overdue catch-up with a friend.

I snapped back to reality when she asked if I'd met someone, a romantic partner, at Oxford. *How does she know?* I wondered.

My eyes went wide at this unexpectedly personal question. If I said no, that would be a lie. If I said yes, it would cause a controversy. I finally mumbled something about hoping to find a person who understands and respects me. Sirin saw how uncomfortable I was and, to her credit, quickly moved on. But I spent the rest of the interview trying to rephrase my answer in my mind. I worried Asser would read it and feel like he didn't exist, that I was writing him out of my story.

The middle of an interview is not the time to plunge yourself into an existential debate about marriage—but that's exactly what I did. The books Sofia and I had read, the chat with my mom, and the pro/con lists in my journal were all circling around in my brain as I answered other questions. When it was clear that Sirin was winding down the conversation, I wanted to try to restate my views on love. I told her that I'd seen a few of my college friends get more serious about their relationships since graduation and start coupling up. What I didn't understand, I explained, was how you could ever trust someone enough to make that commitment. Even if you thought the other person was wonderful, how could you be sure?

With a nervous laugh, I blurted out, "I still don't understand why people have to get married. If you want to have a person in your life, why do you have to sign marriage papers, why can't it just be a partnership?" It wasn't meant to be a statement on the institution of marriage or any sort of call to action—just venting my personal frustrations to an affable stranger. Sirin smiled and nodded, as if she understood exactly what I meant.

That went well, I thought as we took a selfie and said goodbye. I got in the car for the long ride back to Birmingham, feeling glad that I'd agreed to the cover story and relieved that it was over.

WHEN MY ISSUE of *British Vogue* was published and the photos went online, I paused for a moment before looking at them. I've sat for hundreds of professional portraits in my life, and when I see the final images, I often feel like there's a stranger looking back at me. Sometimes she's dressed in lavender parachute pants that I would never wear in real life, the choice of an overambitious stylist. Or her face is suspiciously flawless, the imperfections I see in the mirror airbrushed away. But I loved the woman facing the world from the cover of *British Vogue* in a red headscarf and matching lipstick.

Within minutes, my phone was buzzing nonstop. Friends sent hyperactive, barely coherent texts with lots of emojis. My parents huddled around their iPad, my dad reading the interview while my mom examined the photos. "Did you get to keep the jewelry? Where is it?" she asked, looking disappointed when I told her that everything goes back to the designers after the shoot.

I padded up to my room to read the interview in peace and scanned the page for things that might cause a controversy. The article revealed that I played poker and went to pubs in college, but made sure to include that I don't drink. I thought I'd probably get some sermons about that from pious Pakistanis, but nothing too damaging. Sirin had done a beautiful job with the piece, and I most appreciated that my work for girls' education was the heart of the article.

Asser called to say I looked stunning and that he thought the interview was great. If he was uncomfortable about the way I'd stumbled over the question about whether I had a romantic partner, he didn't mention it. I picked up my phone to share the story on Instagram and found that my dad had already posted an enthusiastic review on his Twitter account. That night I read glowing comments from people all over the world who connected with the words and images.

When I woke up the next day, though, no one was celebrating. #ShameOnMalala was trending in Pakistan, as people had decided that my comments on marriage were "lewd," "un-Islamic," and an "assault on the foundations of society." They claimed I was encouraging adultery, and seized on the word "partnership," as if equality between men and women was unnatural and profane. Thousands upon thousands of tweets were calling me an atheist, a prostitute, a foreign agent intent on destroying the country, everything but what I really was—a twenty-three-year-old asking questions about love and relationships.

The attacks ranged from commentary on my appearance— "too ugly to get a husband anyway"—to saying I should be raped, burned, or strangled. One man wrote that the Taliban's "poor aim" had shamed the entire country. A popular meme showed two dogs having sex, with my name written under the female dog. I scrolled through page after page of replies with only one word: *bitch*.

They wanted me to feel shame, but I was angry. The attack seemed coordinated—like people were deliberately misreading my words to cause a scandal. And in the process of tearing me down, they were sending a message to every young woman in Pakistan: Marriage is not optional.

Over the next few days, the hysteria grew every time I opened my phone. A coalition of independent schools announced that their students would wear black armbands on my birthday. Lawmakers in Khyber Pakhtunkhwa, my home province, debated issuing a resolution against me and demanded a government probe into the interview. They called on my father to offer an explanation, as if I was not worthy of speaking for myself. A cleric gave a sermon promising a suicide attack on me the next time I set foot in the country.

I saw many versions of "She is supposed to be an education activist, not give her opinions on marriage." But what was the point of sending girls to school if they did not become women who could choose their own futures? These people, some of whom claimed to be feminists or liberals, were revealing the limits of their commitment to women's rights: You can go to school, but you can't choose your husband. You can go to college, but you can only have children, not a career. You can use your voice, so long as you never criticize the system.

My parents were assailed with calls and text messages. Our relatives gave breathless reports of the damage, what their neighbors were saying, every stupid meme or WhatsApp message they received. "Why does Malala reject marriage? It's against our religion!" they gasped. An imam from Shangla phoned to lecture them for over an hour.

My dad pressured me to make a statement clarifying my comments. "It's harming our reputation. You need to do it now before the situation gets worse," he said.

I wanted to laugh. How could it get worse? "If I give in to this," I countered, "what will people ask me to explain tomorrow? Every time I speak, they'll come back with their notes." And he had been the first one to share the interview, I pointed out. He was proud of it until the backlash began.

For years, when people asked my dad about how he raised me, he'd always replied, "Don't ask what I did. Ask what I did not do. I did not clip her wings." He often spoke of me as a bird, but sometimes I felt more like a kite—flying high when it served him, pulled back to earth by a string when it did not.

Meanwhile, my mom sobbed and walked around the house like she'd been physically wounded. When she finally spoke to me, it was with an anger that bordered on contempt: "How could you do this, Malala? I wish you'd never opened your mouth."

I knew better than to talk back, so I went to my room and messaged Asser.

> My parents are receiving calls from relatives saying I'm "anti-Islam."

> My mom won't stop crying.

Please tell her not to be sad.

This is just the "outrage of the week" in Pakistan. It's really not that serious.

> I'm 23. Why am I supposed to have all the answers? I should be allowed to be confused.

Can I talk to them? Would that help?

> Up to you.

He called and I walked downstairs with the phone on speaker. "It's Asser. He wants to talk to you."

My parents looked stricken. "Is he upset?" my dad asked.

"Ask him yourself," I said, holding out the phone to them.

"No, of course not—I am not upset," Asser told them calmly. "There's nothing wrong with the interview or with an open discussion on marriage."

"What about your family?" my mom said. "Your mother must be *very* disappointed."

"Oh, my family is fine! My mom loves the photos. Her only comment was how beautiful Malala looked. Please don't even think of it."

Asser paused for a moment and added, "I think the social media reaction is making this seem bigger than it is, especially from afar. The people who won't let it go—the trolls, politicians, radicals—are just using this to build their own profiles. They don't speak for everyone in Pakistan. But even if the whole world was saying this garbage, Malala is not alone. I will always support her."

They talked for a few more minutes, and I watched my mom and dad relax. With Asser's reassurance, they stopped their scolding and prodding for me to make a statement. I could walk around the house again without feeling like a monster.

In the early evening, I called my high school friend Alice. "Let's have dinner," I said. "I need a change of scenery, and I want to go somewhere expensive." We booked a table at one of Birmingham's better restaurants and ordered everything that sounded good to us. Alice kept me distracted and entertained with wild stories about her job as a paramedic. When I got home, I felt more like myself again. But the night out with my friend only reinforced my desire to go farther away, to be with the person I most wanted to see.

I waited until 3 a.m., when it was morning in Lahore, to send the message.

> Let's take a trip, just the two of us, and talk about everything.

> Tell me where and I'll leave now. When I hold you again, I will never let go.

36.

My childhood made me feel so much older than I was, forcing me to contend with violence and physical pain, to provide financial support for my family, and to stand in a spotlight I had not sought out. Then college made me feel like I had plenty of time to grow up, that I should enjoy being young and free. During the pandemic, I was relearning time as a finite thing. The days I slept away passed just the same; I couldn't get them back. Brooding about marriage in the pages of *British Vogue* wouldn't buy me another two years to see if my feelings changed. If I wanted my life to move forward, I needed to make some adult decisions, starting with my relationship.

Due to Covid travel restrictions in July 2021, Asser couldn't come to the UK and I couldn't go to Pakistan. The US would allow us both to visit, so we decided to meet there at the end of the month. On the plane from London, I wrote down all my remaining relationship questions in my notebook. I'd told Asser to think of everything he wanted to ask me as well. This was not a philosophy tutorial that prized the depth of inquiry over conclusions. I was determined to come home with an answer about our future, one way or another.

Asser's flight from Lahore to New York landed hours before mine. He sat outside international baggage claim most of the day, watching people reunite with their loved ones. Nine months had passed since his last visit; when I saw him, my legs wobbled and I almost cried. He wrapped his arms around me, and I pressed my head into his chest. I couldn't hear the luggage carousel rumbling to life or the people shouting all around us, just the sound of his heartbeat, steady as a clock.

After finding our driver, we headed to a resort in Lake Placid, New York. The five-hour drive was a perfect opportunity to kick off the conversation, but I only wanted to look at Asser and hold his hand. We spent most of the ride entertaining each other by trying to pronounce town names like "Poughkeepsie" and "Schroeppel" in terrible New York accents.

Tucked between tree-covered mountains and a sparkling lake, the resort was cozy and quiet. It looked like a good place to contemplate the future. Asser stopped at the front desk and signed us up for a few activities—yoga, tennis lessons, a falconry demonstration from a local bird expert. He also picked up a trail map. "Don't worry," he said, "if we need more time to talk, we can cancel whatever you like. I know we're here for a serious reason, but we should try to have some fun too." I am usually a person who prefers to lounge around all day on vacation, and yoga did not sound at all "fun" to me. But, either because I'd been climbing the walls at my parents' house for more than a year, or because I was just so happy to see him, I smiled and said, "Sounds great!"

It rained from sunrise to sunset on our first full day. I might have seen it as a sign, the universe scrapping our outdoor plans, forcing us to sit inside and address our issues. Instead, I challenged Asser to a game of poker and won three straight hands. Then we played Ping-Pong on a covered porch. Just as I felt like I was getting the hang of it, Asser said, "Should we find a place to sit and talk?"

"Eh, not yet. Can we watch a movie instead? You pick," I replied.

"As you wish."

He chose *Zoolander*, a comedy about male models unwittingly entangled in an international assassination plot. I'd never seen the film—released in 2001 when I was four years old—or even heard of it. Asser spent most of the movie watching me nearly laugh myself off the sofa. As the credits rolled, I asked him how he knew I would love it.

"I didn't, but I hoped you would. I just really wanted to see you laugh," he said.

Whatever I'd imagined when I daydreamed about running away with him in college, this was better. Asser had an infectious enthusiasm to try new things, and over the next two days I found myself waking up in the mornings excited for our next adventure. We watched a falconer send hawks and eagles soaring over the water and return to his arm. In the Adirondack Mountains, we hiked up an out-and-back trail. I walked behind Asser on the narrow path, running my hand along the tree trunks, leaves, and rock outcrops, remembering similar trails outside Mingora. The lookout point felt like standing inside a painting, shades of green, blue, and purple in every direction. In the evenings, we lay on a blanket in the grass watching the sun set over the water and the stars appear in the sky.

On the fourth day, I woke up feeling the heavy burden of time. In a little more than twenty-four hours, we'd be heading back to the airport. We still needed to talk, so I proposed a fail-proof plan: "Let's get a canoe and some lunch and paddle out on the lake. We won't come back to shore until we have an answer about the future. And, whatever happens out there, we'll return as friends." Asser agreed and went off to find a boat.

After an hour or so on the water, we pulled in our paddles for a rest. I opened a Coke and Asser unwrapped a sandwich. Gusts of wind blew across the lake and we drifted through the water as we ate.

"Ready to talk?" he asked when we finished lunch.

"Asser . . ."

"Yes?"

"Where is the hotel?"

We spun around in all directions and could see nothing but water and trees—no trace of the resort, swimmers, or other boats. The shoreline was a bank of massive black rocks. We were lost in the middle of a miles-long lake.

He caught a flash of panic in my eyes. "Just hang on," he said. "We can figure this out. If we pick a direction and paddle, we'll eventually see something, right?"

We headed in the same direction as the wind. About fifteen minutes later, we saw a weathered dock jutting out into the water. We rowed as hard as we could to reach it and clung to the splin-tery pilings.

Just as we were catching our breath, three enormous dogs came rushing down the planks, barking wildly at us. In the years since, I've learned to love dogs, but at the time they terrified me. I had to make a quick decision—be eaten alive by animals or perish at sea. I let go of the dock.

"Malala, no!" Asser cried, still holding on to the piling as the bow drifted away.

"I'm sorry," shouted a woman running up behind the dogs. "Do you need help?" We explained what had happened, and she told us the wind always kicked up in the afternoon. "It's easy to get lost out here. Happens all the time. They'll swing by in a motor-boat and pick up your canoe later." She corralled the dogs, helped us tie down the canoe, and drove us back to the hotel. "I need a nap," I said when we got inside.

In the evening, I sat outside by myself, watching the sunset and wondering if it had been a mistake to set an artificial deadline to determine our future. The intention was right—it wasn't good for either of us to keep agonizing about it. But something was keeping me from the actual conversation. *Maybe it's just happiness,* I thought. *I don't want to break the spell in the little time we have together.*

And maybe I already had the answers I needed. Asser made me happier than anyone else. When I was down, he lifted my spir-its. He was patient and respectful with my parents. Ambitious but not self-serious. And so ridiculously hot; after three years, I still felt dizzy when he smiled at me. Most of all, I loved his kind and gentle heart. When he said he would never intentionally hurt me, I believed him.

As for marriage, I wasn't sure what to believe. Somewhere along the way personal decisions about our future had gotten wrapped up in the patriarchal history and practice of matrimony. That wasn't the point when I'd first considered spending my life with Asser. I only wanted to know that I'd be safe with him.

The next morning, we packed our bags, ate pancakes, and walked down to the lake. I put my feet in the sand and watched the water lap at my toes. Asser sat down next to me. We had twenty minutes until the car arrived to take us back to the airport.

I took a deep breath and looked at him. "Okay, I think I'm ready."

"To talk? You've really left it to the last possible minute," he replied, laughing and shaking his head. "But that's all right, let's—"

I held up my hand to stop him. "Asser, I'm ready to marry you."

37.

Two weeks later, Asser, his sister Ambreena, and his brother-in-law Atif came to Birmingham for the *haan*, a formal visit where the groom's father asks the bride's father for her hand in marriage on behalf of his son. I didn't love the tradition, but I thought it was important for both of our families to know that we were serious. The formal rituals are helpful in legitimizing "love marriages," still rare and frowned upon in most parts of Pakistan.

I suspected my mom would be upset or angry about me getting engaged, as she had shown no signs of relenting in her insistence on me marrying a Pashtun man. When I played out the situation in my head, I guessed that my dad would try to pacify my mom and find a middle ground. "You can marry Asser, if you wish," I imagined him saying. "Just wait a year or two." But I had made my choice, and now I was ready to get on with my life. I decided, perhaps immaturely, that it would be better to rip the Band-Aid off with my parents, rather than preparing them for what was about to happen. So I casually mentioned that Asser and his sister were popping by without revealing the true purpose for the visit.

When Asser's family arrived and my dad saw Atif, he caught on immediately and looked at me with bulging eyes. He showed our guests to the living room and made small talk in Urdu and English, while my mom sat on the sofa looking confused and increasingly agitated, unable to follow the conversation. Then Atif, standing in for Asser's father, turned to my dad and said, "We're so lucky to know Malala. She and Asser make each other very happy, and we would like to extend our formal proposal."

My dad looked down at his lap. For a few frantic seconds, I wondered what he would say. He looked up again with tears in his eyes and raised his eyebrows at me. I nodded. "I am happy for them," he said, and wrapped Atif in an enormous hug. Ambreena presented me with a gold bracelet, a traditional engagement gift.

"What is happening?" my mom snapped in Pashto.

"It's fine, Mom, it's okay," I replied, my hands patting the air, the universal gesture for *please calm down*.

She stood up and tugged at my father's elbow. "Did you just give her away? What have you done? You're here crying and hugging them, congratulating everyone, saying 'Take her! She's yours!'"

Asser and his family didn't understand her words, but they heard the rising panic in her voice. My throat closed with embarrassment and I looked at her with pleading eyes. Then my dad took her hand and, in his most gentle voice, said, "Toor Pekai, I am only the messenger. Malala gave herself away."

⌒

BEFORE WE COULD plan a wedding, I had to complete the final procedure in facial paralysis treatment—the unpleasantly named "debulking surgery." Dr. Hadlock would again cut into my face through my cheek and reshape the muscle and tissue she'd implanted two years ago. This would correct the bulge on my left side and, at last, allow me to see the new nerve at work in my smile. I was relieved to finally complete the reconstructive work on my face; with luck, this would be my last summer of hospital visits.

Covid restrictions limited me to one companion on this trip to Boston. Since my dad spoke English, he was the obvious choice. We boarded the plane in early August and, though we didn't say it out loud, I think we were both relieved to escape my mom's simmering ire over the engagement.

The day before the surgery, the two of us sat on a couch in my hotel room to take a conference call with Malala Fund's partners in Afghanistan. On the line were lawyers, journalists, and educators who used their varied backgrounds to help more Afghan girls access education. There were tech specialists who developed digital lessons and distributed tablets to girls who couldn't go to school in person; researchers who studied the issues contributing to high drop-out rates. Others served as the Afghan equivalent of social workers, advocating on an individual and community level, persuading parents and religious leaders of the importance of education for all children.

My dad and I were concerned about their safety. Since the United States military had begun their withdrawal from the country that spring, the Taliban and Afghan military engaged in firefights almost every day. At first these conflicts were limited to border towns, but the insurgents seemed to be gaining momentum, launching attacks in twenty-six of the thirty-four provinces.

Malala Fund worked in eight countries, and while I cared about each of them, Afghanistan had a special place in my heart. My family's ancestors came from Afghanistan, and Pashtuns like us are the predominant ethnic group in the country. When we lived in Mingora, my dad used to cross the border, only eight minutes' drive from some parts of our province, to attend poetry festivals there. Through Malala Fund, we had invested millions of dollars in girls' education efforts across the country. Now I worried that all our work would be reversed if the Taliban took power.

The Afghan activists on the phone were worried too, but most of them seemed determined to stay in the country. Since the major cities—Herat, Mazar, Kandahar, Kunduz, and Kabul—were still under government control, they believed the Afghan army would prevail. We all prayed it would happen soon, before more civilians were killed. As we said good-bye, my dad told them to keep in touch. "Don't even look at the clock," he said. "If you need help in the middle of the night, call us."

If our Afghan partners did come into contact with Taliban fighters, any connection to me could put them in more danger. Later that night, the team at Malala Fund took their names and photos off our website, and I removed all references to them from my social media accounts.

Before I went to bed, I got out my laptop and opened my old college files. Reading through the notes from my International Security and Conflict course, I searched for a law or treaty or emergency panic button we could push to stop violent extremists from taking over an entire country. When I couldn't find one, it took me back to being a child in Mingora and watching as our city was overtaken by the Taliban, wondering why no one was coming to save us. I played out the worst-case scenarios in my mind, which all seemed increasingly plausible the longer I went without sleep. *It will only get worse*, I thought. *If the Taliban win, people around the world will be shocked. But they have no idea of the barbarity that will follow their victory.*

At five the next morning, we drove to the hospital. The nurses ran through their pre-op checklists, administered injections, and tried to make me comfortable. Dr. Hadlock came in and drew on my face with a Magic Marker, outlining the spots where she would work. I kept my phone with me as long as I could, constantly checking for updates on the conflict. When the doctors injected the anesthesia, I wasn't thinking about the surgery at all; my mind was consumed with worry for Afghanistan. As they rolled me into the operating room, the Taliban held four provincial capitals; when I woke up in the recovery ward a few hours later, they had six.

According to Afghan human rights groups, the Taliban were approaching local imams after taking control of a city or town, instructing them to make a list of all unmarried women between fourteen and forty-five years old. Fathers began arranging hasty marriages for girls as young as ten, telling them a cousin or family friend would be a better husband than a Taliban fighter.

Lying in the hospital bed, I saw a clip of an activist we supported speaking to a British broadcaster from her home in Kandahar. Like me, she was twenty-four and not married. "What will you do if there's a knock on your door?" the journalist asked. "Pray," she answered. I put down my phone and shuddered.

The next day Afghan forces in Kunduz surrendered to the Taliban. Then Herat, Kandahar, and Mazar fell, and everything turned into chaos. Taliban fighters raided the office of a Malala Fund partner who trained female teachers, taking laptops and staff lists. Several of our contacts in rural provinces fled to Iran, Uzbekistan, and Pakistan. But those in the cities were trapped, as the Taliban set up checkpoints along the major roads. Our team in the US and UK began arranging for them to move to safe houses and working on evacuation plans. Just a few days earlier, our partners had planned to stay in their country—now we needed to get them out fast.

I returned to the hotel where I would stay for the following week until the doctors removed my stitches and told me it was safe to fly home. My dad, who has Pakistani contacts in every city in the world, had already filled the fridge in my room with containers of homemade mutton korma and dowdo soup. "My friends have brought us this food, Malala," he said. "Come and eat. I will make a plate for you."

I couldn't even think about food; all I wanted to do was lie in bed and scroll through the latest news. But I could always read my dad's face, and I saw that he was also feeling helpless and scared, exhausted from worrying about my surgery and waiting by the phone at night in case someone called from Afghanistan. "Just soup, please," I said. He smiled and seemed to relax a little as he fiddled with the hotel microwave and set the small tea table with a napkin, spoon, and glass of water.

In response to the Taliban's offensive, the United States sped up its withdrawal plans, pulling out not just military personnel but the embassy staff who were processing visas for their Afghan translators, drivers, and other allies—all in danger and desperate to leave. The Afghan army was running out of ammunition and the will to fight. That night I got in bed and prayed, saying the names of every Afghan man, woman, and child I knew, pleading with God to keep them safe.

When we woke up the next day, the Taliban had control of all land border crossings in and out of the country. Thousands of people gathered on the tarmac at Kabul Airport, pleading to be evacuated. A video from the scene showed a teenage boy holding on to the wing of a US military aircraft at takeoff. As the plane gained altitude, he lost his grip and fell to his death. The camera captured his descent, back down into the city he'd tried to escape. I had experienced violence in my life, but I had never watched someone die. My dad began to pray, his voice shaking; but the shock of it left me speechless and sickened.

Every day the paths for getting Malala Fund's Afghan partners out seemed to narrow. We needed to find a country willing to waive the entry visa requirements, and then get them seats on one of the scarce evacuation planes. With millions of people trying to leave through a single operating airport, it felt like we needed a miracle.

I requested calls and sent urgent emails to presidents and prime ministers in various countries to ask for help, nervously fiddling with the stitches around my ear while I waited for an answer. For years, I'd smiled in pictures with these leaders, shaken their hands, and stood next to them at podiums—but not one of them picked up the phone or replied to my messages now. To the men who ran the world, I was just a photo op, not someone worthy of their time and attention, even when I needed it most.

Women, on the other hand, responded immediately, answering my calls and jumping into action as soon as we hung up. Norwegian Prime Minister Erna Solberg, former US Secretary of State Hillary Clinton, and their teams helped our Afghan partners get seats on the planes leaving Kabul. Lolwah Al-Khater, the assistant foreign minister of Qatar, allowed them to enter the country without paperwork, or even passports in some cases, and provided housing until we could sort out their relocation plans. Lisa Cheskes and Elizabeth Snow, resettlement managers in the Canadian government, guided us through the process of securing refugee visas. I may not personally agree with every opinion these women hold or every decision they made as leaders—but I will forever be grateful to them for helping save so many lives. With their support, Malala Fund helped 263 people evacuate Afghanistan.

All week, journalists requested interviews with me. I declined, hoping things would change and not wanting to speculate about what the Taliban would inflict on the country in the middle of the fight. But the day Kabul fell, we knew it was over. "Complete

Collapse in Afghanistan," the headlines said. I unwrapped the surgical bandage around my head and went on TV from the hotel room.

CNN's Christiane Amanpour mentioned the promises coming from the Taliban, vague statements about ensuring "no discrimination against women within the framework of Islamic law." "Does that give you hope?" she asked.

What I wanted to say: *If they stopped subjugating women and banning girls from school, they wouldn't be the Taliban anymore. Hating us is fundamental to who they are—and only fools believe they will change.*

What I actually said: "It's too early for hope."

When a crisis arises in the world, people often chastise me for not speaking out as early or often as they expect, and not sounding angry enough when I do. It happened the week of my surgery; commenters flooded social media to claim I didn't care about Afghanistan, that I had sold out, that I wasn't "a real activist."

These keyboard warriors didn't have to worry about our Afghan partners hiding in safe houses across Kabul and Kandahar, about the men and women who had publicly associated with Malala Fund, now trapped in their country as insurgents roamed the streets arresting and executing dissenters. They didn't live with the constant dread that their words could put people in even greater danger.

I might have looked calm on TV, but I was outraged. It made me angry that, after decades of using Afghanistan in their proxy wars and killing tens of thousands of civilians, the United States and its allies were leaving millions of women and girls at the mercy of the Taliban. In the early 2000s, President George W. Bush used girls' education to make the case for America's presence in Afghanistan. "In helping the Afghan people rebuild their country, we have placed a central focus on education," he said.

"Education is the pathway to progress, particularly for women." Twenty years later, when President Donald Trump began negotiating with the Afghan government and the Taliban on the US withdrawal from the country, women—who had the most to lose—were not even allowed in the room. Now, under President Joe Biden, the US was leaving Afghanistan with no guarantees on women's rights or girls' education.

Was the US government unable to predict this outcome? Or did they just not care enough to stop it? In my eyes, they exploited Afghan girls when they needed good PR and tossed them aside when the cost of staying in the country got too high.

I also seethed at Pakistani politicians who hailed the Taliban as liberators, using the conflict to hype their one-sided rivalry with America—and at the Afghan leaders who were reportedly fleeing their country for fancy houses in foreign cities, leaving civilians to be slaughtered.

Cowards, all of them.

And I was angry at myself for feeling blindsided and betrayed. All those years that I stood on stages while people clapped and told me, through tears, how my story moved them—I had thought it meant that they wouldn't let this happen to other girls. I believed they would rise up to defend us. Only now, as the world sat back and watched while an entire country was handed over to the men who'd tried to kill me, did I realize I was wrong. While I will always be grateful for the support I received after the Taliban's attack on my life, it was wrenching to know that such an outpouring of sympathy was possible, and then watch as it failed to materialize for other girls.

When I was a child, I thought if I spoke out, things would get better. Surely, once world leaders understood our problems, they would fix them. As a teenager and young adult, I learned that the issues were far more complex. You had to advocate for every policy change and budget increase, sit through hours of negotiations to take a small step forward. Change was slow but steady.

Afghanistan shattered the promise of progress for me. For the first time, I realized the world was not committed to fighting for the rights of women and girls. The worst moment of my life had been not a turning point, but a pause—an opportunity for leaders to act appalled that the Taliban would dare to shoot a child, throw some money into girls' education, and then return to the business of growing economies and winning elections.

Later in the week, I went back to the hospital. Dr. Hadlock took the stitches out and said I should start to see the improvements in my facial mobility as soon as the swelling went down. A few weeks at most. "Congratulations, it's finally over!" she said. It should have been cause for celebration—nine years and dozens of procedures trying to fix my face were now behind me. But it felt meaningless in that moment. So we had repaired some of the damage from one Taliban bullet—what was that compared to the thousands of bullets raining down on Afghanistan, to the suffering of girls whose names we'll never know, whose cries will go unanswered?

On my last night in Boston, I climbed in bed and wept for the first time that week. My chest heaved at the thought of ten-year-olds learning they would soon become wives. I'd spent the last year deliberating over whether to marry a man I loved. Even now, I knew I had the power to walk away if I changed my mind before or after the wedding. I shuddered, picturing little girls held captive by their husbands.

I remembered the long, listless days of the pandemic when I'd yearned to be back at Oxford with my friends. How foolish that seemed in light of the lifetime lockdown facing young Afghan women, years upon years confined to kitchens and bedrooms, their dreams dying in slow motion.

When I was eleven years old, the Taliban began bombing schools in Mingora and throughout Swat Valley. Of the 1,600 schools that existed when they arrived, some 400 were destroyed and many more damaged; 70% were girls' schools. They attacked teachers by splashing acid on their faces or gunning them down in the street—now they had a laptop with the names of hundreds of female teachers in Afghanistan. I cried harder, realizing that we couldn't save all of them.

Between sobs, I struggled to breathe and my lungs burned. A sharp, stabbing pain radiated through my rib cage. When the room began to reel, I saw images of bearded men carrying automatic rifles. *These are just thoughts,* I told myself. *They aren't real. They are just waves on a beach.* But they were real—I'd seen them on TV that day. My nightmares were alive and walking around in the world.

LESS THAN A month after taking control of Kabul, the Taliban prohibited girls from attending school past sixth grade. Today, Afghan women are not allowed to attend university or hold a job. They are banned from public parks, gyms, and swimming pools. If they leave their homes, they must cover their faces and bodies from head to toe and be accompanied at all times by a male chaperone. They must also remain completely silent, as they are forbidden to speak or sing in public. Afghanistan is now one of the only countries in the world where the suicide rate is higher for women than for men.

For months after the fall of Afghanistan, I thought about long nights in the Birmingham hospital, when I would lie awake imagining a conversation with the Taliban. If they would just sit down with me, I had thought, I could reason with them and convince them to end their reign of misogyny and violence. With the pen and notebook I kept by my bed, I wrote down the names of journalists I knew who might be able to broker a meeting and scribbled down talking points. Because the Taliban claimed that their rules and doctrine were "true Islam," I planned to recite all the verses from the Quran that prove girls have a right to education. Then I would show them what a good Muslim I was by listing all ninety-nine names for Allah from memory. I thought they would be impressed by my arguments and moved by my commitment to God. Back then, I didn't understand that their ideology wasn't about faith, but about power and control. I didn't realize that they would never respond to openness and dialogue, especially with a fifteen-year-old girl.

As an adult, reflecting on those nights I spent planning for a meeting that would never happen made me wince a bit. But they also revealed how much I had grown—I could see the Taliban for what they were now, and I knew that we would not defeat them with reason or compromise. The women risking their lives to protest on the streets in Kabul knew it too—and I wanted to stand with them, to amplify their voices, to follow where they led.

I thought back to my last year of college, when all my friends were lining up jobs and applying to grad school, while I waffled about what to do with my life, which path to pursue. At times, these thoughts were egocentric and self-obsessed. Becoming so famous so young left me feeling washed up at twenty-four, searching for ways to prove that I was still worthy of attention, still capable of commanding a room. The fall of Afghanistan clarified all of that for me. I had choices that millions of young women had just lost. To agonize over my place in the world seemed immaterial.

My purpose is the same today as it has always been—I will continue to advocate for girls, to do everything in my power to ensure they can choose their own futures. For me, there is no career path, no ladder to climb. I can only keep trying to make progress.

When I was young and full of hope, I used to say that I wanted to see every girl in school in my lifetime. I don't know if that will happen—most of the time, I feel it won't. But for every day that God gives me, you will find me working in service of that dream.

38.

Neither Asser nor I wanted a grand, expensive wedding; we'd both seen those events that seemed more about proving how much money the couple's families had than celebrating the relationship. So we decided to hold a small *nikah* at my parents' home in Birmingham—a simple ceremony where the bride and groom confirm their wish to wed in front of an imam, then sign the marriage contract. It takes less than five minutes; after that, the union is legal under Islamic law. We settled on mid-September, but the day after Asser landed in the UK, my mother's eldest brother died of Covid. She booked a one-way ticket to Shangla and packed a suitcase big enough for the forty-day mourning period. The wedding would have to wait.

While my mom was in Shangla for my uncle's funeral, Asser stayed at his sister's house, waiting for the wedding to be rescheduled and trying to appease his bosses at the Pakistan Cricket Board.

Once we'd announced the marriage, he planned to resign his position and move to England. To keep our relationship confidential until then, he had asked for ten days off work, telling his managers he needed to see his family in the UK. After he'd been away for three weeks, they were understandably getting impatient, asking why he had overstayed his leave period and when he would return. With a big match against India approaching, the team needed his help to analyze data and develop the best batting lineup against their rival's dangerous bowling line. He spent a lot of time calling in to meetings and working remotely, but he felt the chill from his bosses on the other end of the line.

Forty, forty-five, then fifty days passed since my mom had left. Sometimes I wondered if she was still unhappy about the marriage and planned to stay in Shangla until we gave up and called off the wedding. I still wasn't sure about her true feelings toward Asser, and I didn't know how to ask. During lockdown, I'd felt like I was getting close to my mom for the first time, but our progress had stalled in the year since. The benchmarks of adulthood, like graduating from college and getting engaged, had not reshaped our relationship as I'd imagined they would. All I wanted was for her to be happy for me.

On the fifty-third day, we got good news: My mom was coming home in a week. Asser and I decided that we would be married a few days after her return and jumped into action. We booked the imam, a photographer, and a flight from Lahore for Farida, but I told my mom I would wait for her to help me pick out a dress. She said she would buy my outfit in Pakistan and bring it with her. I knew better than to argue.

She arrived bearing a dusty-pink shalwar kameez with gold embroidery at the sleeves and neck, and a matching dupatta. *It's perfect. I love it. Thank you, Mom.* I had pictured myself in something more modern, a simple silk dress with no embellishment.

But her selection was pretty, and the color complemented my skin tone and hair. As I hung it up in my bedroom closet, I thought, *This might be the last time she picks out my clothes. Maybe after the wedding, we'll be friends, two married ladies sharing a laugh.*

The day before the nikah, Asser and I went shopping to pick up a few final touches—a new pair of heels for me, a tie and pocket square for him. That evening my mom insisted on a dress rehearsal to inspect our clothes. She fussed with my headscarf and studied the jewelry—drop earrings and matching *maang tikka* headpiece—gifts from my soon-to-be mother-in-law. I also wore the custom wedding ring Asser had given me, a Swat Valley emerald set in a simple, delicate gold band. Every time I looked at it, I was amazed that he knew exactly what I wanted to wear on my hand for the rest of my life.

"You're fine," she said, dismissing me and turning her attention to Asser.

In the time we had spent together, I'd mostly seen Asser in casual clothes. Now he stood before me in a midnight-blue three-piece suit, such a handsome and elegant man. I was proud of him and proud of myself for being someone he could love. He winked at me, and I smiled dreamily back at him. We were so lost in our own world that we didn't notice my mom staring at his shoes.

"His shoes are not new," she snapped at me in Pashto.

"You can go change—looking good!" I said to Asser, sensing what was coming and trying to spare him.

"Everyone knows you must have new clothes for a wedding," my mom continued. "What did he buy? Not shoes. Shirt? Suit?"

"Mom, it's fine. He looks nice."

"What is new?" she demanded.

"Only the tie, I think. He already owned everything he needed. But why does it matter?"

"Oh, it doesn't matter? Why doesn't he wear pajamas on the most important day of your life?" I held my tongue and looked at the floor, which only made her angrier. "Does this guy not care about anything? Does he even care about you?"

I felt the tears forming and ran upstairs, already rationalizing her reaction before I reached the second-floor landing. She grew up in a culture where even the poorest farmers were expected to spend several times their annual income on weddings; she was worried that people would criticize our low-key ceremony. She was tired after her long journey home from the funeral. She was frustrated by the language barrier that kept her from having a real conversation with Asser and his family. She was emotional about letting go of a child, and her sadness came out the wrong way.

I reminded myself that my mom meant well, that she only wanted to protect me. Over the years, I had learned to let go of the things she forbade, to forget I'd ever wanted them—jeans, the high school parties where I might have made friends, the freedom to smile for a photograph without thinking how it could be used against me. I loved her, so I tried not to love things that made her angry or scared. Whatever her reasons, she was not happy about the wedding—and I needed to fix it.

My hands trembled as I changed clothes, then went back downstairs and out to the garden where I knew Asser would follow me.

"Is everything okay?" he asked.

"I'm just curious why you didn't buy new shoes."

He cocked his head, confused. "Those are my special occasion shoes. I've had them for a few years, but only worn them two or three times and kept them polished. No reason to let them go to waste when they're practically new."

"That's not the point—my mom says you're supposed to wear new things. She's an expert in—"

"—in men's shoes? Come on, Malala."

When he laughed, my upper lip curled in disgust. "It's not just the shoes. You should have gotten a new suit as well! New everything! People expect it *at a fucking wedding, Asser.*"

I sometimes used curse words in text messages for emphasis, but rarely in speech. Asser looked stunned. Then I dug deeper, kicking up enough dirt to fill the crater of pain my mom had created. "I guess I'm just really surprised that your own family didn't bother to check your outfit. Was it too much trouble for them to make sure you are properly dressed?" As soon as I said it, I wanted to take it back. I loved Farida and Ambreena—but it was too late.

"I don't know what to say. I feel good in those clothes and they look nice, so I didn't see a reason to replace them. But I made that decision, so please don't blame my family."

"Explain that to my mom. She thinks you don't care about me."

His shoulders crumpled and his head fell low. After a few moments, he drew himself back up with a deep breath. "I can't really afford a whole new look right now," he said on the exhale. "The cricket board stopped paying me when I didn't go back to Lahore."

. . . *What?* I scanned through his recent expenses in my mind—multiple round-trip flights, mandatory Covid tests, dinners out with my family, train fares to London, the wedding ring. My stab at sympathy came out as condescension. "Why didn't you tell me? I would have paid for everything you need."

"I think 'need' is what we're debating right now. I would never ask you—or anyone—to buy things for me. It makes me uncomfortable, brings up memories of my dad and all the debts he never repaid. Also, it's . . . embarrassing?

"I have money in a savings account, but it's set aside to support my mom and help us buy a house someday. I don't use it to splurge on unnecessary things. And that's because I *do* care about you."

Now I didn't know what to say. I wanted him to fight back, to justify my cruelty with his own. Or to beg for forgiveness, to promise he would secure suitable wedding attire by morning and never make my mom angry again for as long as he lived.

"Can I ask you something?" he said. "Do you really care about the shoes? When you first saw my outfit, you were smiling and said I looked great."

"I don't care, but it's not about what I think. People will notice and they will talk. Not just the people in the room but everyone who will see the photos online."

"If people talk, I hope they will say how happy we are and how much I love you." He walked back inside, said good-bye to my family, and left. I didn't look up to watch him go.

That night I lay awake for hours, doubts circling above my bed, taking turns to dive-bomb into my brain. *Why didn't Asser tell me he was running out of money? What other secrets is he keeping? Will I ever make my mom happy? Is it too soon to get married?*

The advice Evelyn had given me in college, which once seemed soothing and optimistic, now felt like a curse. *Make the best choice you can with what you happen to know at the time. Don't look back and imagine that there were other better options.* It meant that I had to question everything before it was too late. Until the nikah was over, the decision to marry was open—I could make and un-make it a million times before morning. I could hold my own head underwater and drown myself in a sea of uncertainty.

I believed the problem was with Asser or with marriage itself, that my hesitation signaled danger. That night, I was only begin-ning to understand the truth: For my entire life, people had told me who I was and how I should act. They would not allow me to grow beyond their reach. They taught me not to trust my own choices. Now I felt paralyzed anytime I tried to make one.

39.

In college, I was fascinated by hangovers and the way my friends woke up from them in various emotional states—confused and irritable, sheepish and self-loathing. The most compelling were those who got out of bed with a manic drive to redeem themselves. As soon as they could stand, they were deep-cleaning their rooms, taking five-mile runs with a pounding headache, planting themselves in the library and finishing a week's worth of essays.

On the morning of the wedding, I finally understood that reaction. As soon as I opened my eyes, I was overwhelmed with shame and disgust that I'd fallen asleep doubting Asser's love and my own mind. I came back to my senses, and they all seemed to tremble at the narrow escape. Normally I would wallow in an emotional assault like this, staying in bed for hours replaying my sins. But today I had a mission: I was determined to get married, if Asser would still have me.

I hesitantly picked up my phone, praying not to see a message saying that he'd changed his mind.

7:08 am

Asser

Morning!

7:09 am

Asser

I am soooooo excited!

7:32 am

Asser

Missing you! Can't wait to see you SOON!

7:56 am

Asser

Remember that I love you

Reading his messages filled me with joy at how much he cared about me and fresh remorse over the way I'd treated him the previous night. I replied:

Love you too. I'm sorry for the things I said. I pray to Allah to make this the happiest day of our lives.

8:14 a.m.

Asser

Let's get married

Maria was on her way over to help with the preparations and I texted her next: Bring the hair and makeup crew up to me. To avoid potential distractions and derailments, I decided to stay bunkered in my room as long as possible, not realizing I already had the house to myself. My brothers were still asleep, and my dad was out for a walk. My mom had gone shopping for new dress shoes for Asser—part peace offering, part chokehold.

"What do you think?" the makeup artist asked me an hour later.

I glanced at my reflection and said, "Looks great, thanks." I've never wanted to be vain or self-absorbed. After the shooting, I had spent so many years telling myself that it didn't matter how I looked that it was hard to admit, even to myself, when I felt beautiful. That day, I looked into the mirror and saw a young woman staring back who was glowing, confident, gorgeous. And more important than anything else: She was happy.

At noon I left to meet Asser and the photographer for wedding portraits at the Winterbourne House and Garden, a nearby arboretum. The first time the world saw us as a couple, we wanted to be surrounded by nature—trees and grass, not glitter and gold.

As soon as our eyes met, I knew I was forgiven for the things I'd said the night before. He took my hand and said, "You're stunning, Malala." I blushed.

We were both so relieved about the fight being over and giddy for our wedding day that we could not stop laughing during the shoot. We snickered at his new shoes slipping on the slick stone path, giggled at the security guards turning into bridesmaids as they tried to keep my dupatta from dragging on the ground. We laughed when the photographer asked us to stop laughing so she could get the shot.

I am sure the handful of people at our wedding could give more expansive descriptions of that afternoon, but the day was a blur to me. Here's what I remember: The imam said a few words. We signed the marriage contract. My dad cried. Farida beamed.

My mom smiled for the family portrait. Khushal and Atal brought out a grocery store sheet cake with *Malala & Asser* chicken-scratched in icing across the top. Everything was perfect.

Toward the end of the evening, the photographer pulled me aside to review "selects," three dozen of her best photos from the day, the ones I might want to share when announcing the wedding.

The portraits took my breath away. There we were, tucked in a tall thicket of gemmy reds and quiet greens, looking like fairy-tale lovers on the last page of a picture book. In the next photo, we stood arm in arm under an arch of twisted hazel. We'd just been told to pull ourselves together, but the remnants of laughter lingered in our openmouthed smiles. Then the two of us were glowing against a backdrop of autumnal-gold ginkgo leaves. The otherworldliness of the images somehow made them feel more real, as if they revealed a beauty you couldn't create with anything less than true love. The indisputable proof I'd sought for so long was right here in high-resolution.

I sat with the laptop, flicking through the photos until they became a choppy little film, the two of us turning in to face each other, out to face the world, and back in again. Then I stopped. "This one. This is my favorite," I said.

Asser and my parents drifted over to the couch where I sat next to the photographer. They peered down at the laptop to see the two of us standing on a wide swath of lawn. A bright-orange maple tree appears in the background, framed like a flame between our bodies. I am looking up at Asser as he holds my left hand to his lips and kisses it.

"No, no, no!" my mom exclaimed. "You cannot use it."

She'd never seen a wedding portrait like this. In our culture, weddings are segregated—the men sit in the garden or the largest room of the house, eating a feast that their wives spent all day preparing. The women and girls pile into a smaller space with smaller plates of food. Photos are usually limited to the groom and his male relatives. On rare occasions when there is a picture of the new couple, they will be sitting side by side, several feet apart, not touching or even smiling. A photo showing any physical contact between a man and a woman, even a husband and wife, is prohibited. Where we come from, my parents are considered liberals, yet you will never see a picture of them holding hands or hugging.

I had said the photo of Asser and me was my favorite, not that I intended to make it public. But my mom's reaction made me wonder if it could, in its own way, announce my marriage as the true partnership that it was. After all, these rules weren't handed down by God. If people create culture, they can also change it. I wanted my community to see that men can show affection for their wives, that devotion and love are the highest forms of honor.

My mom shook her head, and my dad frowned. I looked at Asser. "It's your decision," he said.

With apologies to my parents, I shared the photo with the world.

40.

My world today is nothing like what I imagined as a child or even in college, when I pictured my adult self as a nun, dedicating all my time to good works. Nor is it what I feared when I worried about losing my autonomy if I got married. I still have reservations about marriage as an institution—and I probably always will. But my life with Asser is one of freedom and joy.

After the wedding, Asser resigned his job at the cricket board and started working freelance, which meant he could accompany me for speaking engagements and advocacy trips. As we traveled the world together, I found the grind of airports and living out of my luggage more enjoyable in his company. Everywhere we went, Asser insisted that we take time to check out local scenery or restaurants, something I'd rarely done in the past. He scheduled lessons in a sport I'd never tried, like pickleball, skiing, or archery. To my surprise, I learned that I'm a decent athlete. I particularly took to golf, and after six months of lessons, my husband couldn't take a round off me. These outings weren't just aimed at having fun; Asser showed me that taking a break, eating well, moving my body, and getting enough sleep were critical to taking care of myself.

For a while, I worried that, as happy as I was traveling the world with Asser, I would lose touch with my friends. I didn't want to be a person who only hung out with her husband and other couples after marriage. Staying close to them wasn't easy, though, because we all had adult lives and responsibilities now. Many of my friends had moved away and taken jobs in other countries. So whenever they were back in town or in between apartments in London, I invited them to crash at our place. In the first few years after our wedding, Asser often came home from a meeting or a workout to find me on the couch with one of my Oxford pals, eating takeout pad thai, binge-watching *Love Is Blind*, and howling with laughter. I know he sometimes felt like a thirty-two-year-old man living in a college dorm, sharing a bathroom with a revolving cast of my friends, but he rarely complained, remaining as patient with me as he had always been.

He needed an equal amount of patience to deal with my family. One afternoon he and I arrived home after several weeks away. Our flat in London overlooks the Thames, and I couldn't wait to plant myself on the couch with a cup of tea and watch the sun set on the water. As I stood in the kitchen flipping through the mail, suitcase still at my side, Asser called my name from the bedroom. I walked down the hall and gasped at the sight: Our tasteful, neutral-toned bed linens had been replaced by a teal-and-gold duvet set. There were tassels, beadwork, fringe trim, even velvet throw pillows featuring long, wispy peacock feathers. If you have seen Princess Jasmine's room in the animated version of *Aladdin*, you have an idea of what we encountered that day.

It wasn't the first time this had happened. My mom frequently came over to our apartment with a new rug or lamp and attempted to redecorate our space. "You have to tell her not to do this anymore," Asser sighed. But he knew I wouldn't do it. As of this writing, I am twenty-eight years old and I still can't say no to my mom.

Of all our adventures in the first three years of marriage, my favorite was visiting Lahore, Asser's hometown. I'd only been there once before, when I was fourteen years old. It was a quick trip to give a speech and accept an award for standing up to the Taliban, and I didn't get to see the city. Through my friends in college, I had come to understand Lahore as the country's cultural capital, with thriving art and food scenes. But I was most excited about seeing the streets where Asser grew up and imagining the boy he used to be.

At Farida's house, I flipped through old photo albums, delighted by pictures of Asser as a fat, angry-looking toddler. A few of his extended family members stopped by to welcome us. When I heard a child refer to me as "Auntie" for the first time, I nearly jumped out of my skin, surprised at the thought that anyone could see me the way I saw my own aunts. It took me a moment to comprehend that, to Asser's littlest relatives, I was just another grown-up, their favorite uncle's new wife.

Toward the end of our visit to Lahore, I was scheduled to give a speech at an event promoting the Oxford Pakistan Programme, a scholarship fund created by a few members of the old 24 Obs crew. I was so proud of my friends for starting this initiative and happy to give my time to help disadvantaged Pakistani students study at Oxford. On the day of the event, though, I looked in the mirror and noticed that my hair was a mess; the blunt bangs I'd given myself during lockdown two years ago were longer now and sticking out at odd angles. We had been on the road so much that I couldn't remember the last time I'd had a proper haircut. *Was it before Covid?* I wondered in dismay.

Maria, who was traveling with us, tracked down a local stylist who could come to our hotel as security wouldn't allow an unscheduled visit to a salon. As I sat listening to the quiet snip of the scissors on my wet hair, I couldn't stop smiling to myself, surprised by the contentment and joy I felt at doing something as ordinary as getting a haircut in my homeland.

When we were back in London, I shared pictures from the trip on social media. In addition to many kind responses, my post triggered the usual round of hateful comments—"traitor," "bitch," conspiracy theories, insults about my clothing and appearance. One person wrote, "Go away. This is not your home."

That taunt would have hurt me a few years earlier, sending me into a spiral of trying to prove to myself and others that there was still a place for me in Pakistan. Now, though, I knew what home meant to me, what it feels like, how to recognize it. It is the first sip of chai at Farida's house in Lahore, and walks along the Birmingham canals with my mom. The mountains in Mingora, the rooftops of Oxford, the gardens of Islamabad, boats gliding along the Thames in London. It is sitting on the couch, laughing with my friends. It is falling asleep in my husband's arms, anywhere in the world. And no one can take that away from me.

41.

Whenever I experience a period of profound happiness, like my first months at college or first years of marriage, I know it won't last. It's not that I'm a pessimist—but after so much upheaval in my life, I never assume that things will stay as they are. When the change comes, I try not to be afraid and hope I can learn from it.

In December 2023, I was invited to deliver the 21st Annual Nelson Mandela Lecture in Johannesburg. Since I was a girl, Mandela had been a hero to me, and I wanted to honor his legacy by speaking out for women and girls in Afghanistan.

The Taliban had issued more than eighty edicts against the female population in the two and a half years since they took control of the country. Where women and girls had once been university students, government ministers, dentists, and shop owners, now they were erased from public life and confined to their homes. The punishments for those who broke the rules ran from indefinite detention to forced marriage to being stoned to death.

In the months before I traveled to Johannesburg, Afghan activists had been pushing for gender apartheid to be included in the United Nations' new Crimes Against Humanity Treaty. It was, by no means, a perfect solution. Even if they were successful, the treaty would not put an immediate stop to the daily horrors facing Afghans. It did mean, though, that the Taliban and others who commit crimes against women and girls might someday face justice. South Africa was an important player at the UN, and I hoped my remarks would rally their leaders to our cause and bolster the treaty.

The speech went well. At a reception afterward, politicians and influential women pledged their support, promising to use whatever means they had to help bring an end to the Taliban's reign. Their solidarity lifted my spirits, and I left the event feeling hopeful that together we might make some progress for Afghanistan.

At the hotel that night, Asser sat next to me in bed, looking up things to do on the second half of our trip—a short holiday in Cape Town. He suggested we take surfing lessons and visit a wildlife sanctuary called World of Birds. "Can we not just sit on the beach for once?" I said, laughing. "We're back in London in four days, and I need to store up some sunshine to survive the winter."

"The things I'm suggesting are also outside," he countered. "You'll get sun either way. I think what you really want is to be lazy."

"You know what? You're right. I *do* want to be lazy . . . starting now." I kissed him good night, tucked myself into the sheets, and closed my eyes.

I woke up a few hours later, my body soaked with sweat and my heart racing. When I sat upright, the room began to spin.

Breathe, I told myself. *Inhale seven, exhale eleven. Repeat.* I thought the breathing exercise had calmed me down—*You're fine, you just sat up too fast*—and went to use the bathroom. But as soon as my feet hit the ground, I felt like I was falling, like being trapped in a broken elevator and plunging to my death. I dropped to my knees, crawled to the sink, and reached for the tap, but couldn't stand up long enough to turn it on.

"Asser!" I shouted. He jumped out of bed and found me on the floor. He must have asked "What's wrong?" but his voice sounded distorted, unrecognizable. Not being able to understand him, the person I loved most in the world, shocked and terrified me. I didn't even realize I was crying until Asser reached for a tissue and wiped my tears away.

The air pressure in the hotel room kept getting lower, as if I were climbing a mountain. "Balcony!" I gasped, struggling to breathe. Asser ran to open the sliding door, then carried me outside. A warm, thick breeze wrapped around me. I could see the treetops and stars; the night was quiet and still. *It's okay, you're fine.* Then a threatening tightness crept across my chest. I assumed it was from being held, from my body compressed and folded up in Asser's arms. "Inside," I pleaded.

He laid me on the bed and my legs began to shake uncontrollably. Asser tried to hold them still, but then my arms trembled and flailed. That's when he grabbed the phone and called for paramedics. As he spoke, I watched all the color drain from his face.

The medical team arrived quickly, checked my vital signs, and gave me water with electrolytes. The shaking eventually stopped, and I lay on the bed depleted and self-conscious. "We can't find the problem," the paramedics said. They asked Asser questions about potential food poisoning, medications I was taking, allergies, and pregnancy.

But I knew what it was. The only panic attacks I've had since college have involved Afghanistan. Not a day goes by when I don't read something about the horrors that women and girls there are living through. I never scroll past them, no matter how painful it is. If I can do nothing else, I will be a witness to their suffering and their courage.

When I see images of women being beaten in the streets or read about girls who are confined to their homes and losing hope, my own violent memories come crashing through the barriers again, the walls that my mind built to keep them out. It was easier for me when my story was in the past, a thing that happened once years ago, a tale of uncommon brutality by evil men. Sometimes, when I think about it happening today to millions of Afghan women and girls, my body tears itself apart with grief.

42.

The first time I went to therapy, I imagined it would be like tightening a screw—a quick fix for the bad thoughts rattling in my brain. When I started to feel better, I put the flashbacks and panic attacks behind me, not wanting to dwell on terrible times when there was so much happiness in my life.

After Johannesburg, though, I called Evelyn and made an appointment. I didn't want to wait like I had in college, hoping it would resolve on its own. I knew I needed to face the problem before it got worse.

When I stepped into her office, I felt at peace in the familiar setting. There was the same sofa, the side table with a glass of water waiting for me, the soft lighting. I remembered the first time I saw this room—how I was desperate for help, but skeptical and nervous about therapy; how much I eventually learned from it.

"Malala, it's good to see you again," Evelyn began. "I'm glad you called. How can I help?"

I recounted my recent panic attack, the way it caught me off guard, the intensity of it. The breathing exercises hadn't worked, and I didn't understand how I could've gone to sleep feeling content, only to wake up in such overwhelming terror. "It's like I've lost control again," I said. "I mean, I feel fine now, but I don't like knowing that this could happen at any moment."

"I'm very sorry to hear this, but not surprised," Evelyn said. "Mental health is a journey—certain times are easy and others more challenging, just like the rest of our lives. Were you feeling a lot of stress on the trip to Johannesburg?"

"I wasn't stressed at all. My speech went well, and Asser and I were going on a beach vacation the next day. I was happy."

"Can you think of any other triggers that might have been present for you at that time?"

My stomach lurched, and I realized I'd have to say it out loud: "It's Afghanistan. And it's the shooting. My shooting."

Evelyn folded her hands and leaned toward me. "Do you remember several years ago when we spoke about PTSD?" I nodded. "In this case, we have to treat the source, not the symptoms. Breathing exercises and learning to recognize triggers can help manage anxiety and, sometimes, interrupt panic attacks. But those are symptoms of PTSD, not the cause.

"Trauma lives in our bodies, and it stays there until we process it," she continued. "Our brains work hard to keep us from reliving a difficult experience, using disassociation and repression to try to protect us. Unfortunately, that gets in the way of healing. We have to acknowledge and understand our pain before we can move past it.

"The good news is that there are several types of treatment. Before you leave today, I'm going to give you some information to read on EMDR, somatic therapy, and trauma-focused cognitive therapy. We can talk about the options in our next session."

"Will I ever get rid of PTSD? Will I be 'cured' at some point?" I asked. My old resistance to therapy welled up in me. Maybe I'd prefer to take my chances with an occasional panic attack than spend an hour every week talking about my past.

"That's a great question, but not one I can answer, I'm afraid," Evelyn replied. "Recovery is certainly possible, but the timeline can vary from person to person. And some people will have symptoms throughout their lives, though treatment can help to reduce them."

"My life is so happy now—and it's hard to look back."

"Processing does not mean constantly dwelling on painful memories. But when we acknowledge trauma in a safe environment, it helps us to regulate our nervous system and stress responses, leading to better physical and mental health. The goal is to build resilience and give you more freedom to fully experience all the wonderful things in your life."

I thought of Asser and how frightened we both had been in that hotel room. If there was something I could do to get better, I knew I had to try.

⌒

TALKING WITH EVELYN became part of my weekly routine, no matter where I was in the world. We didn't always discuss trauma, as I learned that therapy is for more than healing old wounds, more than a fire alarm to be pulled in emergencies. Evelyn also helped me with the day-to-day stresses that piled up in my life. Through our sessions, I got better at setting boundaries with my family, recognizing when I needed some alone time, and communicating my needs to the people in my life.

A few years earlier, I'd rolled my eyes anytime someone mentioned self-care. To me, it seemed self-indulgent and silly, a hobby for people who didn't have any real problems. But the longer I spent in therapy, the more I realized how my physical and emotional well-being affected my mental health and ability to function in my daily life.

Evelyn might say I became "proactive" about taking care of myself; my friends would call it "nerdy." I started tracking my sleep every night—not just total hours, but efficiency, heart rate, and body temperature. A nutritionist helped me balance my diet, swapping out french fries and pad thai for fresh fish and vegetables. I'll admit, I was pouty at mealtimes for a while, but noticed I felt less sluggish and irritable throughout the day. When I looked in the mirror one morning and saw that my skin was clear and glowing, I knew I could learn to love salmon.

In January last year, I set a secret goal of running on the treadmill for an hour without stopping. At first I could only make it two or three minutes. But I kept showing up at the gym, trying to increase my stamina a little bit each time. One morning in September, I got on the treadmill and just kept going—fifty minutes, one hour, an hour and five minutes. *This is incredible! How far can I go?* I wondered. Starting out, running was just about not giving up. Then I wanted to achieve more and more. When I ran, my body was no longer something I feared, but my teacher, revealing all the possibility and strength inside me.

◆

I HAD LESS success in learning to swim. My muscles tensed up every time I got in the pool and my hands slapped wildly at the water instead of gliding through it. My mind was calm—I just couldn't figure out how to tell my body not to fight. Even in the shallow end, some part of me imagined I would drown.

In a similar way, the panic attacks can feel like a betrayal. After all I've lived through—displacement, violence, physical pain, loneliness, hate—why must I continue to suffer? No matter how much therapy I do or how well I take care of myself, I know someday I might feel the tightness in my chest or the pulse in my ears again. But I've come to understand these episodes as a beacon, a reminder to be gentle with myself, to protect my heart and mind, to resist the urge to shoulder so many burdens alone. To trust that I will continue to change and grow.

At my third swimming lesson, my instructor stood next to me as I tried to float. My legs were stiff, teeth clenched, toes curled. "Allow yourself to relax," she said. "You won't be able to float until you believe that the water will hold you."

43.

I looked down from the helicopter as it hovered above the landing site, a white circle chalked in the dirt. This was the moment
I had been imagining for years, the dream I carried wherever I
went, the prayer I whispered at night before bed: Shangla.

Finally I was going to see the school I'd built, meet the students
and teachers, and talk with the first girls about to graduate—the
first young women to complete high school in these villages. As
Asser reached for my hand to help me out of the helicopter, I remembered what I'd said to him about Shangla on our very first
date: *I'll take you there someday.* I could hardly believe that we were
now here.

The dirt road that led to the school was bounded by mountains on one side and a steep drop into the valley on the other.
Deep potholes could send the car tumbling down into the river if
we drove too fast. Several times a year, classes were suspended

when rainy season landslides or winter snow made driving too dangerous.

Above and below the road, mud houses were built into the mountainside like mushrooms growing up a tree trunk. My dad grew up in a house like this, without electricity or plumbing, nine people in two rooms. I tried to picture him walking this road as a teenager, going to school, out to the fields to tend the buffalo, to the mud mosque to pray with his father. At night he hovered over his books with a kerosene lamp, determined to make it to college. Forty years later, many children here did the same.

In the distance, I could see the walls around the school, twelve feet high and topped with barbed wire, an ugly necessity in a place too familiar with terrorists and thieves. Driving through the metal gates, though, was like entering another world. For years I had pored over photographs of this place. My heart fluttered to finally see it for myself, bigger and more beautiful than I ever imagined. It was a sprawling three-story complex, with white stucco walls and a bright-blue metal roof—a miracle of construction in such a remote and challenging landscape.

In every corner of the campus, girls in their green gingham uniforms were walking to class, shouting to their friends, playing basketball, or reading quietly on the lawn. After seven years in operation, the school now had seven hundred students and forty teachers. When I set out to build the school, people told me that parents in the region wouldn't support education for their daughters. Now our applications exceeded the number of desks available. I've never been prouder of anything in my life.

"Welcome!" the principal said with a big smile. She seemed so proud that we were visiting, as if we were doing them a favor when this day had lived in my imagination for years. As we followed her across the courtyard to the main entrance, I was eager to step inside, but anxiety pecked at the corners of my mind. I had built up so many expectations for what this place could be, and I worried that the reality couldn't possibly match my vision.

I wanted the school to be a place where students didn't feel the limitations of the outside world, where they could dream about the future and believe in themselves. I also wanted to see that the deficiencies in my own education, the things lacking for most Pakistani girls, were remedied here. In schools across Pakistan, biology textbooks often come with the pages on human reproduction glued together so students cannot read them. The boys pry them apart with rulers, but girls wouldn't dare. Were the teachers here covering reproductive health? Did they talk about emotional well-being? Were the students encouraged to play sports and be physically active?

It wasn't acceptable for this place to be equivalent to the local boys' schools or "good enough" for a forgotten, largely illiterate community. I wanted it to be a palace of learning, worthy of the girls' wildest dreams. *Your standards aren't realistic*, I told myself, trying to reset my hopes to "low" and my facial expression to "neutral." As we stepped inside and began to look around, my eyes filled with surprised and happy tears. The school was everything I'd imagined and more.

The principal showed us a sunny library full of books and separate science labs for biology, chemistry, and physics. From the corridors, we heard teachers giving lessons in Pashto, Urdu, and English. We peeked in the art studio, where fourth-grade girls in matching blue aprons were learning to sculpt, covered up to their elbows in clay. The middle school girls were holding a chess tournament; I stopped to play for a minute and quickly lost the game to a twelve-year-old.

In my work, I visit schools around the world. They all look different, but every time I walk the halls, I feel like a child again. In Shangla, I wanted to put on goggles in the chemistry lab, sing with the chorus, join the basketball team, and gossip with the older girls at lunch. I thought of my friends when we were young, how Moniba would have been thrilled to take an art class, how my cousin Nazneen would have checked out every book of poetry in the library. Some of my tears were for us, imagining how we would have thrived in these gleaming halls.

The principal showed us the back garden, where the girls were planting and raising trees, a program aimed at combating rampant deforestation in the region. Then we saw the daycare, which the school provided for the teachers' younger children; it helped in recruiting top educators from all over Pakistan, especially women. We toured the large assembly hall, where all students start the day with free breakfast—eggs, toast, and milky tea—to ensure they have a full stomach before going to class.

When we passed a room labeled COUNSELOR's OFFICE, I poked my head in to see a woman with a heart-shaped face and big brown eyes. She had the look of a sympathetic older sister or young aunt, and told me she'd moved to Shangla from Lahore to be part of the faculty. I asked a few questions about the mental health services she offered to students. "It is the first, and so far only, counseling program of its kind in the entire province of Khyber Pakhtunkhwa," she told me. I knew that was true; when I was a child, having a therapist in a school would have been considered absurd.

The final stop on my visit was a meeting with the "pioneer batch," the twenty-five girls who would graduate in the spring. We sat in a circle outside on the lawn, and I looked at each of their faces, so bright and eager. I began by asking them to tell me what they loved best and least about the school, and how we could improve it for the girls who came after them. They all said they loved their teachers. About a third ranked mental health training as the best part of their high school education. "We can talk to the counselor about anything we want," said Hira, the top student in the class. Then she got a conspiratorial glint in her eye and confessed, "Sometimes she even takes us outside in the woods and tells us to scream as loud as we can!" I could imagine how profound that release must be for girls who lived in a society that disapproved of women expressing their emotions.

"If you're accepted to college next year, what do you hope to study? What are your dreams for the future?" I asked.

The answers worried me: doctor, doctor, cardiac specialist, army doctor, neurosurgeon, programmer. So many Pakistani parents push their children toward medicine or engineering, unable to imagine or accept other professional paths. I thought of Moniba's dream to be a fashion designer and how she'd set it aside for med school. I wanted these girls to know that no matter what path they chose, their education would have value.

A girl named Eman fiddled with her fingernails and brushed her hair out of her eyes. "Honestly, I don't know," she said. "I'm so moody and I change my mind all the time." I swallowed a laugh and gestured for her to continue. "I just want to be a good person, and I'm not too concerned about my profession."

"Well, college is the perfect place to learn all you can and see what sparks your interest," I told her. "You don't have to have all the answers right now. Just be open to new experiences and ideas when you leave this school."

I looked at each of them as I continued, "I know how hard it is to go against thousands of years of tradition and believe that your life can be different. Because of you, other girls in Shangla will see what is possible for their own lives.

"But that can also lead to a lot of stress. You might find yourself thinking, 'My parents allowed me to study, so now I have to perform at the highest level.' But you don't need to get the best grades or be a perfect person to prove yourself worthy of your rights—they belonged to you from the moment you were born."

The principal walked over and said it was time to go as the school day was almost over, but I wasn't ready. There was so much I wanted to ask the girls, more I wanted to say. Were they hurt when their mothers were overbearing or unkind? *Remember that your world is new and unknown to them—and they're afraid of losing you.* What did they think of love and marriage? *If you choose to marry, I hope you find someone who tells you jokes as you drift to sleep at night and clears the dinner plates, a partner who will love you and support your dreams.* Were they worried about losing touch with their friends when they went to college? *Keep them close, as they will always carry a piece of you and help you find your way when you feel lost.*

I wanted to tell them that I understood how easy it is, especially when you're young, to get caught up in an idea of yourself. You might inherit an identity and feel obligated to carry it, even as it crushes you. You may be certain of your path and have every step planned out. It's hard to imagine your allegiances, ambitions, and desires will ever change.

But someday when you don't expect it, the river may rise and carry you away to a new place. You can try to fight it, swim upstream, cling to the rocks on the shore. *It's safer to stay here*, you think. *To hold on to what I know and who I'm supposed to be.* I had those thoughts too, before I understood we are always changing, always growing into an uncertain future.

Let go, I wanted to say. *Trust the water to hold you, trust yourself to float.*

~~~

OVER THE LAST decade, people have often asked me if I would give up my current life to go back to a time before I was attacked. If I could wave my hand and erase the shooting from history, would I want to be the old Malala, knowing what I know now? Would I exchange fame and relative wealth, all my awards and achievements, for the anonymity of life in rural Pakistan?

It's an odd question, and I don't really understand why people ask it. Are they trying to test my goodness and humility? Or do they want to prove that their lives of airports and washing machines are so enviable that I would choose being shot in the head to gain what they have?

For years, I answered yes—I would give up everything to go back. To see my parents surrounded by their lifelong friends. To finish high school with Moniba. To hold my grandmother's hand as she grew old. Who knows what my life would've been like, in that parallel universe? I might've had a job and my own apartment in a city like Lahore, spent my weekends watching cricket matches and meeting my friends for tea. But more likely, my life would be difficult—a never-ending effort to mollify men who felt entitled to determine my future.

As Asser and I walked back to the car to leave, I contemplated these phantom timelines, and what remains when your world is turned upside down. I stopped for a moment to wave good-bye to the school, breathe in the pine-scented air, and look up at the massive White Mountain, covered in snow all year long.

A few minutes into our drive, I spotted the narrow path to Abai's house. "Please stop," I said to the driver. He hesitated, eager to get farther down the road before it filled up with buses taking the schoolgirls back to their villages. "I just need a moment," I promised.

Cut around the rocks and through the forest, the trail led to a sunny clearing in the foothills. As a child, I leapt off the bus that carried my family from Mingora to Shangla, and ran up the path as fast as I could. But on this trip, I took my time, observing the light breaking through the branches and listening to the muffled crack of pine needles under my feet.

On the right side of the clearing, I found her burial site, a small mound of soil surrounded by wildflowers. Seeing her name on the headstone made it real: Abai was no longer here. Yet I felt her spirit all around me, in the warmth of the sun on my face and the memory of her sleeping under the stars.

Kneeling by the grave, I spoke to her. "Thank you for all your prayers and for everything you taught me. You won't be surprised to hear that I still haven't learned to cook . . . but I did get married! You were right about that, and I think you would like him. Today I visited the school, and it was incredible. I wish you had been there with me. The girls would make you laugh—they're a lot like me at that age. Please watch over them and keep them safe. I love you, Abai."

I sat there for a little while, watching the flowers tilt in the warm breeze. When I stood up, I could see the school off in the distance. Girls were spilling out of the gates, singing and laughing, walking arm in arm or racing each other to the bus. Their voices echoed around the mountains and down to the valley. I smiled at how loud they were, unafraid to fill the air with their high-spirited songs, bursting with determination and joy.

Walking back down the trail, I was grateful for the mountains and Abai's meadow, comforted that the places I loved in my childhood remained the same. But I didn't feel sad that I couldn't stay in Shangla. Listening to the chorus of girls in the distance, I changed my answer to the question people always asked me: No, I wouldn't go back to my old life. I would not trade this life for anything. Whatever I have lost or gained, the path that led me here is the one where I belong.

Acknowledgments

I love to read. Sometimes, when I come to the last page of a book, I linger for a while, trying to avoid the head rush that comes with leaving the author's world and returning to my own. If you've just finished *Finding My Way*, can we have one more moment together? I want to thank you for spending time with me, for letting me tell you my story and introduce you to all the people and places I love. If we meet someday, I hope I can return the favor.

Writing this book was a journey of healing in itself. I could not have done it, especially the tough parts, without Taylor Royle being there with me. You have helped me write for many years, and have been beside me on my journey since I was 17. When I decided to write this book, you were the only person I felt comfortable with to help me share my story, and I feel so lucky for our friendship.

To Kate Napolitano, my editor, who brought enthusiasm, joy

and patience to this process and helped me shape this story. You were the perfect person to usher this book into the world and I will never forget your empathy and kindness. To the tireless team at Atria Books—Suzanne Donahue, Hannah Frankel, Alison Hinchcliffe, Karlyn Hixson, Erin Kibby, Jessica Laino, Libby McGuire, Katherine Nintzel, Morgan Pager, Annie Probert, Yaasmeen Sanzar, Lisa Sciambra, Dana Trocker—thank you for believing in me.

To my literary agents, Albert Lee and Meredith Miller, who made this process so fun and exciting from start to finish. Thank you for each emoji and gif, for the last-minute phone calls and long lunches. I love working with you. To everyone at United Talent Agency who helped with this book: Margaret Alisberg, Sophie Baker, Brittany Balbo, Melissa Chinchillo, Eddie Clemens, Edwin Garcia, Katie Harrison, Charlotte Perman, Zoe Neely, Ethan Schlatter, Sam Solomons, Isaiah Telewoda, David Zedeck, and my longtime agent and friend, Darnell Strom.

I know that there are memoirists who write only from their own memory, photographs, journals—but I forget things too easily and needed a lot of support to fill in the details in this book. My friends and family spent hours going through text messages, Snapchat videos, file cabinets, and notebooks to help me find the answers. I can't thank them enough for giving so much of their time throughout the writing process.

I would also like to thank current and former colleagues at Malala Fund, the Shangla school, and my personal team who pitched in: Lena Alfi, Amanda Cosby, Mubashir Hassan, Hannah Orenstein, Leila Seradj, and Tess Thomas. Maria Qanita—few things in my life are possible without you, including this book.

My friends brought laughter, youth, and a sense of home back into my life. I wish I had enough space in this book to share what each and every one of them mean to me, but, at the very least, I would like to tell you their names: Bilal, Ellen, Gabriella, Haroon, Jess, Kia, Maahnoor, Maham, Mehroz, Minahil, Munirah, Nina, Saad, Sarah, Shazil, Talha, Vee, Zahra. Thanks as well to the understanding adults who guided me in and out of Oxford: Mrs. Coley, Margaret Coombe, Robin Harding, Natalie Quinn, Dominic Scott, Fiona Spensly, James Studd, and my therapist.

To Moniba and the Mingora girls who were my first friends—you knew me before I knew myself, and I carry you with me wherever I go.

To my mom and dad—thank you for loving and protecting me. I am so glad to have parents who keep trying to understand me as I change and grow. To my brothers—I am proud of the men you are becoming . . . but I could always be prouder, so keep trying!

Thank you to my husband Asser, my cheerleader and the first reader of this book. Everything in my life changed when I met you.

To Afghan girls, Shangla girls, and every child around the world struggling to go to school and follow their dreams: You are never alone. People you may never meet believe in you, in your right to education, in your future. Do not lose hope.

About the Author

Malala Yousafzai is an education activist, the youngest-ever Nobel laureate, best-selling author, and an investor in women's sports. She was born in Mingora, Pakistan in 1997 and graduated from Oxford University in 2020.

Atria Books, an imprint of Simon & Schuster, fosters an open environment where ideas flourish, best-selling authors soar to new heights, and tomorrow's finest voices are discovered and nurtured. Since its launch in 2002, Atria has published hundreds of bestsellers and extraordinary books, which would not have been possible without the invaluable support and expertise of its team and publishing partners. Thank you to the Atria Books colleagues who collaborated on *Finding My Way*, as well as to the hundreds of professionals in the Simon & Schuster advertising, audio, communications, design, ebook, finance, human resources, legal, marketing, operations, production, sales, supply chain, subsidiary rights, and warehouse departments who help Atria bring great books to light.

EDITORIAL
Kate Napolitano
Hannah Frankel

JACKET DESIGN
James Iacobelli

MARKETING
Erin Kibby
Morgan Pager
Annie Probert

MANAGING EDITORIAL
Paige Lytle
Shelby Pumphrey
Lacee Burr
Sofia Echeverry
Abby Borchers

PRODUCTION
Abel Berriz
Vanessa Silverio
Joal Hetherington
Davina Mock-Maniscalco

PUBLICITY
Alison Hinchcliffe
Jessica Laino

PUBLISHING OFFICE
Dana Trocker
Suzanne Donahue
Abby Velasco

SUBSIDIARY RIGHTS
Nicole Bond
Sara Bowne
Rebecca Justiniano
Germanie Louis